Philosophical Aesthetics and the Sciences of Art

ROYAL INSTITUTE OF PHILOSOPHY SUPPLEMENT: 75

EDITED BY

Gregory Currie
Matthew Kieran
Aaron Meskin
and
Margaret Moore

CAMBRIDGE
UNIVERSITY PRESS

CAMBRIDGE
UNIVERSITY PRESS

Shaftesbury Road, Cambridge CB2 8EA, United Kingdom

One Liberty Plaza, 20th Floor, New York, NY 10006, USA

477 Williamstown Road, Port Melbourne, VIC 3207, Australia

314–321, 3rd Floor, Plot 3, Splendor Forum, Jasola District Centre, New Delhi – 110025, India

103 Penang Road, #05–06/07, Visioncrest Commercial, Singapore 238467

Cambridge University Press is part of Cambridge University Press & Assessment,
a department of the University of Cambridge.

We share the University's mission to contribute to society through the pursuit of
education, learning and research at the highest international levels of excellence.

www.cambridge.org
Information on this title: www.cambridge.org/9781107654587

A catalogue record for this publication is available from the British Library

ISBN   978-1-107-65458-7   Paperback

Contents

Notes on Contributors and Editors

GREGORY CURRIE

Greg Currie is Professor of Philosophy at the University of York. He is an editor of *Mind & Language* and the author of a number of books on the arts and imagination. He is currently writing a book on literature and knowledge.

NIGEL FABB

Nigel Fabb is Professor of Literary Linguistics at the University of Strathclyde. He is an editor of *Journal of Linguistics*, author of nine books on linguistics and literature, and from 2014-17 a Leverhulme Major Research Fellow undertaking a literary linguistic and psychological study of epiphanies and the sublime.

BERYS GAUT

Berys Gaut is Professor of Philosophy at the University of St Andrews, Scotland, and President of the British Society of Aesthetics. His books include *Art, Emotion and Ethics* (OUP, 2007) and *A Philosophy of Cinematic Art* (CUP, 2010). He is currently writing a monograph on the philosophy of creativity.

JONATHAN GILMORE

Jonathan Gilmore teaches philosophy at the City University of New York and is a 2013-14 National Endowment for the Humanities Fellow. He is the author of *The Life of a Style* (Cornell UP, 2000) and several articles in aesthetics and art criticism. He is currently working on emotion and imagination.

GORDON GRAHAM

Gordon Graham is Henry Luce III Professor of Philosophy and the Arts at Princeton Theological Seminary. He is the author of *Philosophy of the Arts* (Routledge, 2005) and *The Re-enchantment of the World: Art versus Religion* (OUP, 2007), as well as papers in *The Journal of Aesthetics and Art Criticism* and the *British Journal of Aesthetics*.

Notes on Contributors and Editors

MATTHEW KIERAN
Matthew Kieran is Professor of Philosophy and the Arts at the University of Leeds. He is the author of *Revealing Art* (Routledge, 2005), numerous articles, editor and co-editor of a number of anthologies and is currently working on creativity.

SHEN-YI LIAO
Shen-yi Liao is an assistant professor of philosophy at Nanyang Technological University and a Marie Curie international incoming fellow at the University of Leeds. He works at the intersections of cognitive science, analytic aesthetics, philosophy of mind, and moral psychology.

MARGARET MOORE
Margaret Moore is a lecturer at the University of Tennessee, Knoxville. She has co-authored a number of articles on aesthetics and the philosophy of music, and is currently working on the topics of imagination and musical sound.

AARON MESKIN
Aaron Meskin is Associate Professor of Philosophy at the University of Leeds. He is the author of numerous articles on aesthetics and other philosophical topics. He co-edited *Aesthetics: A Comprehensive Anthology* (Wiley-Blackwell, 2007) and *The Art of Comics: A Philosophical Approach* (Wiley-Blackwell, 2012).

JENEFER ROBINSON
Jenefer Robinson teaches philosophy at the University of Cincinnati and was president of the American Society for Aesthetics 2009-2011. She is the author of *Deeper then Reason: Emotion and its Role in Literature, Music and Art* (Oxford University Press, 2005). Recent articles include 'On Being Moved by Architecture' and 'Emotions in Music' (with Robert Hatten).

JON ROBSON
Jon Robson is a teaching associate in philosophy at the University of Nottingham. He has published papers on a broad range of topics in aesthetics, epistemology, metaphysics, and the philosophy of religion. His current research centres on the epistemology and aetiology of aesthetic judgements.

Notes on Contributors and Editors

ROGER SCRUTON

Roger Scruton is currently a senior research fellow of Blackfriars Hall, Visiting Professor of Philosophy at the University of Oxford, and a senior fellow at the Ethics and Public Policy Center, Washington DC. He is author of over forty books, including works of criticism, political theory and aesthetics, as well as novels and short stories.

MURRAY SMITH

Murray Smith is Professor of Film Studies at the University of Kent, Canterbury, UK and President of the Society for Cognitive Studies of the Moving Image. His publications include *Engaging Characters: Fiction, Emotion, and the Cinema* (Clarendon, 1995). He is currently at work on *Film, Art, and the Third Culture* (forthcoming with OUP).

DEENA SKOLNICK WEISBERG

Deena Weisberg is a Senior Fellow in the Department of Psychology at the University of Pennsylvania. She earned her Ph.D. in Psychology from Yale University and received post-doctoral training at Rutgers University and Temple University. She studies children's imaginative cognition and its role in their learning and development.

Introduction

The idea that aesthetics could be reconfigured wholly as a science is not seriously advocated in philosophy, and the few scientists who have endorsed the idea seem not to have understood what they were taking on. For one thing, aesthetics is concerned with normative questions which cannot be answered by empirical investigation. But this does not mean that science has nothing to say to aesthetics, or that we need never reconsider our critical standards and practices in the light of empirical results. Take the issue, central to aesthetics, of critical judgement. In many areas adopting the opinions of others is as good as – and sometimes better than – forming your own judgement. Kant, an enemy of scientific aesthetics, confidently asserted the irrationality of judgements of taste formed on the basis of testimony, and others have followed him. Jon Robson argues here that our admitted disinclination to accept testimony about the aesthetic is best explained, not by the irrationality of doing so, but by the fact that we systematically overrate our own aesthetic judgement relative to that of other people, a claim for which he produces a good deal of empirical evidence gleaned from psychological studies. Nigel Fabb argues that poetry is enjoyed partly because its regular pattern makes text-processing easier, thereby inducing a 'feeling of truth'. Conclusions such as this might unsettle our confidence in our ability to justify our aesthetic judgements, since few of us would offer this as a reason to support such judgements .

Kant was also an enemy of the idea that disgust is in any sense an aesthetic reaction. Responding to recent attempts to make sense of the role of disgust in art, Jenefer Robinson argues that an aesthetics of disgust must comprehend the emotional, sensory and cognitive components of disgust illuminated by recent work in the behavioural sciences. Turning to fiction, psychologist Deena Skolnick Weisberg suggests that developmental evidence concerning children's judgements about what holds in a game of pretence helps us understand the mature judgements we make about what is true in a story. Jonathan Gilmore argues that the epistemic standards we use when engaging with fiction do not closely parallel those we use when engaging with reality; he suggests along the way that biases in cognition of which most of us know little account for many of the pleasures of fiction, and are exploited, unknowingly, by their authors to that end. Noting an apparently pro-scientific move in recent aesthetics towards

doi:10.1017/S1358246114000228

Introduction

explanatory rather than analytical ambitions, Shen-yi Liao argues that careful attention to the role of ceteris paribus laws in actual scientific practice is necessary for understanding what a good genre explanation in aesthetics would be like. Murray Smith focuses on a particular genre, modernism, which was founded partly on the belief that our responses to art are not significantly constrained by nature. Is such a view consistent with a Darwinian emphasis on the complex tuning of human psychology by millennia of adaptive pressure? Smith argues that a proper understanding of the developmental plasticity of mind and the interactions of genetic and cultural evolution leave a good deal of scope in art for the challenging innovations characteristic of modernism.

But work across the disciplines is a two-way street; philosophers are not unquestioning recipients of information from the empirical sciences, and sometimes show a talent for reinterpreting the results they are presented with. Asking whether creativity is a virtue, Berys Gaut criticises the claim heard in psychology that there is a close connection between being creative and having intrinsic motivation. Matthew Kieran, arguing that creative excellence depends on the possession of virtuous character traits, suggests we rethink the relations between creativity and talent, mental illness and morality respectively. Roger Scruton, while seeing merit in some empirical work in musical cognition, suggests that it is a philosophical project to discover what makes an experience of sound an experience of *music*, and one that ought to be conducted prior to the investigation of the neural processes which are undoubtedly involved. Striking a note of deeper skepticism, Gordon Graham takes the side of Reid against Hume in arguing for a very limited role for empirical inquiry in aesthetics.

This collection of essays originated in a conference, held at the Leeds Art Gallery in the summer of 2012 under the title *Philosophical Aesthetics and the Sciences of Art?* The editors had by then been working for some time on a research project generously funded by the United Kingdom's Arts and Humanities Research Council and titled *Method in Philosophical Aesthetics: the Challenge from the Sciences* (grant number AH/G012644/1). The conference was a natural culmination of the project's public activities; we thank the Royal Institute of Philosophy for financial support and for the opportunity, given in conjunction with Cambridge University Press, to present a selection of the papers, much revised, here. We also thank all those who participated in the lively debates the conference provoked, and our authors, whose tireless revisions helped to give the volume the unity it enjoys.

The Editors

Aesthetic Autonomy and Self-Aggrandisement

JON ROBSON

1. Introduction

1.1 Introductory insults

You're not as clever as you think you are. Nor for that matter are you as good a driver, teacher or romantic partner as you take yourself to be and, as if that wasn't bad enough, you are also considerably less popular than you have hitherto believed. Finally – and crucially for the argument of this paper – I contend that your abilities as an aesthetic judge are considerably less impressive than you take them to be. To avoid descending into name calling it's worth pointing out that such claims apply to the vast majority of people – myself, somewhat paradoxically, included.

These claims (and others like them) are supported by a wealth of empirical research which has shown that an overwhelming majority of people consistently judge themselves to be above average in a whole range of categories.[1] To use just two examples; studies have found that 94% of academics surveyed judged their work to be above average compared to that of their colleagues,[2] and that their students showed only a modicum more modesty with 87% of them judging their performance to be above average.[3] Additional studies

---

[1] Of course the fact that a large majority of people judge themselves to be above average (even where, as with the majority of these studies, this is the median average) in a domain is, strictly speaking, consistent with only a minority of people in that domain overestimating themselves. There are, however, other results in the studies I cite – concerning for example the large number of individuals who rate themselves in the top 1% – which clearly support the claim that a majority are overestimating their own abilities.

[2] P. Cross, 'Not Can but Will College Teachers be Improved?', *New Directions for Higher Education* 17 (1977), 1–15.

[3] J. Zuckerman & J. Jost, 'What Makes You Think You're So Popular? Self-Evaluation Maintenance and the Subjective Side of the "Friendship Paradox"', *Social Psychology Quarterly,* **64** (2001), 207–223, 208.

doi:10.1017/S1358246114000265

Jon Robson

show similar patterns of judgements concerning the other factors listed above and many more besides.[4] In what follows I will have nothing original to say in defence of the general claim that we are disposed to such widespread self-aggrandisement and will merely take it for granted that it has been sufficiently established by empirical investigation.[5] Even accepting this general pattern, though, it is still possible that you are (contrary to my earlier claims) an exception to these trends; perhaps you are every bit as talented in the various domains listed as you believe. However, in light of the picture sketched above, it would still not be rational for you to believe - in the absence of compelling independent evidence - that you are in this privileged position. Then again, perhaps you do possess such evidence - you are a qualified stunt driver, a member in good standing of Mensa, a possessor of numerous distinguished teaching awards and so forth - if so you can feel free to rest on your (considerable) laurels; this paper is about the rest of us. I will focus on the epistemic standing of individuals who are not accredited experts and, in particular, those of us who are not - in a sense I will explicate later - expert aesthetic judges. In doing so I intend to bring the empirical claims I have discussed so far to bear on a particular issue in aesthetics; the alleged autonomy of aesthetic judgements.

[4] For our tendency to overestimate our abilities as drivers see McCormick I.; Walkey F. & Green D. 'Comparative Perceptions of Driver Ability – A Confirmation and Expansion', *Accident Analysis & Prevention* **18**.3 (1986): 205–8; as teachers see Cross op. cit.; as romantic partners see B. Buunk, 'Perceived Superiority of One's own Relationship and Perceived Prevalence of Happy and Unhappy Relationships', *British Journal of Social Psychology* **40** (2001), 565–574, for popularity see Zuckerman and Jost op. cit. For a general overview of these results see D. Dunning; C. Heath & J. Suls, 'Flawed Self-assessment', *Psychological Sciences in the Public Interest* **5** (2004), 69–106.

[5] The most significant challenge to these claims is the growing body of empirical evidence which seems to suggest that they do not hold cross-culturally but only apply to individuals from prototypically Western cultures. There is at present a lively debate as to whether the evidence in question really does support this contention (see H. Boucher, 'Understanding Western-East Asian Differences and Similarities in Self-Enhancement', *Social and Personality Psychology Compass* **4** (2010), 304–317 for an overview) but I am happy for those convinced by this challenge to take my conclusions in this paper to be restricted to individuals from prototypically Western cultures (this concession is not unduly costly since the claims regarding aesthetic judgement that I will discuss below are ones that have arisen in just such a cultural context).

4

Aesthetic Autonomy and Self-Aggrandisement

1.2 Autonomy in Aesthetics

The label 'autonomy' is a notoriously promiscuous one which may ascribe a number of different features to aesthetic judgements (and aesthetic activities more generally)[6] but I intend to focus exclusively on autonomy of the kind outlined in the following, justly famous, passage from Kant's third critique.[7]

> If someone does not find a building, a view, or a poem beautiful [...] he will refuse to let even a hundred voices all praising it highly, prod him into approving of it inwardly [...] he realizes clearly that other people's approval in no way provides him with a valid proof by which to judge beauty.

This passage serves as the *locus classicus* for a number of influential theses concerning aesthetic judgement; most prominently the oft discussed claim that we cannot achieve knowledge (or perhaps proper belief) in aesthetics on the basis of testimony alone. I have had much to say with regards to testimony elsewhere[8] but in this paper I will focus on distinct - but closely related - issues concerning revisions to our aesthetic judgements on the basis of disagreement. In particular I will discuss two theses apparently endorsed by Kant in the passage above.

Descriptive Autonomy (DA) – we *do not* revise our aesthetic evaluation of an object on the basis of disagreement.[9]

Normative Autonomy (NA) – we *should not* revise our aesthetic evaluation of an object on the basis of disagreement.

I will assume below that DA provides a more or less accurate description of how we – as a matter of fact – respond to aesthetic

---

[6] For example that ethical evaluations of a work should have no bearing on our aesthetic assessment of it or that aesthetic judgements should not take into account any instrumental function of the object judged.

[7] I. Kant, *Critique of Judgement*. Trans. J. H. Bernard (New York: Dover, 1790/2005), 94.

[8] In e.g. J. Robson, 'Aesthetic Testimony', *Philosophy Compass* **7** (2012), 1–10, 6–7 and 'Aesthetic Testimony and the Norms of Belief Formation', *European Journal of Philosophy* (forthcoming).

[9] Although Kant focuses exclusively on judgements of beauty recent discussion has tended to apply the doctrine to aesthetic evaluations more generally. I will have something to say on this subject in §4 but for now I will uncritically follow this trend.

disagreement[10] but argue that the endorsement of this practice in NA is mistaken. When properly understood DA does not reveal any deep feature of aesthetic judgement which would lend support to NA, but is primarily a symptom of the kind of self-aggrandising bias that I have discussed above.

1.3 Summary

In §2 I begin by clarifying some important issues and then go on to lay out the methodology I intend to employ in the rest of the paper. §3 focuses on presenting my own explanation for the widespread acceptance of NA. I argue that our tendency to endorse NA rests on a number of factors including, crucially, the kind of self-aggrandisement I have discussed above. In §4 I consider the most promising rival account to my view – which seeks to vindicate NA by appeal to a certain kind of relativism – and argue that it ultimately fails to account for the relevant phenomena.

2. Disagreement in aesthetics and elsewhere

2.1 An alleged asymmetry

In his insightful discussion of NA Robert Hopkins writes

> When one party finds herself disagreeing with several others who share a view then (a) for ordinary empirical matters this is sometimes reason enough for her to adopt their view, but is never so in the case of beauty. Instead, in the latter case (b) she should place less confidence in her view; and (c) she should, if possible, test the issue by re-examining

---

[10] My own view is that while DA reflects something important concerning our reluctance to revise our aesthetic beliefs it overstates this reticence somewhat; expressing something like the policy we take ourselves to be adopting when we introspect with respect to our own belief revision practices in aesthetics. I argue elsewhere (J. Robson 'A Social Epistemology of Aesthetics' *Synthese* (forthcoming)) that by applying such processes we typically underestimate the extent to which our aesthetic beliefs are formed on the basis of testimony and I think – though I will not argue for the claim here – that something similar applies with respect to revising those beliefs on the basis of disagreement. I will, however, largely ignore these complications in what follows.

the disputed item. The question thus raised is why this contrast holds.[11]

An obvious worry is that the picture I am presenting in this paper will not explain the crucial asymmetry Hopkins highlights; or rather – since I am explicitly not endorsing the rationality of our attitudes towards belief revision in aesthetics – that it will not explain the descriptive version of Hopkins proposed normative asymmetry. I am claiming that while DA correctly describes our practice of belief revision (or the lack of same) in aesthetics this is, in large part, a result of our overestimating our abilities as aesthetic judges. Yet I have claimed above that the tendency to overestimate our own abilities is a general one and, as such, it surely cannot be appealed to as an explanation of the psychological difference between our attitudes to belief revision in aesthetics and elsewhere. In the next section I will respond to this worry by presenting my own account of DA and highlighting what I take to be the relevant differences between aesthetic and mundane cases; differences which are perfectly compatible with our self-aggrandisement being general rather than restricted to the aesthetic domain. First, though, it is important to clarify exactly what is at stake in the autonomy debate.

2.2 Responding to disagreement

To begin let us consider the following pair of disagreements; one aesthetic, the other more mundane

Flute Solo:

I attend a live orchestral performance with ten friends. Later I discuss this performance with one of the friends who says 'the final flute solo was magnificent'. I am in agreement with her on the order of performance but differ with respect to the magnificence and insist that it was, in point of fact, pedestrian at best. I look for support from my other friends but none is forthcoming and they all side with the judgement that the solo was magnificent.

Colourful Birds:

I am with the same group of friends; we pass a flock of birds perched on the grass some metres away and spend a few seconds admiring them before they fly away. Later I discuss

---

[11]   R. Hopkins, 'Kant, Quasi-Realism & the Autonomy of Aesthetic Judgement', *European Journal of Philosophy* **9** (2001), 166–189, 169.

this incident with one of the friends who says 'there were a dozen yellow birds'. I am in agreement with her on the number of birds but differ with respect to their colour and insist that they were, in point of fact, red. I look for support from my other friends but none is forthcoming and they all side with the judgement that they were yellow.

How would I respond to disagreement in these cases? And how should I respond? These are not easy questions to answer for a number of reasons; most obviously because these examples are underspecified in a number of respects and leave a range of potentially relevant questions unanswered. Do my friends have significantly better vision, or aesthetic judgment, than I? What are our track records in these kinds of disagreement? How honest are my friends (and how honest do I take them to be)? How confident was I in my initial belief? How much is at stake for each of us in getting the right answer? And so forth. To prevent such issues complicating matters unduly let us stipulate that in the cases above (and, unless otherwise stated, in any further cases discussed below) all those involved in the disputes are epistemic peers. Peers in the general sense that they possess equivalent 'intelligence, perspicacity, honesty, thoroughness, and other relevant epistemic virtues'[12] and the specific sense that they are alike 'with respect to their exposure to evidence and arguments which bear on the question at issue'[13] as well as with respect to the reliability of the relevant faculties (none of us are colour blind, tone deaf etc.).[14] Furthermore an impartial assessment of the evidence available to each of the disputants would warrant their believing that their interlocutors were their epistemic peers in all these respects.[15] Finally we should assume – in order to focus on the relevance of the 'higher order' evidence arising from the disagreement itself rather than on any 'first order' evidence –[16] that none of the parties puts forward any independent

---

[12]   G. Gutting, *Religious Belief and Religious Skepticism* (University of Notre Dame Press, 1982), 83.

[13]   T. Kelly, 'The Epistemic Significance of Disagreement', *Oxford Studies in Epistemology* **1** (2005), 167–196, 168.

[14]   Thanks to Matthew Kieran for pushing me to clarify this point.

[15]   Though, of course, it is a central claim of this paper that we will not typically assess such matters impartially.

[16]   For more on the distinction between first order and higher order evidence see T. Kelly, 'Peer Disagreement and Higher Order Evidence'. In R. Feldman and T. Warfield (eds.) *Disagreement*, (Oxford: Oxford University Press, 2011, 111–174).

evidence (concerning typical bird populations in the area, the flau-tist's credentials etc.) in favour of their judgements. The extent to which such first order evidence is (and ought to be) significant in aes-thetic disputes is, of course, a controversial issue in its own right but not one I will pursue here.[17]

Even given all these stipulations (and ignoring any peculiarities in-troduced by considering specifically aesthetic judgements) there is still significant controversy regarding how best to respond in the face of disagreement. One thing that is evident from the growing lit-erature on this subject of peer disagreement is that there is no clear consensus as to how we *ought* to respond to disagreement even in straightforward cases like *Colourful Birds*.[18] As such it would be implausible to think that any straightforward comparison of how we ought to act in aesthetic and non-aesthetic cases will be possible. Crudely speaking there are three stances which we could take with respect to disagreements of either kind, we could (i) retain our origin-al belief; (ii) withhold belief endorsing neither our original belief nor that of our opponents; (iii) reject our initial belief in favour of the incompatible belief put forward by our interlocutors.[19]

Although NA (as stated above) does not tell us anything about how we should respond in non-aesthetic cases it is clear that if the propon-ent of NA intends their doctrine to reveal anything interesting about *aesthetics* then they must propose, as does, a marked contrast between the correct response in aesthetic cases and those concerning more mundane disagreements.[20] It is not immediately clear, though, from the quotes from Kant and Hopkins above – nor from other

---

[17]   For discussion of this issue see e.g. R. Hopkins, 'Critical Reasoning and Critical Perception'. In M. Kieran & D. McIver Lopes (eds.) *Knowing Art: Essay in Aesthetics and Epistemology*, (Dordrecht: Springer, 2006, 137–154).
[18]   D. Christensen, 'Epistemology of Disagreement: the Good News', *Philosophical Review* **116** (2007), 187–217 and A. Elga, 'Reflection and Disagreement,' *Nous* **41** (2007), 478–502 for example would claim that we ought to give the judgements of each of our epistemic peers 'equal weight' to our own judgement while Kelly (2005, 2011) and J. Lackey, 'A Justificationist View of Disagreement's Epistemic Significance', A. Haddock, A. Millar, and D. Pritchard (eds.) *Social Epistemology,* (Oxford: Oxford University Press, 2010, 298–325) would, for different reasons, deny this.
[19]   Further complications arise if we introduce - as much of the peer dis-agreement literature does – considerations of degrees of belief or Bayesian credences.
[20]   Hopkins 2001 op. cit. 169.

defences of NA – exactly what the contrast is supposed to be. Certainly that response (iii) is often correct in mundane disputes and never (or rarely ever) with respect to aesthetic disagreements, even if true, though, this doesn't tell us what our response in aesthetic cases *should* be. Should I retain my initial belief or merely refrain from adopting that of my fellow disputants? While the quotes I have marshalled above are perhaps consistent with either interpretation – suspending judgement could, for instance, be construed as one form of placing 'less confidence in' a view – it is clear that advocates of NA standardly take their doctrine to entail the claim that I should retain my initial belief and not merely suspend judgement.[21] From now on, then, I will take talk of revising aesthetic beliefs (or failing to do so) on the basis of disagreement to include not only cases where I adopt my opponent's belief but also those in which I come to suspend judgment on the issue in question. Of these two options I will focus primarily on the latter and argue that the best explanation for our peculiar unwillingness to abandon our aesthetic beliefs on the basis of disagreement is one which does not provide any normative vindication for this refusal. Of course if we do abandon our original belief in cases such as *Flute Solo* this raises the further issue of whether we should also adopt the views of our opponents. However, at this point the discussion becomes primarily concerned with issues surrounding whether (and under what circumstances) one should form aesthetic beliefs on the basis of the word of others; that is with the debate over aesthetic testimony. As mentioned above, though, I do not intend to address issues of testimony directly here and as such will focus almost exclusively on the question of whether we should abandon our previously held aesthetic beliefs on the basis of disagreement. It is important, especially considering the ease with which they are conflated, to stress the differences between these two topics particularly since several prominent arguments for rejecting aesthetic testimony would be clear non-starters if proposed as reasons not to abandon our current aesthetic beliefs. The accounts offered by Robert Hopkins, Philip Pettit, Roger Scruton and Cain Todd,[22] for instance all place additional constraints

---

[21] The discussion in Hopkins 2001 op.cit. 167–9) for example strongly suggest that he interprets the doctrine this way and A. McGonigal, 'The Autonomy of Aesthetic Judgement', *British Journal of Aesthetics* **46** (2006), 331–348, 331 explicitly endorses this interpretation (taking Hopkins, Kant et al as subscribing to it also).

[22] R. Hopkins, 'How to be a Pessimist about Aesthetic Testimony', *Journal of Philosophy* **108** (2011), 138–157; P. Pettit, 'The Possibility of

on the legitimate formation of aesthetic beliefs (or their expressivist equivalents).[23] Constraints which, they allege, prevent beliefs formed on the basis of testimony from being legitimate. Even if such constraints were in place, though, they would only add to the conditions which an aesthetic belief must meet in order to be legitimate and as such they could never justify retaining aesthetic beliefs in circumstances where mundane beliefs would be abandoned.

2.3 Methodology

Now that we have got a little clearer as to the issue at hand, how should we go about addressing it? When discussing disagreements in aesthetics and elsewhere Andrew McGonigal suggests the following line of reasoning which may lead someone to revise a belief – in this case concerning the colour of a particular surface – on the basis of disagreement

(1)   I and my opponents disagree about whether the surface is blue
(2)   One of us is at fault.
(3)   They outnumber me; in general they and I are equally competent in matters of this sort; and we've all tried to access the facts in the same way.
(4)   *The best explanation of the disagreement in this scenario is that I am at fault.*
(5)   So it is likely that I am fault.[24]

With regards to cases of colour disagreement it is easy to see why, as McGonigal suggests, we should accept (5). Let us imagine some third party (Bobby) eavesdropping on my disagreement during *colourful birds* who regards my friends and I merely as systems for producing true beliefs. Further Bobby judges, correctly we will assume, that

---

Aesthetic Realism'. In E. Schaper (ed.) *Pleasure, Preference and Value*, (Cambridge: Cambridge University Press, 1983, 17–38); R. Scruton, *Art and Imagination* (London: Methuen, 1976) and C. S. Todd, 'Quasi-realism, Acquaintance and the Normative Claims of Aesthetic Judgement', *British Journal of Aesthetics* **44** (2004), 277–96.
    [23]   I assume throughout this paper that aesthetic judgements are beliefs but, so far as I can see, none of the arguments I put forward depend on this assumption.
    [24]   McGonigal op. cit. 338. McGonigal further concludes that I should come to believe that it is likely that things are as my opponent claims but I will not consider this claim here.

when it comes to colour judgements – at least those made in normal lighting concerning medium sized objects in our immediate vicinity etc. – we are all extremely reliable. Of course we all make the occasional mistakes and are doubtless not quite as reliable as we think we are but when it comes to differentiating reds and yellows in favourable conditions our judgements are almost beyond reproach. Bobby correctly gauges each of us to judge accurately with respect to such issues, say, 98% of the time; how, then, would he assess the probabilities in the relevant disagreement.[25] Well, the odds of my being wrong are fairly low (one in fifty in fact) but the odds of the other ten all independently being mistaken are, for all practical purposes, virtually zero. It seems clear, then, that absent any further information Bobby should believe that my opponents are correct and that I am mistaken. And so, the argument goes, should I. It may well be that, as a number of those engaged in the peer disagreement debate have tried to show, such arguments oversimplify matters but they are certainly an instructive place to start.[26]

It seems, however, that this line of thought will not preserve the crucial asymmetry – between aesthetic cases and others – appealed to above. If we apply the same line of reasoning to *Flute Solo* we will get parallel results – Bobby and I should believe that my initial judgement was mistaken.[27] How, then, do we explain our unwillingness to defer in the aesthetic case? A proponent of NA would most likely appeal to some additional factor unique to aesthetics – or to aesthetics plus some other problem cases such as ethics[28] – which explains (and justifies) our unwillingness to revise our beliefs in cases such as *Flute Solo*. Of course I do not accept any such explanation but I intend not merely to deny NA but to supplement this denial

[25]   Here and elsewhere I employ artificially precise estimates for the reliability of various belief forming processes but these are meant only as a convenient approximation for illustrative purposes rather than as a serious attempt to assess the reliability of the relevant faculties.

[26]   For a sympathetic discussion of this methodology see R. White, 'On Treating Oneself and Others as Thermometers', *Episteme* **6** (2009), 233–250.

[27]   Assuming that the reliability of my belief forming mechanisms in aesthetic cases (and thus the belief forming mechanisms of my peers) is above chance then an argument parallel to the one above can be offered. I will not consider cases where our reliability is at or below chance since my initial belief would clearly be unjustified in such cases.

[28]   See J. Driver, 'Autonomy and the Asymmetry Problem for Moral Expertise', *Philosophical Studies* **128** (2006), 619–644 and A. Hills, *The Beloved Self* (Oxford: Oxford University Press, 2010).

with a persuasive account of why we typically behave as if NA is true; in other words of why DA holds. This account relies on three central claims which I will defend in the next section; (i) our aesthetic judgements are not very reliable, (ii) a number of factors make us peculiarly unable to accept this unreliability and so enable us to confidently persist in making aesthetic judgements of the relevant kind, (iii) we overestimate our own capacities as aesthetic judges.

3. My account

3.1 Unreliability

I have suggested above that when it comes to making certain colour judgements most of us are extremely reliable. In contrast I maintain that aesthetic judgements – by which I will hereafter, unless otherwise stated, mean the first-hand judgements of non-experts regarding complex artworks – are typically unreliable. That is to say that our judgements are frequently incorrect, far more often than they are with respect to e.g. straightforward colour judgements, to the extent that such judgements (even when correct) frequently fail to achieve the status of knowledge. Further even in those cases where we do attain aesthetic knowledge through first-hand judgement such knowledge is likely to be far more precarious – subject to potential defeaters etc. – than our knowledge concerning ordinary empirical matters.[29]

There is a large and rapidly expanding literature showing that our aesthetic judgements are heavily influenced by a number of biases and distortions; ordering effects, exposure effects, snobbery, belief polarisation, echo chambers and many more besides.[30] Such studies

---

[29] My own preference would be to give a contextualist analysis of such claims e.g. we quite often 'know' such aesthetic claims by low standards but rarely do so by high standards.

[30] For discussion of such factors S. Irvin, 'Is Aesthetic Experience Possible?' In G. Currie, M. Kieran, A. Meskin & J. Robson (eds.) *Philosophical Aesthetics and the Sciences of Mind*, (Oxford University Press, forthcoming), M. Kieran, 'The Fragility of Aesthetic Knowledge: Aesthetic Psychology and Appreciative Virtues'. In P. Goldie and E. Schellekens (eds.), *The Aesthetic Mind: Philosophy and Psychology*, (Oxford: Oxford University Press, 2011, 32–43), D. Lopes, 'Feckless Reason'. In G. Currie, M. Kieran, A. Meskin & J. Robson (eds.) *Philosophical Aesthetics and the Sciences of Mind*, (Oxford University Press, forthcoming), A. Meskin, 'Aesthetic Unreliability', (Manuscript) and Robson op. cit. A. Meskin; M. Phelan; M.; Moore & M. Kieran,

have led some to make rather extreme claims; for example that mere exposure or order effects frequently play a larger role in determining preference than does actual aesthetic quality.[31] I do not, however, propose to argue that the empirical results support such ambitious assertions - nor do I intend to deny this – but merely that they support my earlier claim that aesthetic judgements are unreliable in the sense outlined above. This general unreliability picture, or something very like it, has already been argued for at length elsewhere[32] and I will not rehearse these arguments here. Instead I will focus on some specific aspects of this unreliability picture which will be crucial for my argument.

Consider Aaron Meskin's attempt to show that aesthetic testimony is unreliable as a source of knowledge and, in particular, that it is less reliable than first-hand aesthetic judgement.[33] Meskin argues that very few of us meet, or even approximate, Hume's standards for being a true judge; 'strong sense, united to delicate sentiment, improved by practice, perfected by comparison, and cleared of all prejudice'[34] and that an individual is 'much more likely to know the extent to which he or she meets the requirements for being a true judge than the extent to which another person meets those requirements'.[35] As such she would often have a defeater for aesthetic beliefs based on testimony (the high proportion of testifiers who are not true judges) which is not itself defeated (as it would be if she were able to e.g. establish that a particular testifier were a true judge). By contrast she is able to trust her own judgement provided she has taken the appropriate steps to check that she possesses delicate sentiment, is

'Mere Exposure to Bad Art', *British Journal of Aesthetics* **53** (2013), 139–164) offer some reasons to think that our susceptibility to exposure effects may not generate sceptical consequences but even if their arguments are sound they only apply to one bias amongst many.

[31] V. Ginsburgh, & J. van Ours, 'Expert Opinion and Compensation: Evidence from a Musical Competition', *American Economic Review* **93** (2003), 289–296 make the latter claim with regards to the rankings in a prestigious piano contest. Meskin et al op. cit. consider arguments for the former claim but do not endorse it.

[32] Most comprehensively in Meskin op. cit.

[33] A. Meskin, 'Solving the Puzzle of Aesthetic Testimony'. In M. Kieran and D. McIver Lopes (eds.) *Knowing Art: Essay in Aesthetics and Epistemology*, (Dordrecht: Springer, 2006, 109–125).

[34] D. Hume, 'Of the Standard of Taste', *Essays: Moral, Political and Literary*, (London: Oxford University Press, 1963, 167–182, 177).

[35] Meskin op. cit. 123.

free from prejudice and so forth. A similar story could be told with respect to disagreement in aesthetics. If I am able to tell, through introspection say, that I at least approximate Hume's standards with regards to a particular aesthetic judgement but am unable to make such a determination with respect to my opponents – and indeed possess good statistical grounds to doubt it – then this may explain, and justify, my unwillingness to revise my aesthetic beliefs in many (though doubtless not all) cases of aesthetic peer disagreement.[36]

Yet the situation with respect to such matters is, in fact, very different to that which this argument suggests. As I have stressed at length above we are generally remarkably poor at assessing our own abilities in a whole range of areas and, in particular, tend to overestimate our abilities in comparison to those of our peers. As such we should be very much inclined to doubt – in the absence of any compelling independent evidence – any claim which rests on our ability to successfully gauge our own abilities in some area. Beyond this general picture, though, there are specific reasons to worry about our self-assessment of our fitness to be Humean judges. As indicated above, I am in agreement with Meskin that the source of much of our unreliability concerning aesthetic matters lies in biases and distorting factors of various kinds – order effects, snobbery etc. – which would clearly disqualify us from the role of true judges. The situation with respect to our ability to detect such biases, however, seems to be the exact reverse of that which Meskin's argument requires.[37] Research has repeatedly shown that individuals greatly underestimate their own susceptibility to various biases and distorting factors – including many relevant to unreliability in aesthetics – even in the face of powerful evidence that they are greatly influenced by such biases.[38] They readily accept that the evidence shows such biases to be widespread in others (and even that people typically underestimate their susceptibility to such biases) but resist applying these conclusions in their own case. Such 'bias blind spots' – combined with the

---

[36] I stipulated above that all those involved in the cases I present know their interlocutors to be their epistemic peers but this stipulation was made purely for ease of exposition and is, of course, unlikely to hold with respect to real-life cases for a variety of reasons.

[37] And closer to that which he later defends in Meskin (manuscript) op. cit.

[38] See e.g. E. Pronin; D. Lin & L. Ross, 'The Bias Blind Spot: Perceptions of Bias in Self Versus Others', *Personality and Social Psychology Bulletin* **28** (2002), 369–381.

impressive evidence that such biases play a uniquely (or at least atypically) prominent role in aesthetics - surely give us even more reason to defer to the judgements of others.

3.2 Irrepressibility and Aesthetic Self-aggrandisement

That aesthetic unreliability is largely rooted in such biases is also extremely important for establishing my second claim; that we are curiously irrepressible in our tendency to make aesthetic judgements. Those who suffer from significant maladies which impair their ability to judge colour are, for the most part, well aware of their conditions and as such refrain from making confident first-hand judgements about such matters. Similarly most of us are well aware that our knowledge of various areas – pre-Columbian South America languages, subatomic physics and so forth – is not what it could be and so refrain from confident pronouncements in these areas.[39] The problem in the aesthetic case, by contrast, is that it combines bad judgement with frequent judgement. To see why we exhibit such irrepressibility with respect to aesthetic judgement we need to turn to my third claim concerning self-aggrandisement in aesthetics.

The claim that we standardly overestimate our own capacities as aesthetic judges is, in several respects, central to my overall argument. I have already alluded to the wealth of empirical evidence supporting the claim that individuals typically overestimate their abilities in a range of areas but what evidence is there that we overestimate our ability as aesthetic judges? Firstly, it is not unreasonable to maintain, given our ubiquitous tendency to self-aggrandisement, that the burden of proof is on the objector to show that the aesthetic domain is an exception rather than on me to show that it is not. Secondly, there is direct evidence of self-aggrandisement in areas at least analogous to aesthetic judgement; for example judgements of our ability to 'get' jokes.[40] Finally, if - as I have claimed - our aesthetic

---

[39]   Further, as M. Kieran, 'The Vice of Snobbery: Aesthetic Knowledge, Justification and Virtue in Art Appreciation', *Philosophical Quarterly* **60** (2010), 243–263, 251 points out, those of us not inclined to such humility about, say, subatomic physics constantly run the risk of having our claims exposed as poppycock by a genuine expert whereas it is typically not so easy to provide a straightforward demonstration that an aesthetic claim is mistaken or poorly grounded.

[40]   See J. Kruger, & J. Dunning, 'Unskilled and Unaware of It: How Difficulties in Recognizing One's Own Incompetence Lead to Inflated

judgements are heavily influenced by a number of biases and we are disposed to underestimate the negative effects of these biases in our own case then this alone makes it extremely likely that we would over-estimate the reliability of our aesthetic judgements compared to those of our peers.

There seems to be good reason, then, to accept that we self-aggrandise with respect to our capacities as aesthetic judges. As with many of the biases discussed above, though, self-aggrandise-ment effects show a remarkable resistance to evidence. Those who are well informed about the prevalence of such biases seem no less susceptible to them and even those (myself for example) who spend a great deal of time writing about such biases - explicitly acknowledg-ing that they are as much disposed to be influenced by them as the next person – still find themselves believing in accordance with such biases most of the time.[41] And it is easy to see why such beliefs would develop so as to be insensitive to evidence. Research in-dicates that self-aggrandising beliefs are often highly conducive to psychological wellbeing[42] and, pre-theoretically, it is difficult to imagine that believing yourself to be below average at your profession or as a conversational or romantic partner would give you much motivation to pursue the development of various personal and pro-fessional projects necessary for human flourishing; 'if a job's worth doing, it's worth leaving for someone else who'll do it better' is not the mantra of someone likely to survive and thrive. As such there would be good (non-epistemic) reason to have these self-aggrandizing beliefs hard-wired into us in such a way that they are insensitive to any evidence we have to the contrary. And, luckily for us, this again appears to be exactly the state we are in.[43]

Self-Assessments', *Journal of Personality and Social Psychology* **77** (1999), 1121–1134, 1123.

[41]   For a fascinating and amusing discussion of the predicament of those in this condition see A. Elga, 'On Overrating Oneself ...and Knowing it', *Philosophical Studies* **123** (2005), 115–124.

[42]   See e.g. C. Benight & A. Bandura, 'Social Cognitive Theory of Posttraumatic Recovery: The role of perceived self-efficacy', *Behaviour Research & Therapy* **42** (2003), 1129–1148.

[43]   Matthew Kieran has pointed out to me (in conversation) that a belief's having this kind of evolutionary etiology and thus being insensitive to evidence is consistent with its being eliminable by other means; perhaps paralleling the ways in which Kieran op. cit. suggests we eliminate problem-atic motivations such as snobbery. I tend to think that the beliefs in question are hard-wired to such an extent that these other methods will also prove

Further, given that our self-aggrandising tendencies (along with, I suspect, many of the other biases discussed above) appear to be (at least to some extent) hard-wired, our irrepressibility as aesthetic judges also becomes a simple matter to explain. Since we are incapable of responding appropriately to our own limitations as aesthetic judges we continue to confidently make aesthetic judgements despite significant evidence of their unreliability.

3.4 Explaining the asymmetry

Having presented and defended the three crucial claims on which my account of DA depends it is now time to lay out the account itself. To begin, consider again our hypothetical individual Bobby observing my disagreements but let us now assume that Bobby has fallen into error while attempting to assess the capacities of individuals as systems for producing true beliefs. Specifically Bobby now shares my self-aggrandising beliefs with respect to my own abilities as well as my resistance to revising those beliefs on the basis of evidence. Bobby believes I am every bit as good as I (in my unreflective moments) think I am.

How would this alter things with respect to *Colourful Birds*? Not, I suspect, very much. Let us assume that Bobby judges my friends to be mistaken twice as often as I am and that while he still (correctly) judges them to be 98% accurate with respect to colour judgement he now (mistakenly) believes me to be 99% accurate. He will then judge the situation as follows: One system with 99% accuracy judges that P, ten systems with 98% accuracy judge that Q (where Q is incompatible with P). The odds of the single system judging P when ¬P is the case are one in a hundred. The odds of the ten systems independently judging that Q when P is the case are – as in the original case – too low to be worth considering. As such Bobby will, again, judge that I should abandon my colour belief.

Turning next to *Flute Solo* is there a significant difference here? I think there is but it is one which will require a little unpacking. First, recall that our aesthetic judgements are nowhere near as reliable as our colour judgements; let us assume that they are only a little better than

---

ineffective but I will not argue for this further claim here since the beliefs in question displaying an unusual insensitivity to evidence is all that my argument requires.

chance (say 60% reliable).[44] Further, recall that a great deal of this unreliability is the result of various biases and distorting factors which we are quick to ascribe to others but incredibly reticent to recognise in ourselves. As such it would not be unreasonable to suppose that I (and by extension Bobby) overestimate my superiority in aesthetic judgement to a greater extent than with respect to colour judgement. Let us say that Bobby correctly judges my friends to be 60% accurate but mistakenly judges me to be 90% accurate (that is he mistakenly judges them to be wrong four times more often rather than twice as often as in the colour case). With numbers like this it is easy to see why I would refuse to revise my belief in one on one cases of disagreement – as well as more complex cases where opinion is, more or less, equally divided - but they are not enough to explain why I continue to do so when faced with Kant's hundred voices or even the ten friends in *Flute Solo*. The odds of ten systems with a 60% accuracy all independently being mistaken are, once again, close to zero.[45] Yet in this case, unlike *Colourful Birds*, the odds of all ten of my friends independently being right – given their low level of reliability would also be extremely remote. And here lies the crucial difference between the two cases.

In my discussion above I have been tacitly assuming that Bobby is disposed to treat my friends and I as akin to something like veritistic slot machines. When asked to provide a judgement with respect to a particular subject we will pay out a certain percentage of the time by producing true beliefs and correspondingly true assertions. Crucially, though, there will be no systematic patterns to the pay outs.[46] Yet in a case such as *Flute Solo* this assumption - given the extreme unlikelihood of all ten of my friends returning the same result (whether mistaken or not) on such a model – does not appear to be legitimate. A better response would be to hold that there are certain instances in which the ten systems are very reliable and others in which they are prone to systematic error. Further, given that they all disagree with a system which is 90% reliable in this

---

[44]   Of course in real-life cases our capacities as aesthetic judges are nowhere near this homogeneous (as I will discuss at length below) and, even restricting ourselves to the first-hand judgements of non-experts regarding complex artworks, our reliability is likely to vary greatly from case to case (though, if I am right, we non-experts will never be especially reliable in these kinds of cases).

[45]   Though, of course, this is vastly more likely than with respect to ten systems which are 98% reliable.

[46]   Doubtless the slot machine analogy oversimplifies things in various other respects but I will not explore these here. Again, see White op. cit.

case, we have some reason to think that we are in the latter category but hardly – without some explanation as to the nature or the source of the error – an overwhelming one. Yet again, though, an appeal to the kind of biases and distorting factors prevalent in aesthetic cases can shore up Bobby's reasoning here. Bobby already thinks (correctly) that my friends are susceptible to all manner of biases to which he believes (incorrectly) I am immune. As such he can readily explain our, initially puzzling, disagreement by assuming that the disputed case is one where such biases play a particularly significant role. My friends are all lead astray by snobbery (or by exposure effects or ordering effects or...), as they so frequently are, whereas I remain immune. Such cases, Bobby reasons, are very common and certainly more common than circumstances in which I am mistaken and my friends are unanimously correct. And, of course, the situation in which the fictional Bobby finds himself (given his stipulated beliefs) is intended to be closely analogous to my actual position with regards to the question of revising my own aesthetic judgements.

We have seen, then, that anyone who holds the kind of self-aggrandising beliefs that I have argued we typically hold with respect to our own aesthetic judgement will – in combination with the other factors highlighted above – take themselves to have good reason to refrain from revising their aesthetic belief on the basis of disagreement. Further, their taking themselves to have such a reason provides an explanation for the existences of DA. Given that these beliefs are mistaken, though, the account I have given of DA provides no justification for adopting NA. Of course merely having an alternative explanation of DA – even one which I hope I have shown to be independently plausible – on the table does not in itself demonstrate that NA is mistaken. In the remainder of this paper, then, I will turn to criticise what I take to be the strongest NA account currently available.

4. Relativism

4.1 McGonigal's sensibilities

In my view by far the most promising defence of NA is the relativistic one recently proposed by Andrew McGonigal. Consider again McGonigal's argument from §2 and, in particular, premise (4) that '*The best explanation of the disagreement in this scenario is that I am at fault*'.[47] McGonigal introduces (4) since he thinks that previous

---

[47]   McGonigal op. cit. 338.

arguments concerning belief revision in aesthetics (in particular those offered in Hopkins 2001) are 'crucially enthymematic' as they do not include this vital premise.[48] He contends, further, that in the aesthetic case we can reject this premise since we have an alternate explanation for our disagreements which enables us to avoid the humiliating concession in (5) that our own judgement is most likely at fault.

According to McGonigal a promising rival explanation for our divergences in these cases is that I have a 'different [aesthetic] sensibility' from that of my interlocutors.[49] A sensibility in McGonigal's sense is, at least partially, constituted by dispositions to have certain experiences in certain conditions. Here McGonigal draws an analogy with judgements of deliciousness; someone finds strawberries delicious if they are disposed to take certain kinds of pleasure in eating them and they should not let disagreement from those who lack such dispositions sway them into thinking they are not delicious (though it may perhaps motivate them to check their judgements more carefully).[50] Similarly my judging an object beautiful, on McGonigal's view, is at least partially constituted by my being disposed to have particular positive experiences when viewing that object in relevant conditions and I should not let disagreement from those who lack such dispositions pressure me into retracting my judgement that it is beautiful.

> My being capable of taking a distinctive kind of pleasure in the perceptual appreciation of a given aesthetic object gives me a reason to appreciate it. Say I find that I am so capable. That, in the normal course of events, warrants the judgement that the object is beautiful. This judgement is internally related to the claim that there is a reason to value the object by perceptually appreciating it, that something counts in favour of so doing – for example, in a wide range of cases, the pleasure that results. Of course, if certain people are simply incapable of taking pleasure in the object, however, due to differences in sensibility, then there may be no reason for them to do any such thing. But their incapacity – even were it proved to me – does not entail that I

---

[48]   Ibid., 331.
[49]   Ibid., 345.
[50]   Ibid., 346. Of course some may doubt whether there can be genuine disagreements between those with differing sensibilities but I will not pursue this issue here (for discussion see C. Baker, 'Indexical Contextualism and the Challenges from Disagreement', *Philosophical Studies* **157** (2012), 107–123).

should withdraw my original judgement, any more than the proof that somebody was constitutionally taste-blind would invalidate my claim that a given foodstuff was delicious. Similar considerations apply if I find myself incapable of appreciating certain objects that others take pleasure in.[51]

In essence we can take McGonigal's proposal as introducing a further option into the kinds of aesthetic disagreement discussed above. As well as the standard possibilities – I am mistaken or they are – I can now consider another explanation; that both my interlocutors and I judge correctly *according to our own sensibilities*. I can therefore accept that their judgement is right *for them* (or similar) without having to concede that my own judgement is in error.[52] This new option certainly makes the situation in aesthetics different from that which we find in standards cases of disagreement; however, I think that it is important not to overestimate the difference this third option will make to the debate.

4.2 Relativism and Belief Revision

Let us for the time being assume that something like the relativistic sensibility picture which McGonigal proposes is correct – those who find such relativistic accounts implausible will, of course, have an additional reason to prefer my debunking account of NA to the vindicating account McGonigal proposes - and ask what consequences this will have for belief revision in aesthetics. Consider first some experiments on aesthetic judgment carried out by Chris McManus, and others, which revealed that subjects displayed 'significant and temporally stable, but somewhat idiosyncratic, individual preferences' between simple figures (squares, triangles and so forth).[53] Let us suppose, for the sake of argument at least, that these results carry over to other kinds of indicator besides mere preference and, in particular, that the same pattern applies to judgements concerning beauty. If in such conditions I find squares, on the whole,

[51]   McGonigal op. cit. 345–346.
[52]   As Matthew Kieran has pointed out to me (in conversation) we can accept that people's aesthetic sensibilities differ in some sense without embracing relativism. I will, however, ignore this possibility in what follows since McGonigal's account clearly requires something like the relativistic framework he appeals to.
[53]   C. McManus, 'The Aesthetics of Simple Figures', *British Journal of Psychology* **71** (1980), 505–524, 505.

more attractive than triangles and you have the opposite disposition then it strikes me as extremely plausible that such differences will be accounted for primarily (if not entirely) by appeal to something like McGonigal's sensibilities. This is not to say, however, that we could not be mistaken with respect to such judgements. Any credible relativistic picture will allow that we can be mistaken with regards to our own aesthetic standard just as we can be mistaken about what is delicious according to our own standards. I could mistakenly believe, for example, that strawberries are not delicious according to my standard if I have only ever eaten them immediately after brushing my teeth. Similarly I could be mistaken – even according to my own standards – if my judgements are too heavily influenced by order effects and the like (I assume that few relativists will want to defend a view according to which the order in which I view objects in anyway determines how beautiful they are according to my own sensibilities[54]).

Still, with respect to aesthetic judgements of this kind the new option which McGonigal introduces will frequently be a live option and under certain circumstances we may well be entitled to accept it and thus avoid the need for belief revision. How often this occurs will depend on a number of factors; the reliability of our aesthetic judgements concerning basic shapes, our evidence that others share our sensibilities and so forth. But it does – again assuming the relativistic picture is correct – legitimise some differences between our belief revision practice in aesthetics and our practice with respect to ordinary empirical matters.[55] Yet this result does not appear to fully capture the alleged phenomena. Kant, Hopkins and McGonigal all seem to endorse an unconditional version of NA according to which disagreement is never reason enough to revise one's aesthetic beliefs. Surely, though, there will be cases where such revisions would still be justified on the picture under consideration. Perhaps my belief only barely counts as knowledge such that even the slightest piece of counterevidence would render the belief illegitimate or perhaps I have very strong evidence based on our past judgements that my interlocutors and I share the same aesthetic sensibilities. As such McGonigal's picture cannot be taken to justify an unconditional version of NA. Perhaps, though, the NA

---

[54]   Although such a view could conceivably be proposed, perhaps paralleling the colour-relationist view in J. Cohen, 'Color Properties and Color Ascriptions: A Relationalist Manifesto', *The Philosophical Review* **113** (2004), 451–506.
[55]   Assuming we are not also relativists about e.g. colour.

advocate would be willing to make their position less ambitious and merely claim that (i) disagreement is much more rarely a legitimate basis for belief revision in aesthetics than with respect to ordinary empirical matters (ii) this disparity is explained by some principled difference (in this case whether the beliefs in question are relativistic) between the two domains. Such a position – particularly when combined with a sceptical attitude with respect to testimony in aesthetics - may well be enough to capture the spirit of NA with respect to aesthetic judgements of the kind under discussion here. Such judgements have not, however, been the focus of this paper nor of most extant discussions of NA. Rather these discussions have tended to focus on aesthetic judgements with respect to artworks, and it is to these which I will now turn.

4.3 Artworks and Experts

I have looked above at the prospects for NA with respect to certain simple cases such as aesthetic judgements concerning basic shapes and in many ways this sounds like the kind of case with which McGonigal is primarily concerned; focusing on a certain kind of beauty, talking about 'My being capable of taking a distinctive kind of pleasure in the perceptual appreciation of a given aesthetic object'[56] and drawing frequent analogies with judgements of deliciousness. Yet, many of the aesthetic judgements we make – particularly those concerning artworks on which I have focused above – are of a rather different kind and it is clear from some of the examples he uses that McGonigal intends his conclusions to apply to judgements of this kind also.[57] When it comes to considering such judgements, though, NA becomes significantly less plausible.

A film's being exquisitely plotted, well-acted or original has very little to do with dispositions or, at least, with dispositions of the straightforward kind which would make such judgements interestingly analogous to judgements of deliciousness. They may perhaps correspond to, or even be constituted by, the dispositions of idealised observers in rarefied circumstances, such as Hume's 'true judges' but seem, at most, loosely related to any distinctive kind of pleasure. Of course I am assuming here that we accept, as I think we should,[58] a

[56] McGonigal op. cit. 345.
[57] See e.g. Ibid., 340.
[58] For arguments to this effect see J. Shelley, 'The Problem of Non-perceptual Art', *British Journal of aesthetics* **43** (2003), 363–378.

rather liberal view of aesthetic properties according to which judgements of well-plotedness, originality and so forth are genuinely aesthetic but my argument in no way depends on making this assumption. A similar line of argument can be constructed with respect to those aesthetic properties of artworks which are often treated (incorrectly I believe) as being, in some sense, essentially perceptual; elegance, gracefulness, dumpiness, gaudiness and so forth. In many cases judging that a line of music is elegant, a painting gaudy or a dance graceful is not very closely analogous to judging a cheesecake to be delicious or a square to be attractive. To see why, consider some of the criteria highlighted by, amongst others, Kendall Walton concerning the proper conditions for perceiving aesthetic properties in a work. In order to adequately judge the aesthetic properties of an artwork (and even to perceive it correctly) we have to properly orientate the work with respects to the category to which it belongs, other artworks in that genre, its historical relations to events in the art world and so on.[59] How often do we non-experts really do this though? Not, I suspect, very often. In part because there are so very few art forms for which most of us have anything like the knowledge required to situate works in this way.[60] Given how rarely we are able to do this then – and even more rarely that we actually do do this – we will (even assuming a thoroughgoing relativism) rarely, if ever, be justified in retaining our aesthetic beliefs given disagreement from genuine experts who have employed such knowledge in making their aesthetic judgements.

Notice here the shift in focus. I have been assuming above that our interlocutors are our peers with respect to the judgements in question. Focusing on such cases simplified matters somewhat and allows for fruitful comparisons between the autonomy debate and the epistemological literature on peer disagreement but, of course, many of our disagreements in aesthetics (and elsewhere) are not with our peers. And with respect to such cases it is important to notice that we have an interesting tendency to maintain our aesthetic beliefs even in the face of disagreement from genuine experts (consider that favourite film or beloved author derided by the critics), how are we to explain this?

---

[59] See K. Walton, 'Categories of Art', *The Philosophical Review* **79** (1970), 334–367.

[60] Though we may, perhaps, do so a little more often with works of mass art of the kind discussed in N. Carroll, *A Philosophy of Mass Art* (Oxford: Oxford University Press, 1999).

Jon Robson

Consider two kinds of factor relevant to being an aesthetic expert with respect to particular complex artworks or genres of artwork.[61] First, an expert must have an impressive range of aesthetically relevant knowledge to draw from; knowledge of genres, of art history, of the contemporary artworld and of much more besides. Second, there are those elements of aesthetic character which contribute to an expert's ability to make appropriate judgements with the knowledge she possess; for instance those Hume attributes to his ideal critics such as strong sense, delicate sentiment and an absence of prejudice.[62] Minimally aesthetic judgements – such as those in the shape cases discussed above – in contrast seem to require only the second kind of expertise. As such persistent disagreements between us in these cases will very often be explained either by flaws in at least one of our aesthetic characters (yours of course), by some blameless divergence in sensibilities or some combination of the two. When it comes to the appreciation of artworks, though, the first kind of factor is often extremely important and far more so than we are pre-theoretically accustomed to thinking. Our reluctance to recognise the importance of such factors leads us to mistakenly treat all aesthetic debates as if they were essentially 'taste offs' which – coupled with our ubiquitous mistaken beliefs in the superiority of our own faculties – leads us to be unwilling to revise our aesthetic beliefs on the basis of expert disagreement. In combination these two errors account for our maintaining DA even in the face of disagreement with genuine experts concerning complex artworks; something which the sensibility account (at least in isolation) is unable to do.

This is not to claim, of course, that no aesthetic disagreement with respect to complex artworks can ever be explained by reference to differing sensibilities and the like (nor do I deny that this is the case, I find the relativistic sensibility picture quite attractive but I am not willing to unequivocally endorse it). It may be, for instance, that I regard a play as well-acted when an expert denies this not due to our considerable differences in theatrical knowledge, or even owing to their superior capabilities as an aesthetic judge, but because of difference in our sensibilities. Perhaps I have a sensibility according to which a certain style of acting should be praised as vibrant and expressive whereas she has one which condemns it as histrionic and unrealistic.[63] Still, to return to an earlier point, it seems unlikely that in any given case I will be able to establish that our disagreement

---

[61] The two are by no means intended to be exhaustive.
[62] See Kieran op. cit. for a discussion of such factors.
[63] I owe this point to Matthew Kieran.

finds its root in such factors rather than as a result of her superior aesthetic expertise. As such, disagreements of this kind will frequently serve as a defeater for my aesthetic beliefs even if they do not go so far as establishing that I ought to adopt the beliefs of my interlocutor.

It may be objected that this appeal to aesthetic experts is problematic given that there are no reliable (non-circular) methods for identifying such experts. The only way, the objector maintains, to establish whether someone is an expert in aesthetics would be to look at their track record of getting the right results concerning disputed aesthetic cases and the only way to do this is to use my own judgement. This need not, however, be the case. [64] There may be problems with establishing just who the genuine aesthetic experts are but there is no reason to think that this will not be possible without appealing to our own aesthetic judgements; just as I can (at least to some extent) establish who the experts in physics are despite my very limited knowledge of physics.[65] Of course there may be worries which need to be dealt with in identifying aesthetic experts which do not arise with respect to experts in physics; checking that the alleged expert possesses an appropriate Humean character for example. However, while assuaging such worries might complicate our search for aesthetic experts somewhat I see no reason to think that they create any in principle barrier to our identifying such experts.

4.4. Conclusions

I have argued above that the best explanation for DA is a debunking account which explains our refusal to revise our aesthetic beliefs by appeal to psychological – rather than normative – factors. McGonigal's alternative explanation for DA may justify a modest NA thesis with respect to disagreement concerning simple aesthetic judgements but it will not vindicate NA in cases involving complex

---

[64]   Though see S. Irvin, 'Forgery and the Corruption of Aesthetic Understanding', *Canadian Journal of Philosophy* **37** (2007), 283–304, 284 for reasons to think that such 'bootstrapping' methods may not be so problematic after all.
[65]   For some excellent general tips for a non-expert seeking to identify experts see A. I. Goldman, 'Experts: Which ones should you Trust?', *Philosophy and Phenomenological Research* **63** (2001), 85–110.

Jon Robson

artworks especially those in which a novice maintains her belief in the face of disagreement from genuine experts.[66]

University of Nottingham
jonvrobson@gmail.com

[66] Work on this paper was supported by a generous grant from the Arts and Humanities Research Council of the United Kingdom. Earlier versions of the paper were presented at the work in progress seminar at the University of Nottingham and the Centre for Aesthetics at the University of Leeds. I offer my thanks to the audiences at those meetings for useful feedback and special thanks to Carl Baker, Greg Currie, Matthew Kieran, Gerald Lang, Aaron Meskin and Margaret Moore.

The Verse-Line as a Whole Unit in Working Memory, Ease of Processing, and the Aesthetic Effects of Form

NIGEL FABB

1. Verse

Verse is text which is divided into lines.[1] In this paper I explore a psychological account of how verse is processed, and specifically the hypothesis that the text is processed line by line, such that each line is held as a whole sequence in the limited capacity of working memory. I will argue that because the line is processed in this way, certain low-level aesthetic effects are thereby produced, thus giving a partial explanation for why verse is often a highly valued type of verbal behaviour. The general goal is to address the question of what literary form is, from a psychological perspective, and how the textual presence and psychological processing of form can contribute to particular aspects of the aesthetic experience of verse.

This greater value can be seen for example in Shakespeare's *Henry IV Part 1*, where 'the scapegrace fun is in prose, but when Hal faces the outer world his different status calls for verse'.[2] Similarly, though in a very different context, McCreery describes a Chinese exorcism in which the magician Ong performs a healing ritual in which he speaks to the demons in prose and switches to syllable–counting verse when he speaks to the gods.[3] Turning to written Chinese literature, we find that the genre of *fu* mixes prose and verse, where verse is used in 'the more rhapsodic and emotionally

[1] Thanks to Alan Baddeley, Rip Cohen, Greg Currie, Graham Hitch, Jonathan Hope, Elspeth Jajdelska, Christian Obermeier, Sinead Rhodes, Gary Thoms, Barbara Tillmann, Stefano Versace, and two anonymous reviewers.
[2] A. R. Humphries, (ed.) *The First Part of King Henry IV. The Arden Edition of the Works of William Shakespeare* (London: Methuen, 1960).
[3] John L. McCreery, 'Negotiating with Demons: The Uses of Magical Language', *American Ethnologist* **22** (1995) 144–164.

doi:10.1017/S1358246114000186

Nigel Fabb

charged passages'.[4] It is not only metrical verse which is valued; thus Martin discusses a conversation amongst Mocho speakers in Chiapas Mexico which, when it touches on ritual topics relating to a potential volcanic eruption shifts into verse based on systematic parallelism.[5] Similarly, Forth says that the Rindi (Sumba, Indonesia) type of speaking which is organized into pairs of lines, based on parallelism, is called *bahasa dalam* 'deep, profound speech'.[6]

In this paper I address the question of why the division of a text into lines often correlates with its being assigned higher value, a question which I have elsewhere phrased as 'why is verse poetry?'.[7] In that paper I suggested that verse is composed line-by-line, and that since the line is not a linguistic constituent, this encourages the production of speech or writing in a way which bypasses ordinary semantically-driven and syntactically-driven processes of speech production, and that this has a range of aesthetic consequences. In the present paper, I focus on the role of working memory capacity in processing verse line-by-line. I point to psychological experiments which show that the forms of verse can produce effects of familiarity, truth and pleasure, and I suggest that these are particularly enabled by processing the text line by line, such that each line is processed as a whole unit in working memory capacity. Much of what I have to say in this paper is quite speculative; though it draws on experimental evidence, the experimental evidence produced so far is limited to a few traditions, and touches only a few parts of the great variety of verse in the literatures of the world.

[4]   Burton Watson, Chinese Rhyme–Prose. *Poems in the Fu Form from the Han and Six Dynasties Period* (New York: Columbia University Press, 1971).

[5]   Laura Martin, 'Parallelism and the spontaneous ritualization of ordinary talk: three Mocho friends discuss a volcano', in Kay Sammons and Joel Sherzer (eds.), *Translating Native Latin American Verbal Art: Ethnopoetics and Ethnography of Speaking.* (Washington: Smithsonian Institution Press, 2000) 104–124.

[6]   Gregory Forth 'Fashioned speech, full communication: aspects of eastern Sumbanese ritual language', in James J. Fox (ed.) *To speak in pairs. Essays on the ritual languages of Eastern Indonesia* (Cambridge: Cambridge University Press, 1988) 129–160.

[7]   Nigel Fabb, 'Why is verse poetry?', *PN Review* **36** (2009), 52–57. The philosophical question of the value of verse is also extensively discussed in Alex Neill 'Poetry' in Jerrold Levinson (ed.) *The Oxford Handbook of Aesthetics* (Oxford: OUP, 2003), though not with reference to the issues raised in the present paper.

The Verse-Line as a Whole Unit in Working Memory

A text divided into lines is a text divided into sub-sequences. There are many ways of dividing a text into sub-sequences, not all of which are verse: for example, written prose is in sub-sequences, divided by punctuation marks. In this paper, I focus on metrical and parallelistic verse. These are types of verse in which the sub-sequences which are lines are subject to generalizations, patterns which hold repeatedly over the lines. These generalizations are forms such as metre, rhyme, and systematic parallelism, which hold of the verse text, and which do not hold of prose.

Roman Jakobson makes a useful distinction between the verse design and verse instance of a text (abstracted away from perform-ance) as opposed to the delivery design and delivery instance of the text (the text as performed).[8] I will suggest that the line is a character-istic of the text at the level of verse design/instance, which may or may not be manifested in the text at the level of delivery design/ instance. This distinction is relevant for thinking about the psycho-logical status of the line: it means that at the relevant psychological level, the listener attends to the (abstract) verse design/instance and not on the actually heard delivery design/instance. To clarify the meaning of Jakobson's terms, consider the following four lines from Shakespeare's eighteenth sonnet.

Shall I compare thee to a Summer's day?
Thou art more lovely and more temperate:
Rough winds do shake the darling buds of May,
And Summer's lease hath all too short a date:

These four lines share the same verse design: they are all in iambic pen-tameter, a metre which specifies that the normative line should be ten syllables long and even-numbered syllables should be stressed and which also allows variations on this pattern. Each of the four lines is a different verse instance of that verse design, manifesting the metre in a different sequence of specific words, each word having an invariant stress pattern, which enables us to predict at least part of the overall stress pattern of each line and thus see how it varies from the iambic pentameter of the verse design. The verse design and verse instances for this text have in principle remained the same since the text was composed: verse design and instance do not vary, because they are abstract characteristics of the text, analogous to the linguistic forms of the text, which are not dependent on context of performance.

---

[8] Roman Jakobson, 'Closing Statement: Linguistics and Poetics.' In T. Sebeok, (ed.) *Style in Language*. (Cambridge MA: MIT Press, 1960). 350–377.

Nigel Fabb

In contrast, a text can be realized as any number of different delivery instances, which are the unique and actual manifestations of the text. For example, David Tennant has recorded a performance of these lines pausing in the following places and for the following times (shown in parentheses in tenths of a second):[9]

> Shall I compare thee to a Summer's day? [1.1]
> Thou art more lovely [0.1] and more temperate: [0.8]
> Rough winds do shake the darling buds of May, [0.6]
> And Summer's lease hath all too short a date: [0.8]

In actual performance, if we think of this as a sequence of lines, then this is a sequence of four delivery instances, with slightly different final pauses, and a pause midway through the second line (plus all the other surface features not transcribed here, including specific intonation contours). Another performance is likely to produce four different delivery instances for these four lines. The delivery design is the generalization over the delivery instances, which in this case may be a generalization that there is a pause of half a second or longer at the end of every line (which is not necessarily the case for every performance of this text). We can say that this text as delivered by Tennant is in lines; that is, that lineation is part of its delivery design. This is because there are pauses at the end of every line, and though there is also a pause midway through line 2 it is much shorter and thus clearly differentiated from the line-final pauses. But in principle performance can erase line boundaries, or break lines up, such that it is no longer clear that the text as performed is in lines. Lineation is thus an obligatory characteristic of the verse design/instance but only optionally a characteristic of the delivery design/instance. An originally verse text could be called 'de-lineated' in delivery if divided into sub-sequences which are no longer subject to the types of generalization which are characteristic of verse (essentially, repeated patterns).

When we hear spoken poetry, if lineation is not salient in the speech stream (e.g., by being marked by pauses), then lines will have a special status for working memory only if the hearer can abstract out the verse design/instance from the delivery instance. This leads to the important hypothesis that even when lineation is not salient in the speech stream, it may be extracted during processing. This may be similar to the way in which lexical and syntactic structure can be extracted from speech streams which provide no direct evidence of them: in processing language, the forms that we establish are not

---

[9]   On the CD, *From Shakespeare with Love*. (Naxos AudioBooks, 2009).

directly heard, and they can be unevidenced, partially evidenced or inconsistently evidenced, just like the discrete unit of the verse line in delivery.

2. The Varieties of Verse

Most of the psychological experimental work on verse has been on English, German or other European-language verse which is metrical in rather specific ways (based on syllable counting and stress) and has rhyme. In this section I illustrate two other types of verse, with the goal of illustrating the range of forms, all of which we would expect to be able to explain in a fundamentally similar way.

The first example comes from Classical Sanskrit, which includes many distinct metres, and had significant influence on metrical traditions in India and South-East Asia. Here is a four line stanza in the *sragdharā* metre:

sambhrāntadroṇam udyacchakunikalakalam vihvalolūkasārtham
sadyovikṣiptagulmam kṣapitanṛpataru kṣuṇṇapunnāgapūgam :
addhā nunnāśvakarṇam pramathitavipulaśrīphalam dhūtadhātrī-
cakram cakre saśokāspadam arigahanam prāg aśokābhirāmam.[10]

In this metre, every line must have twenty-one syllables. Syllables are differentiated by syllable weight, into heavy syllables (H) and light syllables (L); a light syllable consists of a short vowel separated by at most one consonant from the following vowel, and all other syllables are heavy. Every line has exactly the same pattern of heavy and light syllables: HHHHLHHLLLLLLHHLHHLHH. The seventh and fourteenth syllables normally come at the end of one of the words, or at a word boundary inside a compound word. This typical Classical Sanskrit metre reminds us how different metrical verse can be from the familiar English pattern. In English, the rhythm is based on stress and can vary from line to line while

[10] 'The garden of the enemy, formerly delightful with its Aśoka trees, he made a place of sorrow, its ravens frightened, with a confused noise of birds flying up, its flocks of owls terrified, in an instant its clumps of trees scattered, its royal trees smashed, its Punnāga trees and betel-nut trees broken, its Aśvakarṇa trees straightway overturned, its thick clumps of Bilva trees crushed, its ring of Myrobalan trees thrown down.' from Rāghavapāṇḍavīya by Kavirāja. This is one of two possible translations of the text, which throughout can always be read with two different meanings John Brough, *Selections from Classical Sanskrit Literature* (London: SOAS, 1978) p.136.

Nigel Fabb

maintaining a roughly periodic pattern (i.e., repeating a small rhythmic pattern throughout the line), but in contrast the Classical Sanskrit metre has an unvarying aperiodic rhythm (i.e., which does not repeat a small rhythmic pattern) based on syllable weight. Prose never has regular aperiodic rhythms of this kind; they are found only in verse.

The second example comes from a petition in the Rotinese language (spoken on the Island of Roti in the Indonesian archipelago).

Lena–lena ngala lemin	All you great ones
Lesi–lesi ngala lemin	All you superior ones
Sadi mafandendelek	Do remember this
Sadi masanenedak	Do bear this in mind:
Fo ana–ma tua fude	Save the froth of the cooking syrup for the orphans
Ma falu–ina beba langa la	And the heads of the palm leaf–stalks for the widows.[11]

The major type of form holding of these lines is systematic 'parallelism'. In parallelistic verse, pairs of lines have similar syntactic structures, usually with some variation in a specific word or phrase. The varying words can form a stereotyped pair called a 'dyad' which can have similar meanings as in the first and second line, or third and fourth line, or different but related meanings such as *ana* 'orphan' and *falu* 'widow' in the fifth and sixth line. The latter is an example of a dyad which has a combined meaning which is idiomatic; for example this pair has a combined meaning of 'the bereaved' of any gender or age. In the literatures of the world, parallelism is certainly found in prose: there are familiar examples in famous English language speeches. But systematic parallelism of this kind appears to be found only in verse, where there is independent evidence for the line as a division of the text, relative to which the parallelism is structured. (English does not have systematic parallelism of this type in verse. Though some poets such as Pope or Dryden use parallelism extensively, they do not use it regularly as a predictable form holding of the verse line.)

Verse is found even in the most ancient or isolated cultures. Some of the earliest preserved texts, in Sumerian, have lines 'laid out on the clay tablet exactly as in modern European poetry'.[12] The Suyá of

[11] From a petition by Old Meno, quoted in James J. Fox, (ed.) 1988. *To Speak in Pairs. Essays on the Ritual Languages of Eastern Indonesia* (Cambridge: Cambridge University Press, 1988), p. 167.
[12] Jeremy Black, *Reading Sumerian Poetry* (Ithaca: Cornell University Press, 1998).

Brazil have songs in lines organized by parallelism (like Rotinese).[13] Songs in Dyirbal (an Australian aboriginal language of the Queensland area) are organized into lines with fixed syllable counts and fixed stress patterns, in a metre which is strict and aperiodic like Classical Sanskrit but based on stress like English.[14] Ku Waru songs from the Western New Guinea highlands have songs in five-beat lines, each ending in an added vowel, and with extensive parallelism, thus combining both metre and parallelism in the same tradition.[15] The associated formal features of verse vary from culture to culture. The characteristic which connects them all is that the sequence of lines making up the text has some pattern, whether metrical or based on sound patterning or parallelism: that is, the texts are all characterized by what Jakobson called a verse design.

3. The Line is Treated as a Whole Unit in Working Memory Capacity

In this section I discuss evidence which suggests that the line is treated as a whole unit in working memory capacity. The hypothesis is that the sequence of words in the currently processed line, from the first word up to and including the last word in the line, are held all at one time in working memory, before moving on to the next line. The account of working memory used here is the model developed by Alan Baddeley and Graham Hitch over the past forty years, which is widely used in psychological research; I use the version described in Baddeley (2012).[16]

---

[13]   Anthony Seeger, 'Oratory Is Spoken, Myth Is Told, and Song Is Sung, But They Are All Music to My Ears', in Joel Sherzer and Greg Urban (eds.) *Native South American Discourse* (Berlin: Mouton de Gruyter, 1986) 59–82.

[14]   R. M. W. Dixon and Grace Koch, G. *Dyirbal Song Poetry: The Oral Literature of an Australian Rainforest People* (St Lucia: University of Queensland Press, 1996).

[15]   Alan Rumsey, 'A metrical system that defies description by ordinary means', in John Bowden and Nikolaus Himmelmann and Malcolm Ross (eds.) *A Journey through Austronesian and Papuan Linguistic and Cultural Space: Papers in Honour of Andrew K. Pawley* (Canberra: Pacific Linguistics, 2010).

[16]   A.D. Baddeley and G.J. Hitch, G.J., 'Working memory.' In *The Psychology of Learning and Motivation: Advances in Research and Theory*, (ed.) G A Bower, 47–89. (New York: Academic, 1984). Alan Baddeley,

Nigel Fabb

Working memory is the system which takes heard or read language as input, and from which meaning and other information is extracted into long term memory. The current model of working memory structures it into four parts: the phonological loop, the visuo-spatial sketchpad, the episodic buffer, and the central executive. The phonological loop takes as input phonological (spoken, heard) material – about as much as can be spoken in two seconds – and the visuo-spatial sketchpad takes as input visual material. Both of these components take sensory input as well taking input from long term memory (which is necessary in order to give form to the sensory input). The material from the phonological loop and visuo-spatial sketchpad are fed into the episodic buffer, which integrates material from different sources including from long term memory. The central executive is an attentional system which manages the holding and transfer of information between the component parts. The parts of particular interest for the argument of the present paper are the phonological loop and the episodic buffer.

The sounds of speech enter working memory via the phonological loop. The phonological loop is maintained by subvocalization: that is, the hearer 'speaks silently' to herself. About two seconds duration of subvocalized speech can be held at one time. However, the actual durations of spoken lines can in fact often be much longer than two seconds. For example, in the performance cited earlier of the first four lines of Shakespeare's sonnet 18, David Tennant produces lines with durations of 2.3, 2.4, 2.8 and 3.1 seconds.[17] When speech is heard, it can in principle be remembered faster than it is spoken: for example, the ten syllables of the sonnet's iambic pentameter line might be delivered at a tempo such that they take 2.3 seconds, but the same ten syllables could be held in the phonological loop by accelerated subvocalization, thus fitting them into the two second loop. Thus the timing of delivery and the timing of memorizing of lines would be partially desynchronized. It is thus not impossible

---

'Working Memory: Theories, Models, and Controversies.' *Annual Review of Psychology* **63** (2012), 1–29.

[17] In a corpus of recorded English poetry (54 poems), consisting of 1155 metrical lines: 59% of the lines are longer than 3 seconds, 40% are longer than 3.5 seconds, and 26% are longer than 4 seconds. See Nigel Fabb, 'There is no psychological limit on the duration of metrical lines in performance: against Turner and Pöppel', *International Journal of Literary Linguistics* (2013). This paper argues against a durational constraint on the line proposed by Frederick Turner and Ernst Pöppel, 'The Neural Lyre: Poetic Meter, the Brain, and Time', *Poetry* **142** (1983), 277–307.

that lines, most of which are longer in delivery than two seconds, could be held as wholes in the phonological loop. But there are several reasons for thinking that this is unlikely. First, it is phenomenologically alien: we certainly do not experience any accelerated sub-vocalization while we listen to verse. Second, as I will shortly discuss, we actually need to hold more than a single line in working memory in many cases, and this puts increasing strain on the very limited capacity of the phonological loop. Third, the phonological loop may not be complex enough in its operations to be able to process the line as a whole, e.g., establishing its metrical form.

Thus on present evidence we should conclude that the line cannot fit as a whole into the phonological loop. However, it could fit into the episodic buffer. This is the working memory component which takes information from the phonological loop, and other sources including long term memory. Information is combined from different sources, and bound into chunks or episodes, with about four or five chunks being held at any one time. The chunks can each contain several words if the words can be bound together (e.g., if they are syntactically related), with the result that 'memory span for unrelated words is around 5, increasing to 15 when the words make up a sentence'. Words in a line of poetry are usually syntactically related, and the upper limit of 15 words is much longer than almost any line of metrical poetry in any language.[18] Each of the four lines of Shakespeare's sonnet, quoted above, could clearly fit as a whole syntactically related sequence into the episodic buffer: at 8 words, 7 words, 9 words, 9 words, they will each individually fit into the episodic buffer limit of about 15 syntactically related words. An important point to note is that each line will fit into working memory with room to spare; some material from a preceding line could be kept as well.

The notion that the line is treated as a whole unit in working memory capacity (or an equivalent mental capacity in some other model) has been proposed by others. Thus Reuven Tsur argues that the line is a whole unit in 'short term memory'.[19] He draws on Gestalt theory to suggest that the line is a psychological whole against which variation is established. One of his arguments involves

---

[18]   Very few metres allow more than 15 syllables to the line, hence no more than 15 words. The major exception is the metres of Classical Sanskrit, as cited earlier; note however that the longest line quoted here is 21 syllables by metre, but only five and a half words long, because of the extremely long words of the language.

[19]   Reuven Tsur, *Poetic Rhythm: Structure And Performance. An Empirical Study In Cognitive Poetics* (Berne: Peter Lang, 1998).

iambic pentameter, an English language metre in which there is some allowed variation away from a regular even-beat binary rhythm. Tsur notes that the variation is more common in specific places in the line: for example, seventh position syllables in iambic pentameter lines are particularly likely to be stressed against the metrical expectation. Tsur comments 'In order to account for this uneven distribution of stress maxima in weak positions, one must assume that the line constitutes a *whole*, that is, a system that determines the character of its parts'.[20] Steven Willett has drawn on Tsur's proposal to argue that in Greek verse, the (multi-line) period is too long to fit into working memory, and hence that a smaller unit such as the line or colon must be the relevant memory unit.[21] Previous accounts of the line as a whole unit in working memory have however underestimated the capacity of working memory. Thus Tsur suggests that short term memory can contain 5–9 monosyllables at a time (i.e., what George Miller called 'the magic number seven plus or minus two'[22]), saying 'that is why the longest verse line that can be perceived as a rhythmic unit without an obligatory break is ten syllables long'.[23] Similarly Hogan (1997: 242) suggests that 'rehearsal memory' contains 'five to nine chunks of information – and thus, typically, five to nine words – at any given time' adding that 'standard line lengths for poetry in a wide range of traditions tend to fall between five and nine words'.[24] Tsur and Hogan thus treat the line as fitting rather tightly into working memory with little room to spare; I will shortly argue that this is incorrect.

I will now develop further evidence that the whole line might need to fit into the episodic buffer in working memory. The most straightforward evidence involves the forms which hold of lines, such as metre. We will later see evidence that the language of a line is more easily processed if it is structured by regular forms (such as metre) and that this produces low-level aesthetic effects; this gives some reason to think that the regular forms of lines, such as metre, are

[20] Op cit. note 19, p.33.
[21] Steven J. Willett, 'Working Memory and Its Constraints on Colometry', *Quaderni Urbinati di Cultura Classica. New Series* **71** (2002), 7–19.
[22] George A. Miller, 'The Magical Number Seven, Plus or Minus Two Some Limits on Our Capacity for Processing Information', *Psychological Review* **101** (1956) 343–352. Baddeley argues against this way of measuring capacity.
[23] Op cit. note 19, p.15.
[24] Patrick Colm Hogan, 'Literary Universals', *Poetics Today*, **18** (1997) 223–249. [p.242]

computed by hearers. Metre is a characteristic of a whole line. If the hearer is to compute the metrical form of the line, the whole line may need to be held in one place: a good candidate for this place is the episodic buffer. There is evidence from the formal analysis of metre that the line must be processed 'quantally' as a whole unit, rather than incrementally as the line proceeds. For example, many metres set a pattern which can be deviated from, with deviation more likely towards the beginning of the line, and less likely towards the metrically rigid end of the line. The conformity of any part of the line with the metre must therefore be assessed relative to where that part is placed in the line as a whole, meaning that the line as a whole must be taken into account in assessing the metricality of the parts: this is essentially Tsur's argument. The theory of metre which Morris Halle and I have developed is founded on the proposal that the line is processed metrically as a single whole unit and not in parts.[25]

Metre is not the only formal characteristic of verse which is best analyzed by processing lines as whole units in the episodic buffer. Dyadic parallelism of the type described for Roti is a characteristic of a pair of lines; in order for the hearer to recognize parallelism, it is necessary to hold the relevant information all in one place, which will often mean holding two whole lines at a time in the buffer. It is notable that in traditions with parallelism of this type, lines are often short and so in principle two lines at a time could be held in the buffer.

Now, consider rhyme. If rhyme is processed by holding the component parts in working memory capacity, then the first word in a rhyming pair must be retained while waiting for the second word to arrive. In some cases, rhymes can be many words apart, adding up to more words in sequence than can fit into the episodic buffer, so it cannot be that every word between the two rhyming words is recalled. Instead, it might be that the first rhyming word is held continuously (perhaps repeating it in the phonological loop) until the second rhyming word arrives, at which point they can be put together in the episodic buffer. This is again a situation where more than just the line must be retained in working memory capacity: in rhyming verse, the line plus a previous rhyming word must be retained. Sometimes more than one rhyming word from different rhymes must be held simultaneously, as in the intersecting rhymes of the Shakespeare sonnet. There is something to be learned here about the line. Rhyming words do not always have to be line-final; there

---

[25] Nigel Fabb and Morris Halle, *Meter in Poetry: A New Theory* (Cambridge, Cambridge University Press, 2008).

are traditions (including some Mediaeval Latin poetry) in which a mid-line word rhymes with a word at the end of the same line, and also traditions in which a final word rhymes with a word mid-way through a different line. Vietnamese six-eight metre offers an example of the latter. In this metre, odd-numbered lines are six syllables long and even-numbered lines eight syllables long; in addition, even-numbered syllables must carry specific tones: this is a tonal metre. The four lines below are two couplets from a long epic poem which is composed in continuous couplets.

Trăm năm trong cõi người ta,	6 syllables
chữ tài chừ mệnh khéo là ghét nhau.	8 syllables
Trải qua một cuộc bể-dâu,	6 syllables
những điều trông thấy mà đau-đớn lòng.[26]	8 syllables

The final syllable in the six-syllable line rhymes with the sixth syllable in the following eight-syllable line (*ta* to *là* and *dâu* to *đau*), and so is an example of a final-to-medial rhyme. In addition, the final syllable in the eight-syllable line rhymes with the final syllable in the following six-syllable line (*nhau* and *dâu*), which is an example of the more common final-to-final rhyme. What is interesting about examples of this kind is that the first rhyming word, the one which must be rehearsed in working memory, is always line-final. A medial word does not rhyme with a final word. This suggests that the word at the end of the line is particularly suited to being rehearsed; the preceding words in the line can be moved out of working memory and only this line-final word retained. This may explain why alliterating words (words beginning on the same consonant) must always be relatively close to one another while rhymes can be separated quite far apart. Because alliterating words cannot be line-final, they are not as easily rehearsed over a span of several lines.[27]

In sum, there are formal reasons to think that the whole line, and often all or part of a previous line must be held at the same time in the episodic buffer. I now explore evidence that the line has in some traditions acquired design features appropriate to its being

[26] 'A hundred years -- in this life span on earth / talent and destiny are apt to feud. / You must go through a play of ebb and flow / and watch such things as make you sick at heart.' Nguyễn Du *The tale of Kiều* lines 1–4. Discussed in Nigel Fabb, 'Formal interactions in poetic meter', in Tonya Kim Dewey and Frog (eds) *Versatility in Versification: Multidisciplinary Approaches to Metrics* (New York: Peter Lang, 2009) 147–165.

[27] Nigel Fabb, 'Verse Constituency and the Locality of Alliteration', *Lingua* **108** (1999) 223–245.

treated as a whole unit by working memory. This relates to the 'recency' effect in working memory, which is that more recently heard material is recalled more accurately than earlier heard material. If the line is treated as a single unit examined all at one time, once it is completely contained in working memory, then (all other things being equal) recall of the most recently heard line-final word might be easier than recall of an earlier heard line-medial word. Thus if our hypothesis is right, then the line should be asymmetrical as far as working memory is concerned. This may relate to the fact that lines show various formal asymmetries. For example, in metrical verse, the end tends to be more rhythmically regular. An example of this is found in the metre of Homer, the dactylic hexameter, where the first two thirds of the line can vary in their rhythm but where the final five syllables have a fixed heavy-light-light-heavy-heavy rhythm.[28] In traditions where there is rhyme, the end of the line is very often a rhyming word. Both final rhythmic regularity and final rhyme have the consequence of limiting the selection space for processing, and this would mean that processing effort is eased towards the end of the line. The 'selection space' is the set of items, e.g., words, which can be chosen to fill a particular slot. If a line must end on a word with a particular phonology because of rhythmic or rhyming expectations, the selection space is thereby reduced. If processing effort is eased towards the end of the line, this could allow processing effort to be redistributed to earlier in the line, thus making it easier to remember the earlier parts. Limiting the selection space at the end of the line thus enables the earlier part of the line to be better remembered. The evidence that the line is designed to be remembered as a whole is that the selection space is systematically restricted at the ends of line; hence this is evidence that the line is taken as a whole unit for working memory. Another example of a formal asymmetry within the line is in the Finnish *Kalevala*, where 'longer words tend to occur towards the end of the line and shorter ones at the beginning'.[29] This would be functional as a way of remembering longer sections of the line word–by–word; if the final word is longer, then more of the line is remembered by remembering just the final unit.

Tsur argues that iambic pentameter lines which have a significant degree of variation away from the basic pattern of stressing

[28] Complicated by the fact that the final syllable can substitute light for heavy ('anceps').
[29] Pentti Leino, *Language and Metre: Metrics and the Metrical System of Finnish* (Helsinki: Suomalaisen Kirjallisuuden Seura, 1986).

even-numbered syllables are performed in ways which articulate word boundaries more clearly: he suggests that the processing of linguistic form is eased by this clearer articulation, in order to compensate for the greater difficulty of processing the metrical form. We might however invert his proposal, to match it to my proposal in the previous paragraph. We could say that when the metrical form is unclear, it thereby fails to ease processing of the linguistic form, and so the linguistic form must be made easier to process by other means, such as clearer articulation. The difference made by my inversion of Tsur's proposal is that the goal of processing becomes always the extraction of linguistic form: metrical and other literary form is not extracted for its own sake, but only to ease the processing of linguistic form.

In this section I have suggested that the line is processed as a whole unit in the episodic buffer in working memory, and that in many cases additional material such as a previous line-final word, or sometimes the whole previous line, must be included at the same time. Unlike earlier proposals, I have suggested that in the Baddeley-Hitch account of working memory, there is sufficient capacity in the episodic buffer to hold this material. Does this have consequences for long term memory of verse (as opposed to prose)? Tillmann and Dowling have reported an experiment in which they show that unfamiliar lines can be recalled verbatim after a stretch of time (whereas similar sections of unfamiliar prose can not). This supports the idea that the line is a whole unit for working memory, since it is whole units which are remembered, but for present purposes it is particularly worth noting that in one of their experiments it is a whole rhyming couplet which is reported verbatim.[30] Long term memory for verse, specifically for oral narrative poetry, is the subject of a major work by David Rubin, who suggests various means by which the forms holding of verse enable memory for content and form.[31] (Rubin does not, however, treat the line as a crucial factor in memorizing verse; instead he allows smaller intonational units to be the remembered items; his approach does not directly engage with many of the issues discussed here.)

In the next section, I discuss some of the experimental evidence which shows that the forms added to verse are able to produce

---

[30]   Barbara Tillmann and W. Jay Dowling, 'Memory decreases for prose, but not for poetry', *Memory & Cognition* **35** (2007), 628–639.

[31]   David C. Rubin, *Memory in Oral Traditions. The Cognitive Psychology of Epic, Ballads, and Counting-out Rhymes* (New York: Oxford University Press, 1995).

effects of familiarity, truth and pleasure, and I consider the relation between this evidence and the possibility that the line is treated as a whole unit in working memory capacity.

4. Ease of Processing and Low Level Aesthetic Effects

In this section, I will summarize some reasons for thinking that the characteristic forms which hold of the line, including rhythm, sound patterning, and parallelism, may produce specific psychological effects, relating to familiarity, truth, and pleasure. I propose to call these 'shallow end' effects since they arise in in the early stages of processing the input, the stages at which the hearer is still identifying which words have been spoken. The shallow end effects and their relation to deeper effects which arise during inferencing are the topic of an interesting survey article by Reber, Schwarz and Winkielman on the ways in which processing fluency can stimulate aesthetic pleasure, published in 2004.[32]

The linguistic material which constitutes the verse text is processed by establishing its two types of form. Like all verbal input, processing determines the linguistic form of the text, identifying the words and their syntactic relations, and producing a meaning from the input. If this processing is made easier, an interesting result follows: the hearer experiences effects of familiarity, truth, and pleasure. This increased ease of processing of the linguistic material is enabled by the processing of the other type of form which holds specifically in verse: the identification of regular literary form in the text, including the metre, rhyme, parallelism, and so on.[33] Because these forms are regular, they enable the hearer to predict what will come next. For example, in a text in rhyming couplets, the second line in each pair

[32]   Rolf Reber, Norbert Schwarz, and Piotr Winkielman, 'Processing Fluency and Aesthetic Pleasure: Is Beauty in the Perceiver's Processing Experience?', *Personality and Social Psychology Review* **8** (2004) 364–382. More recent research in this area is reported in Christian Obermeier, Winfried Menninghaus, Martin von Koppenfels, Tim Raettig, Maren Schmidt-Kassow, Sascha Otterbein, Sonja Kotz. 'Aesthetic and Emotional Effects of Meter and Rhyme in Poetry', *Frontiers in Psychology* **4** (2013) 1–10.

[33]   There is a complex difference between the processing of linguistic form and the processing of literary form. Whereas the processing of linguistic form can depend entirely on covert linguistic processing, the processing of literary form must reflect overt convention: what counts as a rhyme for example can vary from tradition to tradition, and does not simply reflect the sound structure of the word.

must end in a word which rhymes with the final word of the previous line. Because literary form enables prediction, it thereby eases the processing of the text. The final word in the second line must be identified from the incoming speech stream, but when there is an expectation of rhyme the word to be identified is selected from a reduced set of possibilities (the set of words which rhyme with the final word of the preceding line), and so the task of identifying that word is simplified. The selection space for that part of the line is reduced by the presence of rhyme, thus easing processing. Similar consequences are known to follow once the hearer identifies the metre of the line, which reduces the selection space for words by limiting potential syllable counts or rhythms. I do not think there has been any experimental work on parallelistic verse, but I would predict parallelistic verse also to reduce the selection space, so easing processing.

Reber et al. show that there is experimental support for a correlation between easing a subject's processing of language (e.g., reducing processing time) and producing specific effects in the subject, including pleasure and a sense that the content of the text is familiar and true. Where the input is easier to process, there is a 'hedonic effect', where the subject both reports greater pleasure, and manifests this as activity in the region of the so-called 'smiling muscle' (the zygomaticus major, measured by facial electromyography). Subjects also interpret ease of processing as indicating that the content of the text is familiar, or is true. Thus for example McGlone and Tofighbakhsh showed experimentally that aphorisms which rhyme such as 'birds of a feather flock together' were in an experiment considered by subjects to be truer than aphorisms which do not rhyme such as 'rolling stones gather no moss'. McGlone and Tofighbakhsh attribute this differential attribution of truth to the greater ease of processing enabled by the rhyme.[34]

A sense of familiarity is also produced by ease of processing, even for inputs which are in fact not familiar. A person's sense that the information presented to them is familiar involves a feeling of knowing that they have encountered it before; it is distinct from recollection, which is the ability to recall it. Thus for example we may have a sense that we know someone because their face is familiar (familiarity) as opposed to being able to recall exactly who they are. Experiences of familiarity and recollection have different neural correlates, such that it is possible to test for the generation of

---

[34] Matthew S. McGlone and Jessica Tofighbakhsh. 'Birds of a Feather Flock Conjointly (?): Rhyme as Reason in Aphorisms', *Psychological Science* **11** (2000) 424–428.

familiarity versus recollection by using event–related potentials (ERPs).[35] Familiarity can be a 'false alarm' in the sense that we may have the sense that information is familiar when in fact it has not been previously presented to the subject. The particular relevance of this for our purposes is that one source of the psychological effect of familiarity is ease or fluency of processing, which Kelley and Jacoby call the 'fluency heuristic' as a basis for judgments of familiarity.[36] Familiarity feels different from recollection and so the effect of familiarity, which might be generated by verse, can be thought of both as an epistemic and an emotional effect. Effects of familiarity and truth are both part of the 'shallow-end' aesthetic experience of verse, produced in first stages of processing. There are reinforcing or consequential relations between familiarity and truth and pleasure. Thus for example a sense of familiarity can lead to a sense of truth: 'a statement will seem true if it expresses facts that feel familiar',[37] and familiarity can also lead to liking, such that the text is positively valued.[38]

Experimental investigations of how familiarity, truth and pleasure are produced by verse have all involved metrical verse. I now consider the possibility that similar results might be produced in non-metrical parallelistic verse (such as the Rotinese example quoted earlier), where parallelism is a device for framing a pair of words. Rhodes and Donaldson show that there are psychological differences between different kinds of pairs of words in ordinary language.[39] In one kind of pair, two semantically unrelated words form a commonly associated pair: the words 'traffic' and 'jam' form such a pair, in the common association of 'traffic-jam'. In another kind of pair, the

[35] Sinéad M. Rhodes and David I. Donaldson, 'Electrophysiological Evidence for the Effect of Interactive Imagery on Episodic Memory: Encouraging Familiarity for Non-Unitized Stimuli during Associative Recognition', *NeuroImage* **39** (2008) 873–884.

[36] Colleen M. Kelley and Larry L. Jacoby, 'Recollection and Familiarity: Process–Dissociation', in Endel Tulving and Fergus I. M. Craik. *The Oxford Handbook of Memory* (Oxford: Oxford University Press, 2000) 215–228.

[37] Ian Maynard Begg, Ann Anas, Suzanne Farinacci, 'Dissociation of Processes in Belief: Source Recollection, Statement Familiarity, and the Illusion of Truth' *Journal of Experimental Psychology: General* **121** (1992), 446–458.

[38] Hal R. Arkes, Catherine Hackett and Larry Boehm. 'The Generality of the Relation between Familiarity and Judged Validity', *Journal of Behavioral Decision Making* **2** (1989), 81–94.

[39] Op cit. note 35, 883.

words are related semantically but do not form a stereotyped pair: an example would be 'violin' and 'guitar'. Rhodes and Donaldson argue that associated word pairs such as 'traffic' and 'jam' are able to be 'unitized', a term that they use to describe the pair being treated as a unit by the language processor. Unitization enables faster retrieval of the words from memory and thus should produce the ease-of-processing effects described above. Furthermore, they argue that unitization appears to stimulate the effect of familiarity, manifested as the impression that we have seen *this* associated word pair before. This is true both for already-unitized pairs of words such as 'traffic-jam', but also for associated pairs of words which have not been previously seen before (and thus should not actually seem familiar) but which are put into contexts which encourage unitization (and just for this reason appear to be a familiar pair). Rhodes and Donaldson say for example that 'the creation of a sentence that combines two words could lead to a process of placing the two items in the same context, thus creating an association', and hence producing an effect that the association is already familiar.

Though Rhodes and Donaldson do not discuss verse, associated word pairs are very common in verse, and are the basis of many traditions of parallelistic verse. James J. Fox, in his discussion of Rotinese and other Austronesian parallelistic verse, uses the term 'dyad' to describe a pair of words which are characteristically associated and put into similar syntactic contexts in parallel lines. Similarly, the term 'difrasismo' is used by critics for associated word pairs in Mayan and other Central American verse.[40] I suggest that the dyad and the difrasismo are examples of what Rhodes and Donaldson call 'unitization' of an associated word pair. Unitization is a feature of ordinary language which is thus put to special use in parallelistic verse. Strong evidence for unitization of word-pairs in poetry is that in many cases, the pair has a combined meaning which is not derivable from the meaning of the parts. Thus the Nahuatl difrasismo combination *in xochitl in cuicatl*, literally 'flower and song' means 'poetry', while the Rotinese dyad combination of 'widows' and 'orphans' means 'the bereaved'. Though unitized word pairs can be found in prose, the organization of verse into lines is particularly suited to creating rigid contexts within which the pair of words can be inserted: the two lines have identical syntactic structures, differing only in the dyad. It is possible that by treating the line – or perhaps in

---

[40] The term was introduced for Nahuatl literature in K. Angel María Garibay, *Historia de la Literatura Náhuatl* (Mexico City: Porrúa, 1953–1954).

this case the line-pair – as a unit within working memory, the effect of the dyad is enhanced. I predict that we should find that dyads in parallelistic verse produce a range of effects: they should ease processing (with consequential effects), and should also give rise to the feeling that the dyad is familiar.

In this section I have reviewed experimental evidence which directly or indirectly suggests that the added forms of verse are able to produce three types of subjective or phenomenological effect, which can be mutually reinforcing: the effects of familiarity, truth and pleasure. I suggest that these might be thought of as low-level aesthetic effects, either hedonic or epistemic.

In this paper I have proposed that the metrical line – or in the case of parallelism, the line-pair – is held as a whole unit in working memory. Does this contribute to explaining how forms such as metre, parallelism and rhyme produce these low-level aesthetic effects? As one possible answer to this, we might note that though rhythm and sound patterning are found intermittently in prose, they are regular only in texts which are divided into lines. In part this may be for formal reasons: rhythm in language is dependent on counting, and counting requires starting and end points, which are supplied by line boundaries. Similarly, rhyme and alliteration may only be identifiable as regular if they are located relative to demarcated places within a text, which again are supplied by line boundaries. But these formal considerations may lead us to a functional explanation for the association of regular forms with the verse line, which is that these regular forms more effectively ease processing if they are processed relative to the line as a whole unit. I have suggested for example that rhyme requires rehearsal in working memory, and that the final word in a line is more available for rehearsal (once the rest of the line is removed from working memory) than other words. Thus the line boundary enables rhyme to function more effectively, which in turn eases processing, and produces side-effects of familiarity, truth and pleasure. This suggests that the line must be recognized as a bounded unit in processing, and this fits with the notion that the line is recognized as a whole unit when processing verse in the episodic buffer.

5. Inherent and Attributed Literary From, and the Conscious Awareness of Form

I have in other publications argued that literary form may hold of a text in two quite distinct ways, and have proposed a distinction

Nigel Fabb

between inherent form and attributed form.[41] The distinction
between the two kinds of form can be illustrated from ordinary language: a word like 'dog' is a noun in two different ways. On the one
hand, it is processed as a noun by the language processor, the word
being stored in the mental lexicon as a noun; this type of form is
part of the psychology of language, and is 'inherent form'. On the
other hand, a published grammar or dictionary may call the word a
'noun', which is an explicit attribution of a form to the word: this
is 'attributed form'. Inherent and attributed forms can align, as
they do here, and one of the tasks of grammarians is to 'carve language
at the joints': to align inherent and attributed form by discovering
what the inherent forms are, and bringing them to light by explicitly
attributing formal names to them. However, there are also attributed
forms which do not correspond to inherent forms. If we now turn to
literary forms, we might say that they usually exist as attributed
forms, in the sense that users are conscious of them, have names for
them and so on. Some types of literary form seem to hold only as
attributive form, with no corresponding inherent form, and I argue
that this is true of genre: genre names hold of texts only as attributions
and not as facts about the text.[42] However, it is possible that some literary forms exist also as inherent form, a possibility which is fundamental to much linguistic work on literary form, particularly on
metrical form. For the past forty years, generative linguistic approaches to metrics have sought to demonstrate that metrical forms
have much in common with inherent linguistic forms.[43] In the
terms of the present paper, we might say that inherent forms are
those forms which are produced or manipulated while the line is
being processed in working memory capacity. In contrast, attributed
forms are those forms which are assigned to the text as a result of inferencing about the text. A rhyme in a text can be both inherent and
attributed, processed first in working memory, and then explicitly
identified at a later stage as a characteristic of the text.

This has direct relevant to the fact that verse can be 'de-lineated'
in performance. If a verse text is performed such that it is no
longer possible to identify sub-sequences which are subject to the

[41] Nigel Fabb, *Language and Literary Structure: The Linguistic
Analysis of Form in Verse and Narrative.* (Cambridge: Cambridge
University Press 2002). In this book I use the term 'communicated form'
for what I here call 'attributed form'.
[42] Op cit. note 41, chapter 3.
[43] See for example Kristin Hanson and Paul Kiparsky, 'A Parametric
Theory of Poetic Meter', *Language* **72** (1996), 287–335.

generalizations characteristic of verse, then in this delivery it is technically no longer in lines, and thus by the definition of verse as 'text in lines' it is no longer verse. However, such a text can still be inferred as being 'in verse' and so the form of 'verse' can be attributed to it. For example, verse is characteristically performed in a different manner than prose: it is often performed more slowly, with a less varied intonation contour, various speech effects, various irregularly distributed rhythmic effects, and so on.[44] All of these elements of performance are clues that the text is verse, even if it is difficult or impossible to establish line boundaries. As noted earlier, there is an unexplored question how verse which is de-lineated is processed. We might look to linguistics for an answer: we know that hearers are able to extract linguistic form from spoken texts which do not display these forms on their surface. For example, the speech stream does not saliently indicate every word boundary, but words can still be reliably extracted from it. Lines are different from words, because unlike words, lines do not already exist in a stored memory; however, similar principles of establishing line boundaries, particularly when forms such as metre or parallelism hold of them, may still exist. This suggests that even when verse is performed in a way which blurs line boundaries, lines may still be extracted out as wholes for processing in working memory: this would mean that even when verse is de-lineated in performance, it might still have lines as inherent forms which are processed as such.

In summary, consider a performance of metrical verse in which lineation no longer exists in the speech stream, in the sense that the boundaries of the metrical lines are not signaled by pausing or any other effect. Such a text might still have 'verse' as an attributed form because of the way it is performed, in a manner which communicates that verse is being spoken (e.g., slower tempo, stylized intonation, etc.). And at the same time, the metrical lines may be extracted out and treated as wholes in the episodic buffer in working memory, perhaps below the level of consciousness (like inherent linguistic form): in this sense, the text is also in inherent lines. Thus it is inherently verse as well as being attributively verse, both despite its being performed in a manner which does not overtly mark the metrical line boundaries.

---

[44] Prudence P. Byers, 'A Formula for Poetic Intonation', *Poetics* **8** (1979), 367–380.

Nigel Fabb

Conclusion

In this paper I have proposed that the line of metrical or parallelistic verse is processed as a whole unit in working memory, and have shown that this is both feasible and necessary in order to explain the formal properties of the verse. One side-effect of treating the line as a whole unit for processing the forms of metre, rhyme and parallelism is to produce low-level aesthetic effects, and thus provide a partial explanation for why verse is often especially valued as a type of verbal behaviour. The processing of the text as in lines may proceed in this manner even for performances in which the text as delivered is not in clearly demarcated lines. This is an account of aesthetic form, and of aesthetic experience, which relies on experimental psychology, the psychological theory of working memory, and draws on generative approaches to linguistic (and literary-linguistic) form which allow form to be assigned to a text which on the surface provides no obvious evidence for it. This paper addresses the philosophical interest in cognitive aspects of aesthetic form and experience, drawing on new kinds of psychological evidence which have not previously been the topic of discussion in philosophical aesthetics.

University of Strathclyde
n.fabb@strath.ac.uk

Aesthetic Disgust?

JENEFER ROBINSON

Une Charogne
— *Charles Baudelaire*

Rappelez-vous l'objet que nous vîmes, mon âme,
Ce beau matin d'été si doux:
Au détour d'un sentier une charogne infâme
Sur un lit semé de cailloux,

Les jambes en l'air, comme une femme lubrique,
Brûlante et suant les poisons,
Ouvrait d'une façon nonchalante et cynique
Son ventre plein d'exhalaisons.

Le soleil rayonnait sur cette pourriture,
Comme afin de la cuire à point,
Et de rendre au centuple à la grande Nature
Tout ce qu'ensemble elle avait joint;

Et le ciel regardait la carcasse superbe
Comme une fleur s'épanouir.
La puanteur était si forte, que sur l'herbe
Vous crûtes vous évanouir.

Les mouches bourdonnaient sur ce ventre putride,
D'où sortaient de noirs bataillons
De larves, qui coulaient comme un épais liquide
Le long de ces vivants haillons.

Tout cela descendait, montait comme une vague
Ou s'élançait en pétillant;
On eût dit que le corps, enflé d'un souffle vague,
Vivait en se multipliant.

Et ce monde rendait une étrange musique,
Comme l'eau courante et le vent,
Ou le grain qu'un vanneur d'un mouvement rythmique
Agite et tourne dans son van.

doi:10.1017/S1358246114000253

Jenefer Robinson

Les formes s'effaçaient et n'étaient plus qu'un rêve,
Une ébauche lente à venir
Sur la toile oubliée, et que l'artiste achève
Seulement par le souvenir.

Derrière les rochers une chienne inquiète
Nous regardait d'un oeil fâché,
Epiant le moment de reprendre au squelette
Le morceau qu'elle avait lâché.

— Et pourtant vous serez semblable à cette ordure,
À cette horrible infection,
Etoile de mes yeux, soleil de ma nature,
Vous, mon ange et ma passion!

Oui! telle vous serez, ô la reine des grâces,
Apres les derniers sacrements,
Quand vous irez, sous l'herbe et les floraisons grasses,
Moisir parmi les ossements.

Alors, ô ma beauté! dites à la vermine
Qui vous mangera de baisers,
Que j'ai gardé la forme et l'essence divine
De mes amours décomposés!

A Carcass

My love, do you recall the object which we saw,
That fair, sweet, summer morn!
At a turn in the path a foul carcass
On a gravel strewn bed,

Its legs raised in the air, like a lustful woman,
Burning and dripping with poisons,
Displayed in a shameless, nonchalant way
Its belly, swollen with gases.

The sun shone down upon that putrescence,
As if to roast it to a turn,
And to give back a hundredfold to great Nature
The elements she had combined;

And the sky was watching that superb cadaver
Blossom like a flower.
So frightful was the stench that you believed
You'd faint away upon the grass.

The blow-flies were buzzing round that putrid belly,
From which came forth black battalions
Of maggots, which oozed out like a heavy liquid
All along those living tatters.

All this was descending and rising like a wave,
Or poured out with a crackling sound;
One would have said the body, swollen with a vague breath,
Lived by multiplication.

And this world gave forth singular music,
Like running water or the wind,
Or the grain that winnowers with a rhythmic motion
Shake in their winnowing baskets.

The forms disappeared and were no more than a dream,
A sketch that slowly falls
Upon the forgotten canvas, that the artist
Completes from memory alone.

Crouched behind the boulders, an anxious dog
Watched us with angry eye,
Waiting for the moment to take back from the carcass
The morsel [s]he had left.

— And yet you will be like this corruption,
Like this horrible infection,
Star of my eyes, sunlight of my being,
You, my angel and my passion!

Yes! thus will you be, queen of the Graces,
After the last sacraments,
When you go beneath grass and luxuriant flowers,
To molder among the bones of the dead.

Then, O my beauty! say to the worms who will
Devour you with kisses,
That I have kept the form and the divine essence
Of my decomposed love!

— William Aggeler, *The Flowers of Evil* (Fresno, CA: Academy Library
Guild, 1954)[1]

---

[1]   English translation by William Aggeler, used by permission of
Geoffrey Aggeler.

Jenefer Robinson

Introduction

In paragraph 48 of the *Critique of Judgment*, Immanuel Kant claimed that 'only one kind of ugliness cannot be represented in accordance with nature without destroying all aesthetic satisfaction, hence artistic beauty, namely that which arouses disgust.' However, from Baudelaire to Damien Hirst, there have been artists who delight in arousing disgust through their works, and many of these disgusting works, such as Baudelaire's *Une Charogne*, have high aesthetic merit.[2] In her splendid new book, *Savoring Disgust*, Carolyn Korsmeyer rejects Kant's suggestion and argues that there is something called 'aesthetic disgust,' that is, 'the arousal of disgust in an audience, a spectator, or a reader, under circumstances where that emotion both apprehends artistic properties and constitutes a component of appreciation.'[3]

Although Kant rejects the disgusting as too unpleasant to be a source of beauty, he acknowledges that the sublime depends upon displeasure, although ultimately it induces a kind of *respect* for the human rational faculty of free will.[4] Similarly, Edmund Burke wrote that 'the passion caused by the great and sublime in *nature*, when those causes operate most powerfully, is *Astonishment*,' which is 'that state of the soul, in which all its motions are suspended, with some degree of horror,' although the 'inferior effects' of the sublime are 'admiration, reverence and respect.'[5] These remarks by Kant and Burke suggest that there is a paradox of the sublime: the experience of the sublime includes respect and admiration but depends essentially on less pleasant emotions. Similarly, Hume identifies a paradox of tragedy, noting that 'it

---

[2]   Many thanks to Julien Zanetta at the University of Geneva for introducing me to this disgusting poem.

[3]   Carolyn Korsmeyer, *Savoring Disgust: The Foul and the Fair in Aesthetics* (Oxford University Press, 2011), p. 88.

[4]   Immanuel Kant, *Critique of the Power of Judgment* trans. Paul Guyer and Eric Matthews (Cambridge University Press, 2000), Paragraph 27, p. 141. In his introduction to the *Critique of the Power of Judgment,* Paul Guyer describes the 'displeasure' associated with the mathematical sublime as 'frustration at the inability of the understanding to grasp an absolute whole.' p. xxxi. With respect to the dynamical sublime it is displeasure at the realization of our 'insignificance in relation to' the 'vast forces in nature.' ibid.

[5]   Edmund Burke, *A Philosophical Enquiry into the Origin of Our Ideas of the Sublime and Beautiful* ed. J. T. Boulton (Prairie State Books, 1993), Part 2, section 1, p. 57.

seems an unaccountable pleasure, which the spectators of a well-written tragedy receive from sorrow, terror, anxiety, and other passions, that are in themselves disagreeable and uneasy,' adding that paradoxically 'the more [the spectators] are touched and affected, the more are they delighted with the spectacle.'[6] At a less exalted level, Noël Carroll has discussed the paradox of horror, why it is that people enjoy horror movies and novels despite – or even because of – their horrific content.[7] Korsmeyer christens these paradoxes 'paradoxes of aversion,' and she includes in this category a paradox of disgust.[8] After all, many people actively enjoy disgusting movies, photographs, paintings, sculptures, poems and so on. And even if most disgusting movies do not rise to the level of great art, there are paintings by Goya and Francis Bacon, poems by Baudelaire, and many contemporary artworks – films, photography and installation artworks – which do.

Traditionally the paradoxes of aversion have been articulated as paradoxes about aesthetic pleasure in, enjoyment of, or positive emotional reactions towards subject-matter that is fearsome or terrible (the sublime), deeply sorrowful – pitiable and frightening – (tragedy) or horrific (horror).[9] By analogy, the paradox of disgust can be expressed as the paradox that sometimes people take pleasure in or have a positive emotional experience of works of art that are disgusting.[10] In this paper, I will argue that, although the disgust that an artwork arouses is sometimes outweighed by some other more

---

[6]   David Hume, 'Of Tragedy' in Eileen John and Dominic Lopes eds., *Philosophy of Literature: Contemporary and Classic Readings* (Oxford: Blackwell, 2004), p. 25.

[7]   Noël Carroll, *The Philosophy of Horror, or Paradoxes of the Heart* (New York: Routledge, 1990) p. 10.

[8]   Sometimes Korsmeyer uses the phrase 'paradoxes of aversion' for all these paradoxes e.g. *Savoring Disgust* p. 40 and p. 72. Sometimes she confines its use to what I am calling 'the paradox of disgust' e.g. p. 11.

[9]   Notice that the appropriate response to all three includes varieties of fear. Burke defines the sublime as arousing fear. Tragedy, according to Aristotle, should arouse (a catharsis of) pity and fear. And, according to Carroll, 'art-horror' is a blend of fear and disgust. If we think of disgust as a special kind of fear – fear of contamination or fear of death and disintegration – then all the paradoxes of aversion involve fear. But, as we will see later, the mechanisms of disgust and fear are quite different.

[10]   This can also happen in ordinary life. See, for example, Matthew Kieran's discussion of gurning competitions in which the challenge is to 'pull the most distorted and ugly faces possible,' *Revealing Art*, (New York: Routledge, 2005), p. 85.

positive or pleasant emotion, to the extent that disgusting artworks are disgusting, they *cannot* be sources of pleasure, because the characteristic elicitors of disgust and feelings of disgust are deeply unpleasant. For the same reason, disgust cannot *convert* into an 'aesthetic attraction' or change its valence, as Korsmeyer claims. Furthermore, there is no special emotion of 'aesthetic disgust.' It's just that sometimes disgust, like other negative emotions, can be a source of insight, and thus indirectly contribute to aesthetic appreciation. *Une Charogne* is an excellent example, and I will conclude the paper with an analysis of this great but disgusting poem.

Implicit in my argument is the methodological claim that solving – or dissolving – the paradox of disgust requires not only (1) conceptual analysis of what the paradox is and critical assessment of the various suggested solutions to it, and (2) interpretation of specific disgusting artworks, but also (3) attention to the relevant empirical facts, in this case, facts about disgust. I therefore begin with a brief sketch of the science of disgust.

Disgust as a Basic Emotion

Disgust is widely agreed to be a *basic* emotion, an emotion common to all cultures, even though cultures differ greatly in how many and which non-basic emotions they recognize.[11] Certain emotions are thought to be *biologically* basic in that they develop in all normal functioning human beings. The psychologist Paul Ekman, following Darwin, describes basic emotions as pan-cultural emotions with distinctive facial and vocal expressions as well as distinctive action tendencies and physiology, which 'evolved for their adaptive value in dealing with fundamental life tasks,' such as losses (sadness), offenses (anger), and threats (fear).[12] Different cultures may regard different

---

[11] According to the main contemporary experts on disgust, Paul Rozin and his colleagues, 'disgust is on almost every list of basic emotions that has at least four emotions in it, from Darwin onwards.' Paul Rozin et al, 'Disgust,' in Michael Lewis and Jeannette Haviland-Jones eds., *Handbook of Emotions* 2nd edn., 2000 (London: Guilford), p. 638.

[12] Paul Ekman, 'An Argument for Basic Emotions,' *Cognition and Emotion* 6/3–4 (1992), p. 171. See also Ekman's *Emotions Revealed: Recognizing Faces and Feelings to Improve Communication and Emotional Life* (New York: Henry Holt, 2003), and Jesse Prinz, *Gut Reactions: A perceptual theory of emotion* (Oxford University Press, 2004), especially pp. 86–97, 110–115. The basic emotion approach has its critics. In particular, James Russell and Lisa Feldman-Barrett deny the existence of basic

specific things as losses but everyone responds to what they appraise as a loss in the same way: with the facial and vocal expressions and physiological symptoms characteristic of sadness. Ekman's defense of basic emotions originated in his discovery of pan-cultural facial expressions for certain emotions such as sadness, happiness, anger, fear, surprise, and ... disgust.[13]

Confirmation that disgust is biologically basic comes from those who lack a functioning disgust system and have characteristic neurological deficits. Huntingdon's disease affects the striatum, a region of the basal ganglia, and people with HD have been found to be impaired with respect to recognition of facial expressions of disgust. Moreover, if you have 'the HD mutation,' you have a disgust impairment even before any HD symptoms have emerged. Obsessive-compulsive disorder (OCD) and Tourette's Syndrome also show 'marked impairments in recognizing facial expressions of disgust' but people with Tourette's only show this impairment if they also have obsessive-compulsive symptoms. It seems that 'the presence of OCD' is 'a defining feature of the disgust deficit.'[14] As with some other emotions, losing one's ability to *recognize* disgust in other people's faces is correlated with the ability to *experience* disgust. Hence there seems to be a 'genuine emotion-specific deficit' for disgust.[15]

---

emotions and defend a 'dimensional' approach, according to which all emotions have dimensions such as valence and arousal, but specific emotions are 'configurations constructed on the fly out of more fundamental ingredients,' James Russell, 'Core Affect and the Psychological Construction of Emotion,' *Psychological Review* **110**/1 (2003), p. 167. Dimensional theorists tend to be impressed by the great number and variety of emotions in different cultures, whereas basic emotion theorists are more struck by the commonalities among emotions in different cultures and even among other animals. I do not have space here to adjudicate this dispute here. Suffice to say that the basic emotion approach is in my view for many reasons more plausible than its rivals.

[13]   Ekman's list of basic emotions has varied over the years, but he has consistently classified these six emotions as basic. It is probable that further basic emotions will be confirmed, especially if we consider criteria for basicness other than facial expression. Affiliation or love would be one plausible candidate.

[14]   Andrew Calder et al, 'The Neuropsychology of Fear and Loathing,' *Nature Reviews Neuroscience* **2** (2001), pp. 359.

[15]   Another of Ekman's proposed criteria for the basic emotions is that they are emotions that we share with other primates, or some other primates, or more generally with animals lower down the phylogenetic scale. This is more controversial with respect to disgust. There is evidence that both

Jenefer Robinson

Jesse Prinz argues that basic emotions are also *psychologically* basic in the sense that they contain 'no other emotions as parts,' or, more generally, are 'not *derived* from another emotion.'[16] Thus unlike anger, fear, and sadness, jealousy would appear to be psychologically non-basic in that it is constructed *out of* anger and/or sadness, and/or fear. Prinz thinks disgust is a psychologically basic emotion since 'there is no obvious account of how it might be built up from other affective states that are more basic.'[17] Furthermore, disgust can serve as a building block for other more complex emotions. Noël Carroll, for example, has identified *horror* with a mixture of disgust and fear.[18] Later we will see that in our culture disgust can also mix with positive emotions such as amusement, although it is not hard to conceive of cultures in which the disgusting would never be amusing.

Perhaps it might be objected that disgust is a variety of *fear* – since fear of *contamination* is often cited as at the root of disgust. However, Andrew Calder and his colleagues have shown that the neural circuitry for disgust and fear is significantly different.[19] So even if disgust is (from the point of view of 'conceptual analysis') a variety of fear, it is a distinct variety and uses distinct neural mechanisms. Whereas fear has been linked to the amygdala, the amygdala has rarely been reported as a neural correlate for

---

monkeys and small children (under the age of 3–4) experience and express distaste, as in aversion to a bitter or a sour taste, but that they do not recognize the full range of elicitors or exhibit the full range of physiological symptoms of mature human disgust. In *Yuck! The Nature and Moral Significance of Disgust* (MIT Press, 2011) Daniel Kelly argues that the reason why human disgust is peculiar to human beings is that in humans – unlike other species with only the 'distaste' mechanism – there is not one mechanism but two different ones which, as he puts it, have become 'entangled' over the course of evolution to produce modern human disgust. However, as I explain shortly, I find it more plausible that disgust probably originated as having a simple set of elicitors, shared by humans and other primates, but that in humans it evolved by expanding its elicitors, in the way characteristic of other emotions.

[16] Prinz, *Gut Reactions*, pp. 87–88.

[17] Jesse Prinz, 'Disgust as a Basic Emotion,' *Emotion Researcher*, 16/4 (2002), pp. 7–8. But Prinz does not agree entirely with Ekman's list of basic emotions.

[18] Carroll, *The Philosophy of Horror*, p. 28.

[19] Calder et al., 'Neuropsychology of Fear and Loathing,' *Nature Reviews Neuroscience* 2 (2001), pp. 352–363.

recognizing disgust expressions or for appraisals that something is disgusting.[20] However, all the fMRI imaging studies of people viewing disgust expressions have implicated the insula and the basal ganglia nuclei, especially the putamen and the pallidum. Interestingly, the anterior insulate cortex is sometimes referred to on independent grounds as the gustatory cortex, which is 'active in processing offensive tastes in both humans and other primates.'[21] Moreover, electrical stimulation of the insula in conscious human beings (who were undergoing surgery) produced 'sensations of nausea, unpleasant tastes and sensations in the stomach.'[22] Crudely put, because the neural mechanisms for fear and disgust are distinct, the emotions themselves are distinct, and disgust cannot contain fear as a 'part.' All the so-called 'negative emotions' are *aversions* of some kind or another, but there are different types of 'basic' aversion. As we will see, disgust is distinctive insofar as it focuses specifically on contaminants rather than other types of danger.

Analyzing Disgust

Emotions are processes, which are initiated by an 'appraisal' of the world that (1) presents some situation, event or person as vitally significant in some distinctive way to my survival and/or well-being or that of my 'group,' and that (2) instantly readies the person or animal to deal with the situation, event or person, as so appraised, in a fast and automatic way, by generating autonomic nervous system changes, hormonal changes, postures, gestures, and action tendencies. Specific facial and vocal expressions are also generated, which communicate the emotion to conspecifics and can sometimes alert them to the situation that caused it. (3) Emotions then typically motivate more reflective monitoring or 'regulation' of the emotion, including strategies for *coping* with the situation as appraised. Finally, (4) in human beings the physiological changes induced are often experienced as emotional feelings, which may provide further - conscious - information about the

---

[20]   But compare David Sander who identifies the amygdala as a general *relevance detector*. See David Sander et al, 'The Amygdala: An Evolved System for Relevance Detection' *Reviews in the Neurosciences* **14** (2003), pp. 303–316. But in this article disgust is not explicitly referenced.

[21]   Kelly, *Yuck!* p. 17.

[22]   Calder et al, 'Neuropsychology of Fear and Loathing,' p. 359.

Jenefer Robinson

situation.[23] Basic emotions, such as disgust, can be characterized in terms of relatively distinctive appraisals, action tendencies, physiological changes, expressions, and emotional feelings.

(1) The emotional appraisal of disgust

What is the 'fundamental life task' – what the psychologist Richard Lazarus calls the 'core relational theme' – that disgust evolved to deal with?[24] There is wide – although not universal – agreement that disgust evolved to begin with as a defense against eating poisonous food. Paul Rozin and his colleagues, borrowing from Darwin and from the psychoanalyst Andras Anygal, have identified what they call 'core disgust' as 'revulsion at the prospect of (oral) incorporation of an offensive object.' They then identify these 'offensive objects' as 'contaminants;' that is, 'if they even briefly contact an acceptable food, they tend to render that food unacceptable.'[25] The fear of *ingesting* a contaminant is clearly very powerful, witness some well-known experiments conducted by Rozin, in which, for example, people refuse to drink from a brand new bedpan or to drink milk in which a sterilized cockroach is gently floating. Both bedpans and cockroaches in their different ways come into contact with things that are among the most central cases of disgust: feces, urine, dirt and disease.[26]

It seems likely, however, that disgust does not always focus on 'oral incorporation,' or contamination via the mouth, but extends to smells and olfactory incorporation, as well as to the sense of touch. Robert Plutchik sees disgust as originating as a defense against

---

[23] I am here defining *episodes* of emotion, rather than long-standing traits or dispositions. See also *Deeper than Reason: Emotion and its Role in Literature, Music, and Art* (Oxford University Press, 2005), especially chs. 1–3, where I defend a similar account.

[24] Lazarus himself suggests that the universal theme for disgust is: 'Taking in or being too close to an indigestible object or idea (metaphorically speaking),' which is not very perspicuous. See Richard Lazarus, *Emotion and Adaptation* (Oxford University Press, 1991), p. 122.

[25] Paul Rozin et al, 'Disgust,' p. 637. In this passage they quote from Paul Rozin and April Fallon, 'A Perspective on Disgust' *Psychological Review* **94**/1 (1987), p. 23.

[26] Rozin et al, 'Operation of the Laws of Sympathetic Magic in Disgust and Other Domains,' *Journal of Personality and Social Psychology* **50**/4 (1986), pp. 703–712.

disease and infection, with *the skin* as its main medium.[27] Similarly, Judith Toronchuk and George Ellis observe that 'avoiding contact with infectious substances provides greater safety than merely avoiding ingestion.' They propose that 'touch, olfaction, and taste were all involved in the evolutionary development of the DISGUST system, as early aquatic vertebrates likely had, in common with many modern fish, widespread chemoreceptors on their body surface, an adaptation that allows not only avoidance of ingestion but even earlier avoidance of contact with infectious or noxious substances.'[28] In general, it is widely agreed that, although disgust may have originated as a distaste response, it then expanded to cover many other elicitors, so that today there is 'a qualitative difference' between distaste and disgust: they 'now constitute distinct psychological categories.'[29] Moreover, the way that, according to this story, a 'primitive' emotional response expands to take on more and different elicitors is typical of emotions in general, and not peculiar to disgust.

In earlier work Rozin and his colleagues focused on animals and meat as the elicitor category of core disgust, but more recently they have proposed that the fundamental elicitor of disgust is not food or animals but rather 'reminders of our animal vulnerability.'[30] Anything that reminds us of our 'fragile body envelopes' and the inevitability of death is a potential disgust elicitor: at heart disgust is 'a defense against a universal fear of death.' Disgust is the 'body and soul emotion:' insofar as humans behave like animals, 'the distinction between human and animals is blurred, and we see ourselves as

---

[27] Robert Plutchik, *Emotion: A Psychoevolutionary Synthesis* (New York: Harper and Row, 1980).

[28] Judith Toronchuk and George Ellis, 'Disgust: Sensory affect or primary emotional system?' *Cognition and Emotion* **21**/8 (2007), p. 1802. Toronchuk and Ellis cite Valerie Curtis and Adam Biran as arguing for the 'evolutionary origins [of disgust] in more general protection of organisms from infection' (ibid., 1801). This hypothesis is supported by a 'massive international survey that disgust is universally elicited by disease-salient contact stimuli such as bodily secretions, viscous substances, vermin, and sick or dirty people' (ibid., 1801). Likewise, in his discussion of disgust Steven Pinker comments that 'feces, carrion, and soft, wet animal parts are home to harmful microorganisms and ought to be kept outside the body.' *How the Mind Works* (New York: Norton, 1997) p. 382.

[29] Rozin et al, 'Disgust,' p. 639. Toronchuk and Ellis agree. See 'Disgust: Sensory affect or primary emotional system,' pp. 1800–1802. Compare Kelly, *Yuck!* who argues that disgust and distaste are distinct but became 'entangled' over the course of evolution.

[30] Rozin et al, 'Disgust,' p. 642.

lowered, debased, and (perhaps most critically) mortal.'[31] Dan Kelly christens this theory the 'terror management theory' of disgust.[32]

Paul Bloom rightly argues that Rozin's theory 'misses the physicality, the sensuality, of disgust.'[33] It is not death that's disgusting but rotting corpses. Likewise William Miller points out that the animals that disgust us do not disgust us because they are animals – lots of animals are not disgusting at all – but because they have characteristics that we find disgusting, such as sliminess. Disgusting animals remind us of the cycle of generation and decay, in other words *of life,* 'oozy, slimy, viscous, teeming, messy, uncanny life.'[34] For Miller 'the central themes of disgust elicitation [are] the eternal recurrence of viscous, teeming, swarming generation and the putrefaction and decay that attend it.'[35] In other words, Rozin may have been closer to the truth in his earlier work: the characteristic appraisal in disgust – its core relational theme – seems to be that something is *putrid* and *tainted, contaminated* and *contaminating.*[36] Confirmation for this view comes from the fact that *pan-cultural* elicitors for disgust include disintegrating corpses or carrion, 'violations of the body envelope' such as feces, blood, vomit, pus, oozing sores, spittle, snot, and so on, all potentially infectious, disease-carrying substances.[37]

[31] Ibid.

[32] Kelly, *Yuck!* p. 44.

[33] Paul Bloom, *Descartes' Baby* (London: Heinemann, 2004), p. 171. Korsmeyer (personal communication) points out that according to the 'the embodied appraisal' approach to disgust, 'this 'conceptual' recognition is achieved by means of the automatic reaction of the sensual response.' Rotting corpses are not only disgusting, but also 'viscerally-arousing signals of death.'

[34] William Miller, *The Anatomy of Disgust* (Harvard University Press, 1997), p. 50. *In Savoring Disgust* Korsmeyer defends a similar view: fundamentally what disgusts is death, but it is death appraised not as a mighty, awesome force but as the 'reduction – of [even] the noblest life to decaying organic matter in which all traces of individuality are obliterated' (134).

[35] Miller, *The Anatomy of Disgust*, p. 64.

[36] There is some dispute about the type of appraisal that sets off the emotion process. Many theorists (e.g. Robert C. Solomon and Martha Nussbaum) think that in human beings the appraisal is 'cognitive,' whereas others (e.g. Jesse Prinz and myself) think it is 'embodied' in some sense. I do not have space to discuss this issue here, but it is perhaps worth pointing out that disgust would seem to be a poster child for the 'embodied appraisal' theory, given the immediate, attention-grabbing, visceral way in which it registers its objects.

[37] Not all objects of disgust are *in fact* contaminating, just as not all objects of fear are in fact dangerous. Thus although cockroaches are bearers

(2) Disgust Responses

A typical expression of disgust includes 'the facial movements that precede or accompany retching, the behavior from which the expression is thought to derive.'[38] Darwin says that 'moderate disgust' can be expressed by the 'gape face': 'the mouth being widely opened, as if to let an offensive morsel drop out; by spitting, by blowing out of the protruded lips, or by a sound as of clearing the throat' (Ach or Agh). 'Extreme disgust is expressed by movements around the mouth identical to those preparatory to vomiting.'[39] And sometimes of course the extreme disgust reaction is simply to vomit. But a typical expression of disgust also includes a pronounced nose wrinkle, which suggests that disgust responds also to noxious smells.[40] Ekman thinks there are two distinct facial expressions for disgust, 'nose wrinkling and raised upper lip,' which often occur together: possibly the two expressions originated in disgusting tastes and smells respectively. Moreover, skin-crawling would seem to be a disgust reaction centered on touch.

As for autonomic responses, disgust, unlike sadness, fear or anger, produces a (slightly) lowered heart rate and shows other signs of parasympathetic activation 'which plays a broadly inhibitory role in the functioning of the organism.'[41] The disgust response is typically an immediate and visceral *withdrawal* reaction.

---

of disease, slugs are presumably no more contaminating than ladybugs, although far more disgusting. Moreover, human disgust often expands its elicitors to other people, who are thus appraised as dirty and contaminating, as violating purity norms. William Miller studies the way that disgust marks out social hierarchies: the low tend to be equated with the dirty and disgusting; after all they do the dirty and disgusting jobs. According to Martha Nussbaum, in her study of the horrendous events in Gujarat in 2002, interpersonal disgust is a typical accompaniment of genocide. Appraising other groups of people or individuals as 'disgusting' is a motivator to crush or exterminate them as one would a cockroach, which, incidentally, was the term of choice for the Hutu when describing the Tutsi during the 1994 Rwanda genocide. See her *Hiding from Humanity: Disgust, Shame, and the Law* (Princeton, NJ: Princeton University Press, 2004).

[38]   Kelly, *Yuck!* p. 16.

[39]   Charles Darwin, *The Expression of the Emotions in Man and Animals*, ed. Paul Ekman, Oxford University Press, 1998, p. 256.

[40]   Ekman, *Emotions Revealed*, p. 184.

[41]   Daniel Kelly, *Yuck!* p.16. See Robert Levenson on autonomic differences among emotions in Paul Ekman and Richard Davidson eds., *The Nature of Emotion* (Oxford University Press, 1994), esp. pp. 255–6.

Jenefer Robinson

(3) Monitoring the Disgust Response

The initial emotional appraisal of CONTAMINATED, although difficult to eliminate or moderate, at least in extreme cases, can, like other emotions, be regulated to some degree, but once disgust has become a bodily habit, it is very difficult to eradicate. Disgust has its coping strategies: if we are nauseated by something, we may need to focus our attention elsewhere or try to regestalt what we are seeing or smelling as something benign. However, the fact that this is so difficult to do may be why disgust is an especially recalcitrant emotion.

(4) Feelings of Disgust

Bodily feelings of disgust are visceral feelings of nausea (wanting to vomit or actually vomiting), and more or less violent feelings of withdrawal, of action tendencies to escape the noxious smells, tastes, sights and feels that have invaded one's senses, by expelling or eliminating their source. We wash our hands after inadvertently touching a slug, or tending someone's carbuncle. We throw up whatever tastes disgusting, and we move away as fast we can from disgusting smells. Jonathan Haidt writes that all disgust includes a motivation to 'avoid, expel, or otherwise break off contact with the offending entity, often coupled to a motivation to wash, purify, or otherwise remove residues of any physical contact that was made with the entity.'[42] This is clearly adaptive with respect to bacterial contamination of foods, but it is also a reaction to *moral* turpitude (for example, people react with disgust if asked to wear Hitler's – newly cleaned – sweater).

In general, disgust functions like other basic emotions, in that a simple and relatively stereotyped set of responses is elicited by a core relational theme, which I have identified as the 'contaminated and putrid,' with a universal elicitor being the cycle of life – of generation and decay – and in particular the decaying human body after death when consciousness and humanity have been eliminated. This core relational theme is then extended to other people, actions, and objects that are appraised as contaminating.

[42]   Jonathan Haidt, 'The Moral Emotions,' in Richard J. Davidson et al eds., *Handbook of Affective Sciences* (Oxford University Press, 2003), p. 857.

Proposed Solutions to the Paradox of Disgust

We have seen that the object of disgust is the contaminated and/or putrid and that the characteristic *feelings* of disgust include feelings of nausea, and/or of wanting to violently *withdraw from* the disgusting object. In view of this analysis of disgust, there certainly does seem to be a paradox of disgust: how can such an unpleasant emotion contribute in any way to pleasurable aesthetic experiences? Broadly speaking, there are four main species of suggested solution to the various paradoxes of aversion, which I will attempt to apply to the paradox of disgust. Like Korsmeyer, I believe that there is a great variety of disgusting artworks and no one-size-fits-all solution to the 'paradox of disgust.' Mere 'entertainments' such as gross-out movies, need to be treated differently from works of 'high' art, such as Baudelaire's poem, *Une Charogne*. However, some of the suggested solutions do not work well even for works of 'low' art.

(1) The 'Pleasurable Disgust' Solution

One suggested solution is that there is *a special kind of pleasurable disgust*. The idea that disgust can be pleasurable in the right circumstances takes at least three forms.

(i) 'Pleasurable disgust' might be disgust that is under our *control*. Marcia Eaton argues that 'we seek out tragedies (and other art works) in the belief that a *controlled experience* (my italics) will excite, enrich, purge and/or sensitize us in certain ways, and we take genuine pleasure in this experience.'[43] Similarly, perhaps, with respect to disgust: if we are engaged with a disgusting artwork, we are in control of our disgust and it is therefore not unpleasant: after all, it is up to us whether we continue to engage with the disgusting artwork or not.

This proposed solution seems to me to be a non-starter. First, the proposed solution does not explain why controlled disgust would bring positive pleasure rather than merely a lessening of the displeasure that disgust normally brings. It certainly does not explain why we

---

[43]   Marcia Eaton, 'A Strange Kind of Sadness,' *Journal of Aesthetics and Art Criticism* **41**/1 (1982), p. 60. Similarly, John Morreall has stressed that, like fear on a roller-coaster (for those who feel in control in such situations), fear of a monster in a horror movie can be pleasant because 'we retain overall control of the situation' insofar as we know it is only a fiction: we can 'snap out of it' if we so desire. John Morreall, 'Enjoying Negative Emotions in Fiction,' *Philosophy and Literature* **9**/1 (1985), p. 97.

would seek out disgusting art rather than art with a more benign subject-matter. Secondly, even when the disgust reaction is in our control, insofar as we can leave the movie or stop reading the poem whenever we like, as long as we are actually engaged with the movie or poem, and we are experiencing disgust, the experience is going to be, to that extent, an unpleasant one.

(ii) A second version of the *pleasurable disgust view* suggests that disgust can be pleasant when it is a special kind of *distanced* disgust. Edward Bullough famously described the 'aesthetic attitude' as the result of a psychological act of 'distancing:' when we are focused on the aesthetic aspects of a situation, we put ourselves 'out of gear' with the practical aspects of the situation and focus on its purely aesthetic qualities.[44] So perhaps when encountering a disgusting work of art or an artistic representation of something disgusting, we can distance ourselves from its practical implications so that we do not respond as we would in a disgusting real-life situation. But disgust is difficult, if not impossible, to 'put at a distance:' one can try to redirect one's attention, but if the disgusting taste or smell or sight or touch is salient enough, it will inevitably invade one's consciousness. George Dickie argues persuasively that the so-called act of 'distancing' is simply a matter of refocusing one's attention.[45] But when there is a stinking animal carcass in front of us in the road (or being vividly described to us by Baudelaire), it is hard, if not impossible, for most of us to simply ignore it.

(iii) A third version of the *pleasurable disgust view*, which has recently been revived by Nico Frijda and Louise Sundarajaran, holds that in aesthetic experience one experiences only a *refined* version of the emotions.[46] This often goes along with the idea that in aesthetic experience one savors the emotional (aesthetic) quality, such as the sadness of a piece of music, rather than reacting as one would to a genuinely sad situation in real life. But however plausible this view might be for sadness, it clearly will not do for disgust: savoring the disgusting – reveling in the disgusting smell or taste or touch –

---

[44]   Edward Bullough, 'Psychical Distance as a Factor in Art and an Aesthetic Principle,' reprinted in Morris Weitz ed. Problems in Aesthetics, 2nd edn. (London: Macmillan, 1970), pp. 782–92.
[45]   George Dickie, 'The Myth of the Aesthetic Attitude,' *American Philosophical Quarterly*, 1/1 (1964), pp. 56–65.
[46]   Nico Frijda and Louise Sundarajaran, 'Emotion Refinement: A theory inspired by Chinese Poetics,' *Perspectives on Psychological Science* 2/3 (2007), pp. 227–241.

seems to be possible only for those who enjoy the pleasures of deviance (such as, perhaps, Baudelaire).[47]

The 'pleasurable disgust' solution is highly implausible in all three versions. As we have seen, disgust is a basic emotion and its universal core relational theme is *contamination*. There is nothing pleasant about this. Likewise, the disgust *response* is to (tend to) vomit or spit up (something appraised as noxious), to purify ourselves, to close off the nostrils, and, in general, to refuse – with more or less violence – access by the noxious substance to any of our senses. The feelings of these visceral reactions are correspondingly unpleasant and seem to be designed to bring to conscious awareness first the visceral rejection response and second the presence of the noxious substance that caused it.

It seems to me that distancing, savoring, and controlling disgust are not *types of disgust* but rather potential modes of 'cognitive coping' with disgust.[48] As is the case with any emotion, we can try to 'distance' ourselves from the disgusting object or scene by focusing on other aspects of the situation, or we can try to control our response by 'regestalting' the situation if we can. But as a matter of fact, this is particularly difficult with respect to disgust. All emotions capture our attention, but disgust does so in a particularly visceral and unpleasant way. As for 'savoring disgust,' we could in theory try to change our focus from the disgusting object itself and onto its sensory properties, its look, smell, taste, or feel. But, again, this strategy will not work very well with respect to disgust, since disgust is primarily induced by smells, tastes, sights and feels.[49]

---

[47] The title of Korsmeyer's book is *Savoring Disgust*, and she suggests that we do savor the disgusting in certain foods, as when we notice the faint taste of urine in kidneys, but in her examples of this sort the disgust is always mild. As we will see later, she also argues that sometimes disgust *converts* into pleasure – and hence presumably can be savored. I will argue against this particular claim.

[48] This term is derived from Richard Lazarus who has identified several '*cognitive coping* strategies,' which do not actually change anything in the relationship between a person and his or her environment but instead 'change its *meaning*, and therefore the emotional reaction' (Lazarus, *Emotion and Adaptation*, p. 112). For example, 'if we successfully avoid thinking about a threat, the anxiety associated with it is postponed. And if we successfully deny that anything is wrong, there is no reason to experience the emotion appropriate to the particular threat or harm' (ibid.).

[49] Of course disgust responds not just to nasty smells, feels, and so on, but also e.g. to people who are appraised as having other 'disgusting'

Jenefer Robinson

(2) The Weighting View

One advantage of examining the nature of disgust before considering disgust in aesthetic contexts is that it allows us to rule out all the proffered solutions to the paradox of disgust that imply that somehow disgust itself can be pleasurable. The second type of solution, which I call *the weighting view*, is more successful, however, in that it does, I think, explain some instances of the paradox. This view recognizes that disgust is an unpleasant emotion, but it explains the paradox of disgust by saying that the unpleasant disgust reaction is *outweighed* by some other pleasant experience that the disgusting artwork affords. Loosely speaking, there are at least four versions of the weighting view. (i) Disgust can be outweighed by pleasure in the form or structure of a work; (ii) more generally, the disgusting quality of an artwork can be outweighed by some more enjoyable property that it also possesses; (iii) the disgust evoked by a work can be outweighed by the satisfaction we take in being the sort of person who can endure disgust; or (iv) the unpleasant emotion of disgust can be outweighed by a positive emotion that the artwork arouses, such as fascination or amusement.

(i) When writing about the paradox of tragedy, Hume suggests that we can take pleasure in the formal aspects of an artwork even if its subject matter is aversive: the 'force of imagination, the energy of expression, the power of numbers, the charms of imitation' are all, he says, 'of themselves delightful to the mind.'[50] Similarly, for Noël Carroll, the pleasure we get from a horror narrative is also in part pleasure in the structure of the narrative.[51]

Aristotle famously remarked that we can get pleasure from an artistic *representation* of an unpleasant object even if the object itself in real life would arouse an unpleasant reaction such as disgust. Presumably this is because we can take pleasure in how the subject matter is represented, even if the subject matter itself is disgusting. Thus, Géricault's paintings of severed heads can be enjoyed for their formal properties

---

qualities such as amputations or bodily disfigurements. Although such properties are clearly not contaminating, people with disfigurements are often, unfortunately, treated as though diseased and contagious.

[50] Hume, 'Of Tragedy,' p.27.

[51] But in *The Philosophy of Horror* Carroll emphasizes more the satisfaction of curiosity and the fascination we experience for the monsters in the horror fiction as the sources of our pleasure, which compensates for the disgust we feel for the monsters themselves.

and powerful expressiveness – the painterly style, the masterly use of color, and so on – despite their unpleasant subject matter. Korsmeyer, however, disputes this claim for disgust, arguing that disgust is 'transparent:' it automatically transfers from an object to a representation of the object.[52] Thus if we are disgusted by seeing severed heads, we will also be disgusted by seeing a clear and accurate picture of these same severed heads. Korsmeyer claims that the paradox of fiction can therefore not take hold with respect to disgusting works of art. There is no puzzle about why we react emotionally to a representation as well as to what it depicts, because both are disgusting. Even if it's 'only a picture,' the disgust response remains.

There is some truth to Korsmeyer's claim, insofar as a realistic representation of a disgusting object may well be nearly as disgusting as the object itself. But although Géricault's severed heads are relatively realistic, we can also appreciate Géricault's skill in representing them and the *style* and *expressiveness* of these paintings, qualities that severed heads in real life will normally lack. When we come to non-visual arts such as poetry, the point becomes even clearer: it is true that we are likely to be disgusted by the vivid poetic description of a carcass that we find in Baudelaire's 'Une Charogne.' But if are appreciating the poem aesthetically, we are also appreciating its formal mastery, which *outweighs* the disgust that the work also arouses. Even so, we might wonder whether the utilitarian calculus would not mandate that we engage only with formally pleasing works that are *not* disgusting.[53]

(ii) 'Gross-out' movies are not notable for their formal sophistication but they may have other positive properties that outweigh – for some audiences – their disgustingness. Movies in which young men vomit after over-indulging in booze and food, or the evil slimy Blob oozes over the world lingering lovingly in people's bodily crevices do not usually lay claim to great art status, and many are aesthetically nugatory. The whole point seems to be to elicit *shock* and *disgust*. But if the main emotion induced is repulsion and if there are few redeeming aesthetic features to compensate for the repulsion, why would anyone engage with such works?

---

[52] Following Aurel Kolnai, Korsmeyer claims that disgust 'can be induced by the presentation of qualities alone, regardless of whether one believes in the existence of the object possessing those qualities' (*Savoring Disgust*, p. 55).

[53] The Weighting View does not seem to have a good response to this objection, but later we will see that disgust in response to an artwork can be a means of insight, in a way that no non-disgusting artwork can provide.

Jenefer Robinson

One plausible suggestion is that popular disgust movies are enjoyable because *transgressive*, without being threatening: in the real world we do not like watching people throwing up, but in the safe movie context audiences can enjoy feeling free from social conventions. Such movies are usually trying to push the boundaries of what is socially acceptable. Disgust has been called the 'gatekeeper emotion,'[54] which serves to help uphold our norms of civilized behavior and our purity norms.[55] Table manners, for example, have been developed partly to keep disgust at bay.[56] Some people enjoy the spectacle of the socially transgressive, especially in a safe context where no transgression actually takes place. On the other hand, many people despise such movies. This is presumably because for those audiences such movies do not provide enough – or any – compensation for their disgustingness.

(iii) Susan Feagin has proposed that the pleasure we take in tragedy is a meta-pleasure, namely pleasure that we are the sorts of people who respond to tragic events in an appropriate way.[57] Similarly, we might take pleasure in a disgusting artwork because we are pleased to be the sorts of people who can tolerate or even enjoy the disgusting, and our feelings of self-satisfaction may outweigh and compensate for the disgusting experience of the artwork itself: the overall experience is pleasant *despite* the disgust we feel. One might doubt whether Feagin's view explains the attraction of great tragedy, but it surely does help to explain the appeal of the kind of disgusting movies I am currently discussing. The psychology seems to be that if I can sit through the disgusting scenes before me, I can take satisfaction in my emotional toughness. Disgusting movies test the boundaries of our tolerance, getting us to feel not only disgust but also curiosity about what our limits are for what is socially taboo. This is not unlike what Rozin has entitled 'benign masochism:' in a safe setting we prepare ourselves to meet disgusting situations in real life.[58]

---

[54] Susan Miller, *Disgust: The Gatekeeper Emotion* (Hillsdale NJ: Analytic Press, 2004).
[55] See also Mary Douglas, *Purity and Danger: An Analysis of the Concepts of Pollution and Taboo* (London: Routledge, 1966).
[56] See Shaun Nichols on etiquette books in 'On the genealogy of norms: A case for the role of emotion in cultural evolution,' *Philosophy of Science* **69** (2002), pp. 234–255.
[57] Susan Feagin, 'The Pleasures of Tragedy,' *American Philosophical Quarterly* **20**/1 (1983), pp. 75–84.
[58] See Bloom, *Descartes' Baby*, p. 182. I suspect too that it is a lot more fun to see these movies if you are in a group all of whose members are reacting in the same way: social solidarity – we in our group are capable of

(iv) Another variation on the weighting view suggests that disgusting artworks arouse not only disgust but some other more positive emotion (or emotions) which can outweigh the 'negative' emotion of disgust.[59] An enjoyment of transgression is probably part of the appeal of Damien Hirst's undeniably disgusting work 'A Thousand Years.' The work is disgusting in that it emphasizes a key elicitor of disgust, the cycle of life and decay described so vividly by William Miller. But this work also arouses *curiosity* and *fascination* in comprehending audiences. In a recent review of a Damien Hirst retrospective at the Tate Modern, Julian Bell describes this work which is a recreation of an original from 1990.

> [In] A Thousand Years, ... the insects are behind glass and anything but exotic: flies in their hundreds, trapped in a garage-sized vitrine with an interior box shelter in which their maggots hatch. On the floor lies their food, the head of a freshly killed cow. From the ceiling dangles their fate, the chill UV striplights of an insect-o-cutor, into which they are drawn and die. I stand outside watching the process, which is full of *strange fascination* (my italics): the sudden swarmings of the flies, the way their dead bodies accumulate, the winding puddle of blood that has welled from the cow's neck over the gallery's oak floor. I sense the closedness of the cycle—and for a moment I am inside there, with the flies, caught up in a kind of grisly living poem. Then a detail returns me to spectatorhood: the way the blood trail concludes with a tiny island drip, like the dot of an exclamation mark.[60]

Bell reports that he felt fascinated by the piece, and it sounds from his description that his fascination outweighed the disgust he also

---

enduring disgust – seems to be part of the appeal, like kids' enjoyment of fear-inducing daredevil games. (But I have no empirical proof of this.)

[59] (iv) and (ii) are clearly related. (ii) focuses on the disgusting properties of an artwork that can be outweighed by other positive properties. (iv) focuses on the emotion and emotional feelings of disgust experienced by an audience, which may be outweighed by a more positive emotion or emotional feelings. But (ii), which is a generalization of (i), is not confined to *emotional* properties.

[60] *Damien Hirst:* an exhibition at Tate Modern, London, April 4–September 9, 2012, reviewed in the *New York Review of Books*, Vol. 59, no. 9, May 24, 2012, by Julian Bell.

experienced.[61] In a different vein, Paul McCarthy's giant sculpture *Complex Shit* (2008) is simultaneously disgusting – this is a representation of a giant dog turd, after all – and *amusing*: the sculpture is inflatable and huge (as big as a house).[62] Here again we have a case where the weighting view seems plausible: our amusement at the giant inflatable turd may outweigh our disgust.

(3) The Integrationist View: The Disgusting as Amusing

Gary Iseminger has distinguished between two proposed solutions to the paradoxes of aversion. According to the 'Co-Existentialist View,' the 'feeling of pleasure with reference to distressful fictions is a case of one feeling's being strong enough to overcome the other.'[63] This is essentially what I have been calling the Weighting View. By contrast, according to the 'Integrationist View,' the very distress that we feel for 'the events [persons, situations, or objects] depicted' *contributes to* the pleasure we take in the [artwork].'[64] Iseminger's example is melodrama where (he claims) it sometimes happens that 'one is saddened by the events depicted and the very sadness contributes to the pleasure we take in the fiction.' By analogy, there might be cases in which 'when one derives pleasure from a [disgusting artwork], one is [disgusted] by the events [persons, situations, or objects] depicted, and the very [disgust] contributes to the pleasure we take in the artwork.'[65] Since I am interested in a broader range of 'positive' qualities and emotions than merely pleasure, I prefer a more inclusive version of the 'Integrationist View' with respect to disgust. Instead of restricting the response to pleasure, I suggest that the Integrationist View should be construed as the view that the disgust I experience when faced with a disgusting artwork 'contributes to' a *positive experience* of the work, where by 'positive' I

[61]   Similarly, Noël Carroll has emphasized how a disgusting and fearsome monster in a horror movie is nevertheless an object of intense curiosity and fascination.

[62]   It memorably escaped its moorings at an exhibition at the Paul Klee Center in Berne, Switzerland, in 2008, breaking windows and bringing down a power line!

[63]   Gary Iseminger, 'How Strange a Sadness,' *Journal of Aesthetics and Art Criticism* **42**/1 (1983), p. 191. The term 'Co-Existentialist' is unfortunate. What Iseminger seems to mean is that two feelings, pleasure and distress, *co-exist* in our reaction.

[64]   Ibid.

[65]   Ibid.

mean an experience that one would want to have, and once achieved, one would want to continue, other things being equal.[66]

To say that disgust can 'contribute' to pleasure or a positive experience, however, is very unclear. After all, if I am pleased by my tolerance for the disgusting (as in Feagin's solution), then the disgusting 'contributes to' my pleasure. But in such cases I am not responding positively to the disgusting artwork itself, but only to my own ability to tolerate it. I suspect that Iseminger's 'integrationist' view is more perspicuously described in relation to disgust as the view that sometimes when I have a positive experience of a disgusting artwork, what I enjoy is something about the *disgusting itself*. Consider, for example, enjoyment of the transgressiveness of a disgusting gross-out movie. What we enjoy (if we do) is not simply transgressiveness, but the transgressiveness of something disgusting, such as watching people vomit or defecate in public. In many popular disgusting movies our enjoyment (if any) is in the disgusting *appraised as transgressive*. The disgust is *integral* to the enjoyment because it is the contaminating and putrid – the object of disgust – which is appraised as enjoyably transgressive.

Similarly, where an artwork arouses the unpleasant emotion of disgust as well as some positive emotion such as fascination or amusement, sometimes the positive emotion is directed towards an object or event that is appraised as not simply amusing but amusing partly *because* it is also contaminating and putrid. In such cases the disgust is 'integral' to the experience in that what I enjoy is the fascination or humor *of* something disgusting. Not all amusing things are disgusting, of course, and not all disgusting things are amusing. It is only when I am amused by something disgusting *because* it is disgusting that disgust is 'integral' to my amusement. Interestingly, Nina Strohminger and her colleagues have found empirical evidence that in 'contexts where we are evaluating something for its humor,' disgust 'makes targets seem funny rather than revolting.' (Her example is masturbating with a chicken carcass.) As they put the point, 'disgust enhances the funniness of humor.'[67]

Strohminger and her colleagues claim that in such situations people *find disgust enjoyable*. But this cannot be right. As we saw in

[66] Compare Korsmeyer on pleasure: an 'aesthetic pleasure' should be reconstrued as 'an intense absorption in an object that induces us to continue rather than halt an experience,' *Savoring Disgust*, p. 124. See also footnote 83.
[67] Nina Strohminger et al, 'Disgust enhances the funniness of humor,' Manuscript under review, p. 6.

the discussion of the 'Pleasurable Disgust' solution to the paradox of disgust, people do not enjoy feeling disgusted. It is not *disgust* that people enjoy but *the disgusting*, and because the disgusting is unremittingly repulsive, it cannot be the disgusting *as such* that people enjoy but rather the disgusting object viewed as humorous or as fascinating or as having some other positive quality.[68] Similarly, when I feel thrilled or exalted by the sublime, I am not thrilled or exalted by the *terror* that I feel, but by the *terrible*.[69] The object of terror – such as the vastness and power of nature – is also the object of thrilled exaltation. The terror is *integral* to the thrilled exaltation because it is the terrible vastness and power of nature that is appraised as thrilling and exalting, and it is thrilling and exalting partly *because* it is terrible.

As we saw earlier, disgust is a basic emotion in the *psychological* as well as the biological sense, hence it is able to serve as a 'building block' for mixed emotions or blends of emotion. When an artwork is amusing partly *because* it is disgusting, it is reasonable to think that the appropriate response is a mixture of disgust and amusement. Something normally viewed as contaminating, such as an enormous turd facsimile, can be both disgusting and amusing, and amusing partly *because* disgusting. Similarly, in an experience of the sublime we feel mixed emotions of terror and admiration or reverence, and our admiration or reverence is directed towards the terrible. For example, the vastness and power of nature arouses terror and at the same time admiration or reverence for its 'terribleness.' In English we call this mixture of reverence and terror 'awe.'[70] There is no comparable term for a mix of amusement and disgust, but in our culture it is an instantly recognizable emotion. One can imagine, however, that some other cultures might find this mix of emotions very puzzling. Although disgust is a pan-cultural 'basic' emotion, this does not

[68] This is true for disgust in real life as well as disgust responses for artworks.

[69] This is a point emphasized to me by Alex Neill.

[70] Keltner and Haidt also emphasize (like Kant) how 'prototypical awe involves a challenge to or negation of mental structures when they fail to make sense of an experience of something vast.' Dacher Keltner and Jonathan Haidt, 'Approaching awe, a moral, spiritual, and aesthetic emotion,' *Cognition and Emotion* **17** (2003), p. 304. Some prefer to talk about emotion blends rather than mixed feelings of two or more emotions. I do not have space here to defend my preference for 'mixed feelings' over 'blends.' However, one problem with the idea of emotion blends is that the responses characteristic of each of the emotions in the 'emotion blend' may interfere with one another rather than blend. In mixed emotions, the two (or more) emotions may remain to some extent distinct.

mean that all cultures have the same *attitude towards* the emotion of disgust: indeed, the idea that the disgusting can be amusing might well seem bizarre even to some people in our own culture.

Strohminger suggests that perhaps 'emotions can have multiple appraisals which come more or less to the fore depending on context.'[71] Thus in mixed feelings of amusement and disgust, perhaps the appraisal characteristic of disgust (it's tainted and/or putrid) 'recedes' as the appraisal of humor comes 'to the fore.' (Presumably in someone who is not amused, the reverse would be true.) If this means that in responding to something that is both disgusting and amusing, the tainted quality of the object may be more or less salient than its amusing qualities, this seems very plausible.[72] Different aspects of an object can be more or less salient, and in a mix of disgust and amusement, the disgusting object can be appraised as more or less disgusting, and more or less amusing. However, in cases where we are amused by something partly *because* it is disgusting, the disgust response would seem to be primary in that it is a requirement for the amusement response.

Things are a little different with respect to disgust and fascination, however.[73] Whereas the disgusting is not always amusing, it seems as though the disgusting almost invariably has a fascinating aspect. However, the intentional objects of fascination and disgust seem to be inconsistent – being attractive and repulsive respectively – and the characteristic responses of fascination and disgust are also inconsistent – magnetic attraction versus more or less violent withdrawal. But although the 'attractive' is often identified with the pretty and endearing, some things attract us even though 'unattractive' in the usual sense.[74] Human beings seem perfectly capable of simultaneous attraction to and repulsion for the same object, such as Hirst's 'A Thousand Years'. Indeed, it seems as if we are fascinated partly *because* we are repelled. I suspect that in such cases the intentional objects of the emotions are subtly different. The actual set-up – the

[71] Strohminger et al, 'Disgust enhances the funniness of humor,' p. 6.

[72] Sometimes Strohminger seems to be saying that an appraisal of taint 'recedes' in the sense that it tends to vanish, but in amusing-but-disgusting artworks or real life situations, the appraisal of taint must be present alongside the appraisal of incongruity (or whatever).

[73] It might be questioned whether fascination is a bona fide emotion. However, it has the marks of one: it involves an appraisal of something perceived as very significant to me; it appears to have a characteristic response (attraction and fixation of attention) and expression (the gaze); and the initial appraisal can be monitored for appropriateness.

[74] Thanks to Alex Neill for this insight.

insects feeding on the cow's blood, their dead bodies lying around, and so on – is undeniably disgusting, but Hirst's clever dramatization of the inexorable cycle of death and decay is also fascinating: this is our own fate unfolding before us.[75]

The upshot of this discussion seems to be that the 'Integrationist View' is simply another version of the Weighting View, in which a positive emotion is directed towards a disgusting object, situation or event appraised as not only disgusting but also as having some more positive property *because* it is disgusting. Thus eating dog feces (orally incorporating what is viewed panculturally as highly contaminating) is a paradigm elicitor of disgust, but in the context of the famous scene in the John Waters film *Pink Flamingoes*, the very disgustingness of the situation may also elicit amusement. And sometimes – for some people – in such 'integrated' cases of mixed emotions, the positive emotion will over-ride the negative, although both are present.

(4) The 'Conversion' View

Hume claimed that in our experience of tragedy, not only are we delighted by formal qualities, but also the unpleasant emotions aroused (by the subject matter) are *converted* into pleasant ones: '... the uneasiness of the melancholy passions is not only overpowered and effaced by something stronger of an opposite kind; but the whole impulse of those passions is converted into pleasure, and swells the delight which the eloquence raises in us.'[76] By analogy, although disgust is unpleasant, in aesthetic contexts perhaps it can be *converted* into aesthetic pleasure.[77] In Hume's formulation, however, the conversion solution is highly implausible: disgust cannot 'convert' into pleasure without losing its character and ceasing to be disgust. Both the core relational theme for disgust and the disgust response with

---

[75] Compare Korsmeyer, *Savoring Disgust*, p. 24, where she writes that reflecting on the idea that all mortals will die and disintegrate inspires 'curiosity' and 'fascination.'

[76] Hume, 'Of Tragedy,' p. 26.

[77] Sometimes Strohminger writes as if she endorses this view, for example, when she says 'people find disgust enjoyable in certain contexts' as though sometimes disgust can somehow transform into pleasure. 'Disgust enhances the funniness of humor,' p. 1. Strohminger (personal communication) holds that 'you can change one dimension of an emotion (e.g. valence) while still retaining the other dimensions (e.g. a sense of yuckiness, beliefs about contamination).' I would question this assertion, at least for basic emotions.

its concomitant feelings are unremittingly unpleasant. At best a disgusting object can be appraised as fascinating or amusing or pleasurable *as well as* – and sometimes *because of* – being repellent, but if the object is disgusting, then, even if it has other more pleasant properties as well, the response to it will normally be, at least in part, deeply unpleasant.

Korsmeyer claims that 'aesthetic disgust,' which 'apprehends artistic properties and constitutes a component of appreciation,'[78] can be a 'component of recognition' of the *value* of an artwork, and 'a significant feature of aesthetic judgment.'[79] Here Korsmeyer rightly emphasizes that the *aesthetic value* of artworks outstrips pleasure, so that even if disgust is not pleasurable, it can have *aesthetic value* in art contexts. The traditional model for the paradoxes of aversion was set in the 18th century when both beauty and the sublime were held to produce different varieties of aesthetic *pleasure*. But today we recognize that pleasure is not the only value that the experience of works of art has to offer us. Even artworks that are not primarily designed to provide pleasure can have cognitive value, and for many contemporary thinkers, cognitive values are important *aesthetic* values. As Flint Schier has argued with respect to tragedy, we '*spontaneously* seek – without utilitarian forethought – experiences painful in themselves which we nonetheless value.'[80]

There is an important distinction between disgusting works that are designed primarily for pleasure or entertainment and disgusting works that are primarily aimed at *insight*, which is both a cognitive and an aesthetic value. Clearly most gross-out movies do not repay reflection, whereas the greatest works of disgusting art invite 'cognitive monitoring' of the disgust they arouse. Thus Aaron Ridley has stressed that we attend great tragedies even though they contain extremely painful events, such as the death of Cordelia or the blinding of Oedipus, because they raise deep and important issues which we find valuable to reflect upon.[81] What Ridley says about great tragedies applies equally to great disgusting artworks. They too raise

[78] Korsmeyer, *Savoring Disgust*, p. 88.
[79] Ibid., p. 89.
[80] Flint Schier, 'Tragedy and the Community of Sentiment,' in Eileen John and Dominic Lopes eds., *Philosophy of Literature: Contemporary and Classic Readings* (Oxford: Blackwell, 2004), p. 199.
[81] See Aaron Ridley, 'Tragedy' in Jerrold Levinson ed., *The Oxford Handbook of Aesthetics* (Oxford University Press, 2003), p. 419. For this reason he claims that it is absurd to think that the paradox of tragedy is in any way parallel to the 'paradox of horror.' For the importance of 'cognitive monitoring' of emotions in art contexts, see my *Deeper than Reason*.

deep questions about life and values that are important for us to reflect upon.[82]

Korsmeyer argues that 'in its more profound uses, at the root of the apprehension afforded by the arousal of disgust is recognition of the aspects of death that are the least heroic: stench and bodily disintegration presented with particular intimacy and nearness.'[83] She sees the basic elicitor of disgust as the decay and disintegration of organisms, especially ourselves, and she emphasizes the power of the insight that comes from a powerful visceral disgust response. There is a big difference between simply telling me that one day my body will disintegrate – something I surely already know – and presenting that insight in a poem such as *Une charogne* by eliciting a powerful disgust response. But notice that with respect to such cases of 'aesthetic disgust,' the paradox of disgust simply dissolves: there is nothing paradoxical about the fact that an unpleasant emotion can be a means towards knowledge or insight. In ordinary life, jealousy and grief, for example, can both lead to insights about what I truly value. And when artworks successfully try to instill insights by arousing unpleasant emotions, this *cognitive* value may be an important part of their *aesthetic* value.[84]

[82] Of course, it is not always clear to which category a particular work belongs. Thus Andres Serrano (author of the infamous 'Piss Christ') has recently completed a series of giant photographs of animal shit. They have such titles as 'Self-Portrait Shit' and 'Hieronymous Bosch Shit.' Such art can lay claim to being adventurous and transgressive, like gross-out movies, but no doubt the defenders of serious 'shit art' would claim that it also carries some more profound meaning ('a meditation on the corporeality of existence' perhaps), i.e., to invite not just an emotional response of shock and/or disgust but also reflection on the meaning of these reactions and what it is about the artwork that prompts such reactions. See Donald Kuspit, 'The Triumph of Shit' (2008) for a vigorous attack on the pretensions of such art. http://www.artnet.com/magazineus/features/kuspit/kuspit9-11-08.asp

[83] Korsmeyer, *Savoring Disgust*, p. 127.

[84] Korsmeyer says that the 'disgust remains aversive' (130) but 'the knowledge gained by means of it affords enjoyment' (130). She argues that aesthetic 'pleasure' or enjoyment is best identified with 'what absorbs attention in artworks' (118), and tries in this way to link pleasure to the cognitive value of artworks. But, as Mitchell Green pointed out in his comments on Korsmeyer's book at the *American Philosophical Association* Pacific Division meetings in Seattle, April 2012, this account of enjoyment requires qualification: one can enjoy chewing gum even though it is not a very absorbing activity.

Korsmeyer, however, wants to go further, suggesting that in some cases of great art, 'what is ordinarily an aversion sometimes may *convert* in affective tenor to an aesthetic attraction.'[85] She proposes a new aesthetic category, the sublate, which is designed to parallel the sublime.

> As a rule, aesthetic emotions (i.e., those that constitute appreciative arousal) are varieties of everyday emotions: anxiety, sorrow, dread, anticipation, happiness, and so forth, although they may alter in their aesthetic form from the ordinary variety.... With certain emotions, however, aesthetic transformation is so profound that an entirely new affective experience is brought into being.[86]

According to Korsmeyer, in the experience of the *sublime*, terror is 'transmogrified into powerful and transportive aesthetic delight,' the recognition of 'might, magnificence, and the ineffable endlessness of the cosmos.'[87] Analogously, in the *sublate*, disgust is *converted* into 'insight,' specifically the insight that even 'the noblest life' will be reduced to 'decaying organic matter in which all traces of individuality are obliterated.'[88] When disgust 'converts' to the sublate, it grasps insights about mortality and putrefaction 'with palpable somatic resonance.'[89] The sublate is the contrary of the sublime: rather than exalting the spirit (or the rational will), it rubs our noses in the fact that we will all one day be eaten by worms.

The experience of the sublime, however, is not a matter of a 'negative' emotion, terror, *converting* into a positive emotion, admiration or reverence. Rather, the very same object is appraised as both terrible and admirable, and as admirable partly *because* terrible. This explanation avoids the Humean difficulty of explaining how a negative emotion can 'convert' into a positive. But Korsmeyer's account of the sublate is subtly different from her account of the sublime: in the sublate disgust is converted not into another (positive) emotion but into *insight*. How does the Conversion Account fare on this new interpretation?

---

[85]   Korsmeyer, *Savoring Disgust*, p. 130.
[86]   Ibid. p. 131.
[87]   Ibid. p. 133.
[88]   Ibid. p. 134.
[89]   Ibid.

Jenefer Robinson

Aesthetic Disgust?

According to Korsmeyer, an experience of the sublate 'gives rise to an apprehension ... of an idea that is so embedded in affective response to the work that provokes it as to be virtually inseparable.'[90] Just as, she thinks, the sublime converts terror into admiration and respect, so the 'sublate' converts disgust into an intensely satisfying experience of 'insight in a bodily, visceral response.'[91] Disgust is converted into 'an aesthetically significant quality [the sublate] that has an emotive tone all its own.'[92] However, fear (in the experience of the sublime) and disgust (in the experience of the sublate) do not lose their nature altogether 'in the process of aesthetic conversion,' such that 'in their aesthetic form they are no longer members of those classes of emotion.'[93] What changes is the *valence* of disgust.

> What is converted is not the emotion itself but its valence; the insight it affords by means of the particular artistry with which it is delivered is central to its aesthetic import and value.[94]

Korsmeyer's book contains a treasure-trove of insights about the nature of disgust and the many different ways it can operate in our responses to works of art, but there are a number of reasons for denying that there is a special aesthetic category of the 'sublate' as she describes it. While she is correct to point out that a disgust reaction to a work of art may well be a source of insight, it does not follow that disgust can ever 'change its valence' in an aesthetic context while still remaining disgust. As I have emphasized throughout this paper, disgust is a basic emotion. The valence of the disgust appraisal is negative not only insofar as the core relational theme for disgust is highly disagreeable (the tainted and putrid), but also because the disgust response and the bodily feelings of that response are also highly disagreeable. Disgust 'converted' into a positive emotion is no longer disgust. More importantly, in order to give us the kind of insight Korsmeyer identifies, it is essential that disgust remains itself, the basic emotion I described earlier. Korsmeyer is right that we get insight in a peculiarly immediate and visceral way through

90   Ibid.
91   Ibid. p. 131.
92   Ibid. p. 139.
93   Ibid. p. 132.
94   Ibid. p. 139. In this quotation we seem to be back with the 'pleasurable disgust' solution to the paradox of disgust.

experiencing disgust, but the insight, if any, depends essentially on the experience of disgust. If the experience were not so unpleasant, we could not receive the relevant insight.

Korsmeyer is at pains throughout her book to emphasize that 'aesthetic disgust' comes in many varieties: 'it can be funny, pathetic, contemptible, sympathetic, and uneasy:'[95] 'aesthetic emotions are individuated not just by characteristic traits of a type of object but also by specific artworks.'[96] But this way of putting things is misleading on two counts. First, as I have commented before, *disgust* is not funny or contemptible or pathetic or whatever; it's *the disgusting* which can be characterized in these ways, not disgust itself. Because disgust is a basic emotion, the feelings (*qualia*) that result from an experience of disgust are relatively fixed, and when Korsmeyer claims that the *qualia* of disgust vary from one disgusting artwork to another, I think what she is drawing attention to is rather the subtle mixtures of emotions that artworks can arouse, in which disgust is but one element. Thus some artworks are horrific, terrifying and disgusting, whereas others are disgusting and amusing or disgusting and pathetic. Artworks educate us sentimentally partly by enlarging our repertoires of emotional states.

Secondly, the whole idea of 'aesthetic disgust' as a special sort of disgust, that which 'apprehends artistic properties and constitutes a component of appreciation'[97] seems to me misleading. There is no special aesthetic type of disgust; disgust is the same emotion whether elicited by ordinary life or by art. And like any other emotion – positive or negative – it can sometimes provide illumination, again both in life and in art. The visceral spasm that teaches me what human mortality really means can be caused by seeing a carcass in the road or by Baudelaire's poem about a carcass. Of course there are differences between disgust in life and in fiction. Perhaps the main difference is that Baudelaire can control our response in a way that situations in life cannot, so that we likely learn a more nuanced truth from his poem than from seeing actual roadkill.[98] By the same token, there is no special aesthetic category of the sublate in which somehow aesthetic disgust is converted into insight. Joy, sorrow, pity, anger, anxiety can all be aroused in artworks in such a way as to provide insight, but there is no reason to

[95] Ibid. p. 98.
[96] Ibid. p. 101.
[97] Ibid. p. 88.
[98] See my *Deeper than Reason*, e.g. chs. 6 and 7.

think that there is a special aesthetic category for each of these emotions.[99]

Of course, as with other emotions, we need to monitor what our bodily reactions are 'telling' us, in order to ensure that our disgust reactions are appropriate. As in life, disgust in art can be used to manipulate us in ways that can be morally questionable. In some fiction, for example, the mutilated, the disabled, and people with different bodily types or eating habits from ourselves are presented as not only disgusting but evil, and evil *because* disgusting.[100] In *Deeper than Reason* I argued that the greatest artworks among those that set out to arouse emotions, do not *merely* arouse emotions: they encourage their audiences to *monitor* their emotional responses *cognitively*. In other words, we are not only encouraged to experience powerful emotional reactions of disgust (say) but also given sophisticated guidance by the creator of the work in how to reflect on the emotions we are experiencing, whether they are justified or not, and what it is about the work that has made us react in this way.[101] In this respect there is nothing special about the way artworks can give us insight via the arousal of disgust: *all* emotions are potentially able to enlighten us about ourselves and/or the world in which we live, and *all* emotions can play a role in aesthetic understanding. Nevertheless, Korsmeyer is quite right to emphasize that because disgust is such a visceral emotion, it can deliver its insights in a particularly powerful, bodily way.

Baudelaire's 'Une Charogne'

I conclude by showing how Baudelaire's 'Une charogne' ('A Carcass') from *Les Fleurs du Mal* illustrates in a condensed form the two most promising solutions to the paradox of disgust: (1) the Weighting Solution in one of its various forms, including the 'integrationist' version; and (2) the idea that disgust can provide insight, which,

[99] Although certain genres can be defined in part by the emotions they aim to elicit. See e.g. Noël Carroll, 'Film, Emotion and Genre' in Carl Plantinga and Greg M. Smith eds., *Passionate Views: Film, Cognition and Emotion* (Baltimore: John Hopkins University Press, 1999), and my 'Sentimentality in Life and Literature' in Kathleen Higgins and David Sherman eds. *Passion, Death, and Spirituality: the Philosophy of Robert C. Solomon* (New York: Springer, 2012), pp. 67–89.

[100] Frankenstein's monster, for example. See Colin McGinn, *Ethics, Evil, and Fiction* (Oxford University Press, 1997).

[101] This is a theme that runs through my *Deeper than Reason*.

even if unpleasant to contemplate, is nevertheless an important cognitive value of art.

Baudelaire's poem is undeniably disgusting, yet so beautifully structured that we can take pleasure in its formal aspects even if we recoil from its content. The form of the poem is masterly: Baudelaire uses a familiar trope – the poet who will immortalize his beloved after her death – but instead of the elegiac tone one expects, the tone is bitterly ironic. The imagery, as always in Baudelaire, is vivid and often shocking: the legs of the carcass are thrust into the air like 'une femme lubrique;' flies buzz around the 'putrid belly' of the carcass from which come 'de noirs bataillons / De larves, qui coulaient comme un épais liquide / Le long de ces vivants haillons;' as for these worms that have invaded the corpse, 'on eût dit que le corps, enflé d'un soufflé vague, / Vivait en se multipliant.' And at the end of the description of the carcass, a grisly detail: a dog is waiting behind a rock for the lovers to go by so that she can recapture the morsel she had to let drop when the lovers appeared. The poem is structurally tight-knit with an a-b-a-b rhyme scheme – as well as many examples of half-rhymes – that help to convey the meaning of the poem with maximum economy. Thus, the beloved – 'Mon âme' is immediately in the first stanza linked to the 'charogne infâme' as well as – less obviously – to the 'beau matin' which is about to be disrupted. Later the poet exclaims that the beloved, 'soleil de ma nature,' will one day be 'semblable à cette ordure, and 'mon ange et ma passion' will be reduced to an 'infection.'

The poem is also deliberately transgressive. Baudelaire, well-known as a 'bad boy' of literature, invites us to enjoy the transgressive aspects of the poem even as we are disgusted by it. And perhaps we will be pleased with ourselves for enduring the disgust we feel in order to appreciate a modernist masterwork. Moreover, the emotions that the poem invites are not restricted to simple disgust. I think that the poem is also in a grim way *amusing* in the way that Baudelaire juxtaposes the image of the beloved's beauty with the disgusting decaying corpse on the ground, full of multiplying larvae. Indeed we are amused partly *by* the disgusting images that Baudelaire has conjured. He has turned the typical love poem upside down: instead of lamenting the passing of beauty, he seems to take a grim, ironic satisfaction in its eventual decay. And the final lines – 'Tell the vermin who will eat you up with kisses that I have preserved the form and divine essence of my decomposed loves!' – is amusing because the sentiment is so *un*romantic, and so unlike what de Musset or Lamartine might have made of this scenario. Is there also a hint of tenderness here, in the emphasis on the concrete details of the beloved's corporeal

Jenefer Robinson

disintegration by contrast with her present blooming beauty? We know that Baudelaire fluctuated between affection and contempt for Jeanne Duval, about whom the poem was written, and the final lines seem to me to encompass both these feelings.

Although amusing in a bitter way, the poem is not designed primarily to amuse, however, like some more trivial works of disgusting art. Rather it is a vivid expression of a complex emotional mixture of feelings of love and tenderness on the one hand, and disgust and a kind of bitter, half amused, half contemptuous satisfaction on the other. Baudelaire does not lament the fact that only his verses will survive to preserve 'la forme et l'essence divine / De mes amours décomposés' but seems to take an almost vindictive pride in this fact. And he seems to want to arouse in his readers a complex mixture of emotions in which disgust, shock and grim amusement are perhaps the most salient.[102] Most importantly, however, these emotions alert us to what the poem is expressing and help us to understand the tone and the 'message' of the poem. The disgust we feel provides aesthetic *insight*.[103] The poem teaches us in a visceral and shocking way about a very unromantic view of love. The beloved is not an ideal; her beautiful body will disintegrate and rot, and the worms will devour her. And love itself is not an ideal, but is governed by 'the eternal recurrence of viscous, teeming, swarming generation and the putrefaction and decay that attend it.'[104] Faced with this visceral insight into love as part of a disgusting cycle of life and decay, it is inappropriate to take an elegiac tone. For Baudelaire, all it is appropriate to feel is bitter amusement and contemptuous disgust. And with this insight, Baudelaire also signals the arrival of a new poetic sensibility. The visceral spasm of disgust the poem arouses in comprehending readers also alerts us to the fact that Modernism has arrived and that Romanticism is itself decomposing and will soon be fit only for the worms![105]

University of Cincinnati
robinsjm@ucmail.uc.edu

[102] As well as admiration for Baudelaire's poetic powers.
[103] Presumably, for Korsmeyer this would be an example of the 'sublate.'
[104] Miller, *The Anatomy of Disgust*, p. 64.
[105] Many thanks to Matthew Kieran, Carolyn Korsmeyer, Aaron Meskin, and Alex Neill for interesting and helpful comments on an earlier draft of this paper. Thanks also to the Charles Phelps Taft Research Center which partially supported this research.

The Development of Imaginative Cognition[1]

DEENA SKOLNICK WEISBERG

Introduction

Over the last ten years or so, many cognitive scientists have begun to work on topics traditionally associated with philosophical aesthetics, such as issues about the objectivity of aesthetic judgments and the nature of aesthetic experience. An increasingly interdisciplinary turn within philosophy has started to take advantage of these connections, to the benefit of all. But one area that has been somewhat overlooked in this new dialogue is developmental psychology, which treats questions about whether and to what extent children's intuitions about various aspects of aesthetic experience match those of adults, as well as the origins and developmental trajectories of these intuitions. The current paper reviews some recent work in developmental psychology that has the potential to inform philosophical research on a variety of topics – not necessarily because of this work tells us directly about what children think, but because learning what children's aesthetic intuitions are and how they develop can help us to better understand why adults have the intuitions that they do.

For example, consider the paradoxes of tragedy and horror: Why do we as adults enjoy fictions that make us feel sad, horrified, or even disgusted? One possibility is that these preferences are the result of cultural pressure or the output of a highly developed aesthetic sense. A different possibility is that we are attracted to these kinds of aesthetic experiences even as children. This latter option would suggest that the existence of these paradoxes result from some basic facts about how our aesthetic preferences work. Some suggestive recent work indicates that this might in fact be the case, since even

[1] The author would like to thank the organizers and attendees of the 2012 AHRC workshop on "Method in Philosophical Aesthetics: The Challenge from the Sciences" for their insightful comments and questions. Thanks also to Paul Bloom, Joshua Goodstein, Alison Gopnik, Alan Leslie, David Sobel, Lu Wang, and Michael Weisberg for their support of the projects reported in this paper.

doi:10.1017/S1358246114000289

Deena Skolnick Weisberg

6-year-olds report liking scary and sad stories[2]. This is just one example of how empirical data about development can help to inform debates within the field of aesthetics.

This paper provides another, more extended, example of how recent empirical findings in developmental psychology can inform issues in philosophical aesthetics. The topic under consideration is that of how the imagination works. How is it that we are able to interact with stories and scenarios that do not reflect the truth of reality, and that we know to be fictional in this way? What is the nature of this cognitive capacity early in development? More importantly, how can knowing these origins inform our understanding of the ways in which this capacity changes (or remains the same) over the course of development? Answering these questions can provide fresh insight into two philosophical topics: how people decide which propositions hold true in fictional worlds, and under what circumstances people experience imaginative resistance. After reviewing recent empirical work that bears on these topics, this paper closes with some thoughts about the role that imaginative cognition plays in development.

What is imaginative cognition?

Roughly speaking, there are two kinds of cognitive acts: those that are aimed at reality, and those that are not. Into the former category fall those processes that help us to navigate the real world, such as our perceptual abilities. Into the latter category fall those processes that allow us to think about scenarios that do not necessarily reflect the truth of the real world, of which imagination is the primary example.

It is important to note that this distinction is based on what goal is currently driving the cognitive act, rather than on an actual categorical distinction between different types of cognitive processes. To see why this is the case, consider that most of our cognitive processes can be used for both types of act. For instance, we form memories of both real events and of events that we have merely imagined, and we draw inferences about events that happen in reality and events that happen in a fictional story using basically the same cognitive apparatus[3].

---

[2]   L. Guillot & P. Bloom 'Are children interested in negative stories?' Poster presented at the biennial meeting of the Cognitive Development Society (2011).

[3]   This is known as the "single code theory." See F. M. Bosco, O. Friedman, & A. M. Leslie, 'Recognition of pretend and real actions in

86

The Development of Imaginative Cognition

Even still, there is a class of cognitive abilities that seem to be designed to operate without taking into account whether the scenarios they consider are true or false in the real world. This is sometimes described as the contrast between believing and pretending[4], although this class encompasses far more activities than just pretending. We can not only pretend, we can also create thought experiments, or suppose for the sake of argument, or tell a fictional stories, or envision a future possibility. All of these abilities are deployed for different reasons and have their own unique features. But what they have in common is precisely the fact that they can operate independently of what we take to be true. This kernel of commonality is the *imagination* – the ability to engage with entities and events that are not real. Given its role in this wide variety of cognitive tasks, it is clear that the imagination is a ubiquitous tool we use for understanding and interacting with the world around us. Being able to imagine what could possibly happen in the future can help us to plan and make decisions, and being able to consider an alternative past can help us to understand why things happened the way they did[5].

In considering the imaginative capacities of young children, pretending and comprehending fictional stories are the two imagination-based abilities that are studied most often, since these are the abilities with which children are most explicitly familiar. Hence the conclusions that are drawn from this research apply most directly to these kinds of representations. But because the same underlying cognitive mechanism – the imagination – is responsible not only for pretending and story creating, but also for all of the other activities

---

play by 1- and 2-year-olds: Early success and why they fail,' *Cognitive Development*, **21** (2006), 3–10; T. S. Gendler & K. Kovakovich, 'Genuine rational fictional emotions,' in M. Kieran (Ed.), *Contemporary debates in aesthetics and the philosophy of art* (Oxford: Blackwell, 2005); S. Nichols, 'Imagining and believing: The promise of a single code,' *The Journal of Aesthetics and Art Criticism*, **62** (2004), 129–139.

[4]   A. M. Leslie, 'Pretense and representation: The origins of "Theory of Mind,"' *Psychological Review*, **94** (1987), 412–422; S. Nichols & S. P. Stich, *Mindreading: An integrated account of pretense, self-awareness, and understanding other minds* (New York: Oxford University Press, 2003).

[5]   A. Gopnik, C. Glymour, D. M. Sobel, L. E. Schulz, T. Kushnir, & D. Danks, 'A theory of causal learning in children: Causal maps and Bayes nets,' *Psychological Review*, **111** (2004), 3–32; D. Lewis, 'Causation,' *Journal of Philosophy*, **70** (1973), 556–567; D. S. Weisberg & A. Gopnik, 'Pretense, counterfactuals, and Bayesian causal models: Why what is not real really matters,' *Cognitive Science*, **37** (2013), 1368–1381.

Deena Skolnick Weisberg

mentioned above, discovering how children respond to pretend scenarios and fictional stories can shed light on this wider class of representational activities.

What's the difference between reality and fiction?

One of the first questions we must ask when considering how young children cognize and respond to imagined scenarios is whether they understand that these scenarios are indeed imagined. If a child fails to understand that the events in a story have not actually happened in real life, he or she cannot really be said to be *imagining* the story[6].

Luckily, several decades of diligent work in developmental psychology have discovered that children do make a robust reality/fiction distinction[7]. Most of these studies use explicit response measures to draw this conclusion, for example, by asking children to label pictures as "real" or "make-believe," or by asking children to sort pictures into different boxes that represent the two categories. These studies rely on the fact that children understand and properly use words like "make-believe" or "fictional"[8]. Some recent work has begun to rely on more spontaneous or implicit measures of children's understanding, which has permitted the field to test children's understanding of the nature of the reality/fiction distinction at younger and younger ages. In one of these

[6] See J. Piaget, *Play, dreams and imitation in childhood* (New York: Norton, 1962).

[7] For example, A. Bourchier & A. Davis, 'Children's understanding of the pretence-reality distinction: A review of current theory and evidence,' *Developmental Science*, **5** (2002), 397–413; C. Golomb & R. Kuersten, 'On the transition from pretense play to reality: What are the rules of the game?' *British Journal of Developmental Psychology*, **14** (1996), 203–217; A. Samuels & M. Taylor, 'Children's ability to distinguish fantasy events from real-life events,' *British Journal of Developmental Psychology*, **12** (1994), 417–427; J. D. Woolley & V. Cox, 'Development of beliefs about storybook reality.' *Developmental Science*, **10** (2007), 681–693. For review, see D. S. Weisberg, 'Distinguishing imagination from reality' in M. Taylor (ed.), *Oxford Handbook of the Development of Imagination* (New York: Oxford University Press, 2013).

[8] J. D. Woolley & H. M. Wellman, 'Young children's understanding of realities, nonrealities, and appearances' *Child Development*, **61** (1990), 946–961.

studies[9], researchers presented three-year-olds with a pretend scenario in which a puppet used an object functionally in a game, rather than according to its pretend identity. For example, an experimenter would establish a pretense whereby a pen was a toothbrush, and then the puppet would draw with the pen. Children tended to object to the puppet's actions, but only when the puppet had been present for the establishment of the pretend identity. When the puppet was absent for the establishment of the pretend identity, children did not object. These results demonstrate that three-year-olds understand that the rules that govern pretend games are context-specific and should not spill over into reality. Several studies have also used data about the duration or direction of children's spontaneous looking to determine how they think about different kinds of pretend scenarios[10].

More work should be done at the younger end of this age spectrum to determine more precisely when this distinction is in place, although such work cannot rely on verbal measures and is thus hampered by difficulties in interpreting children's spontaneous responses. For example, suppose a child laughs or expresses surprise at someone drinking tea from an empty cup. Is she demonstrating her understanding that this is a non-literal scenario, or merely registering the fact that this is an odd example of a drinking event? Answering this question has the potential to tell us whether children learn at some point that there are different types of representations, only some of which are meant to reflect reality, or whether this type of understanding is in some sense a basic, unlearned property of our cognitive systems. Unfortunately, we currently lack a good method for telling the difference between these two options.

Nevertheless, the overall message of this body of work is that children do understand the difference between imagination and reality, at least by the age of three, and likely earlier. This is itself a substantial cognitive achievement, but recent work in my lab and others has discovered that children's understanding of the difference between reality and fiction is even more nuanced than this. Not only do young children separate the real world from the realm of the

---

[9]   Study 1 of E. Wyman, H. Rakoczy, & M. Tomasello, 'Normativity and context in young children's pretend play,' *Cognitive Development*, **24** (2009), 146–155.
[10]   K. H. Onishi, R. Baillargeon, & A. M. Leslie, '15-month-old infants detect violations in pretend scenarios,' *Acta Psychologica*, **124** (2007), 106–128; D. S. Weisberg, L. Wang, & A. M. Leslie, 'How do young children conceptualize socially constructed pretend scenarios?' (under review).

Deena Skolnick Weisberg

imagination, they also make separations between multiple imagined worlds[11]. In this study, we presented a group of four-year-old children and a group of adults with pictures of fictional characters and real people and asked them three types of question. The fantasy/reality questions probed these participants' ability to tell who was real and who was fictional, from the participant's own point of view: "Is Batman real or is he make-believe?" The within-world questions then shifted their perspective to that of one of the fictional characters and asked what that character would think of a secondary character within the same story: "What does Batman think about Robin? Does Batman think that Robin is real or make-believe?" The fantasy/fantasy questions retained this focus on a fictional character's beliefs but asked participants to report this beliefs about a character from a different story: "What does Batman think about SpongeBob? Does Batman think that SpongeBob is real or make-believe?"

Children and adults responded to these questions in the same way: Batman is in fact fictional, but he believes that Robin is real and he believes that SpongeBob is fictional. This latter response is particularly intriguing, since it suggests that Batman views SpongeBob in the same way that we view SpongeBob: as a fictional character, a denizen of fictional world that is separate from his own. Children and adults thus see the realm of fantasy as populated by multiple, separate fictional worlds. Contact between them is no more possible than it is between our world and any of the many fictional worlds we know about.

However, as argued earlier, understanding fictional stories is not the only way in which our imaginative capacities are deployed; they're also used for creating and understanding a wide variety of non-real scenarios. Given this, one would expect the intuition that different representations are separate to extend beyond fictional stories to other types of representation.

Several examinations of children's interactions with pretend games shows that this is indeed the case. Children create separate representations for the different pretend games that they play in addition to doing so for the different fictional stories that they know about[12].

[11]   D. Skolnick & P. Bloom, 'What does Batman think about SpongeBob? Children's understanding of the fantasy/fantasy distinction,' *Cognition*, **101** (2006), B9–B18.
[12]   P. L. Harris & R. D. Kavanaugh, 'Young children's understanding of pretense,' *Monographs of the Society for Research in Child Development*, **58** (1993); D. S. Weisberg, L. Wang, & A. M. Leslie, 'How do young children

In our first study of this issue[13], two experimenters set up two different pretend games with a group of three- and four-year-old child participants. Within each pretend game, there was a stuffed animal character, controlled by the experimenter. There was also a pile of colored blocks within easy reach of the child, which were used throughout the experiment as pretend objects within the games. First, the experimenters asked for each child's help in setting up the two pretend games, in sequence. For example, the first experimenter asked the child to help her doll to take a bath. The child decided what the doll needed for her bath, such as a towel, and pretended that one of the blocks was a towel within that game. The second experimenter then set up an analogous game with a teddy bear who needed to take a nap.

To test whether children represent these two games as separate, as they do with fictional stories, we set up a situation that could potentially have involved a crossover. For example, the second experimenter announced that it was time for the bear to take a bath, so he needed a towel. On hearing this, children had a number of choices of how to respond. One option was to move the towel from the doll's game into the bear's game. Although this would be a simple and parsimonious way of responding to the situation, it would involve breaking the boundary that potentially exists between the two games. If children represent the games as separate, the doll's towel is inaccessible to the bear, no matter how appropriate it is to solve his current problem. If this is how children see things, then they should select a new block to serve as the bear's towel. This is exactly what they did.

This response tendency is especially interesting because children create and have control over these pretend interactions in a way that they do not for fictional stories. The experimental setup involved both experimenters sitting with the child in the same physical space, so that everyone could see what was going on in both games. Given this, it would have been quite easy to cross an object from one game to the other. But that's not what happened; children preferred to invest a new object with the appropriate pretend identity and keep the two games distinct.

---

conceptualize socially constructed pretend scenarios?' op. cit.; E. Wyman, H. Rakoczy, & M. Tomasello, 'Normativity and context in young children's pretend play,' op. cit.

[13] Study 1 of D. S. Weisberg & P. Bloom, 'Young children separate multiple pretend worlds,' *Developmental Science*, **12** (2009), 699–705.

Deena Skolnick Weisberg

This line of research shows that children understand not only the difference between reality and fiction, but also what would be fictional from the point of view of a particular fictional world. That is, they separate different imagined representations. This is a substantial cognitive achievement that develops early and does not appear to change over the course of development. Although these two facts cannot be taken as definitive evidence that these abilities are unlearned, they do suggest that these response tendencies arise from some basic capacity that is common to all types of imaginative cognition, including fictional stories, pretend games, past and future counterfactuals, and so on.

These results additionally bear on questions of how we know which propositions hold true within the context of a given fictional scenario. Specifically, they suggest that children (and adults) import information about relationships between worlds into imagined representations. The fact "SpongeBob is a fictional character" is true in reality, so when we create a representation of Batman's world, this fact is included in that representation. That is, Batman believes SpongeBob to be fictional because we do; his beliefs about what is fictional are parasitic on ours. This obviously cannot be the whole story: The fact "Batman is a fictional character" is also true in reality but should not hold in Batman's world. Nevertheless, this analysis suggests that our decisions about what is true in any given fictional world are generally based on our understanding of reality. This paper next turns to a broader analysis of this claim.

What belongs in an imagined scenario?

The research just reviewed shows that children and adults understand the relationships that hold among different imagined scenarios. But what are their intuitions about the content of any given imagined scenario? How much of the real world is imported into an imagined scenario, how much comes from the scenario's explicit setup (e.g., counterfactual premise, fictional text), and how much is created out of whole cloth? These issues have been treated extensively by philosophers[14], who generally agree that fictional worlds are based on reality. One simple implementation of this argument is the

[14] For example, G. Currie, *The nature of fiction* (Cambridge, UK: Cambridge University Press, 1990); D. Lewis, 'Truth in fiction,' *American Philosophical Quarterly*, **15** (1978), 37–46; K. L. Walton, *Mimesis as make-believe* (Cambridge, MA: Harvard University Press, 1990).

Principle of Minimal Departure[15], which argues that a given fictional world should be as similar to reality as possible, differing in only those parts of the world that are necessary for implementing the story. This principle works quite well to address the issue raised above: The people who inhabit Batman's world should not believe that Batman is fictional, even though the people who inhabit reality should. So when we construct Batman's world, we need to modify our representation to delete this real-world fact from that representation. There is no reason to delete similar facts about other fictional characters, though, which explains why the fact "SpongeBob is a fictional character" still holds true for the people in Batman's world.

Does this principle capture how people actually decide what is true in a fictional world? Previous studies about people's intuitions about the content of imagined scenarios in the adult psychological literature have generally answered this question in the affirmative; people bring to bear their normal psychological tools and their expectations for how the real world operates to their understanding of imagined words[16]. Our first study[17] was designed to determine more specifically the degree to which this was the case.

This study presented adults with three stories that varied in their similarity to the real world: one in which no laws of reality were broken, one in which the main character had special powers but which was otherwise realistic, and one in which many laws of reality were broken. We then asked adults to judge whether a set of facts, all of which were true in the real world, were also true in the world described by the story. These facts fell into four categories: contingent (e.g., who the current President is), conventional (e.g., what people usually eat for dessert), scientific (e.g., which direction the sun travels across the sky), and mathematical (e.g., $2 + 2 = 4$).

Overall, across all types of stories and all types of facts, our participants judged that the real-world facts would remain true in the fictional world. When considered by story, our participants judged that most real-world facts remained true in the realistic story, and

[15]   M. Ryan, 'Fiction, non-factuals, and the principle of minimal departure,' *Poetics*, **9** (1980), 403–422.
[16]   For example, R. J. Gerrig, *Experiencing narrative worlds: On the psychological activities of reading* (New Haven, CT: Yale University Press, 1993); E. J. Marsh, M. L. Meade, & H. L. Roediger, 'Learning facts from fiction,' *Journal of Memory and Language*, **49** (2003), 519–536; D. A. Prentice, R. J. Gerrig, & D. S. Bailis, 'What readers bring to the processing of fictional texts,' *Psychonomic Bulletin & Review*, **4** (1997), 416–420.
[17]   D. S. Weisberg & J. Goodstein, 'What belongs in a fictional world?' *Journal of Cognition and Culture*, **9** (2009), 69–78.

the number of facts judged true in the story fell off linearly as the stories became less realistic. We found the same linear pattern when considering types of facts: Mathematical facts were the most likely to hold true across all three stories, followed by scientific, conventional, and contingent facts, in that order.

These results demonstrate that adults do not construct fictional stories out of whole cloth; facts that are true in reality also tend to hold true in stories. These results also demonstrate that adults have clear and consistent intuitions about aspects of story worlds that are not explicitly defined by a story's text, and indeed that are not even relevant to the events of the story. Further, these results suggest that the Principle of Minimal Departure, or similarly simple ways of capturing truth-in-fiction, does not tell the whole story. Although our participants did generally judge that real-world facts remained true in fiction, their likelihood of doing so was affected by how different the fictional world was from the real world. The sun still rises in the east and sets in the west, even in our most fantastical story, but this was seen as less likely to be the case in this story than in the wholly realistic one. Thus, any theory about truth-in-fiction should take into account something like story genre. Adults, at least, have some expectations about how stories work in general (e.g., worlds with some violations of real-world structure may contain others), and this knowledge combines with real-world facts to determine what holds true in any given fictional world. The same is true when it comes to thinking about the type of fact itself: Adults know that contingent facts are more variable than mathematical ones, for example. This means that the former are generally less likely to hold true in a story and more vulnerable to being deleted from a story world than the latter, even if no specific information is provided about either.[18]

Our next step was to ask where these intuitions come from. Do children behave like adults with respect to these issues, as they do with the reality/fantasy distinction? Are some aspects of their performance adult-like and some immature? Or are their intuitions at odds with those of adults, suggesting a longer and possibly more complicated developmental trajectory?

To answer these questions, my colleagues and I presented four-year-old children with a similar task to the adult one just described[19].

---

[18]   I am grateful to Gregory Currie for his insightful discussion of these issues.

[19]   D. S. Weisberg, D. M. Sobel, J. Goodstein & P. Bloom, 'Young children are reality-prone when thinking about stories,' *Journal of Cognition and Culture*, **13** (2013), 383–401.

The Development of Imaginative Cognition

Although we had asked adults to use a scale to make an explicit judgment about the content of a story world, we anticipated that this kind of response would be difficult for our preschool-aged subjects, so we changed the design somewhat. Children in this study were presented with one of three types of story: a Realistic one, in which all of the events could possibly happen in reality, a Fantastical one, in which many laws that govern reality were broken, and a Letter, which presented the same text as the Realistic story but which was described as being an explicit reflection of something that had actually happened. The text of these stories presented the same sequence of events, but the way in which these events came about different by condition. For example, the main character decides to go to the ice cream store in both stories. In the Realistic story and the Letter, he walks to the store; in the Fantastical story, he teleports to the store.

Once we set up story world by reading the child a few pages, we pretended that the next page of the book (or letter) had fallen out and had gotten mixed up with pages from other books (or letters). We told the child that his or her job was to help us figure out which page came next in the story that we had been reading. Although not explicitly stated, the goal of this question is the same as the goal of the questions in the adult study: Given what has already happened in this story, what other sorts of events belong within this context? Children's choices were always between a possible event, which did not break any real-world laws, and an impossible event, which did. Once they chose an event, we thanked them without giving any positive or negative feedback and continued reading the story.

There were eight places over the course of the story where children were asked to choose which event should come next. We averaged these eight responses together to obtain an overall measure of how children in each condition responded. We also tested a group of adults in exactly the same procedure to provide a direct comparison for children's responses.

We found that children and adults did not differ in their responses to the Letter. Participants in both age groups judged that only possible events, not impossible ones, belonged in this context. This suggests that children understood the task of filling in the event sequence with appropriate events, lending credence to their behavior in the other two conditions. Here, performance differed markedly between the adults and the children. As would be expected from their behavior in the previous study, adults tended to choose the possible pictures to continue the Realistic story and the impossible pictures to continue the Fantastical story. This demonstrates their understanding that the two stories set up different types of worlds in which different events are more or less likely to happen.

Children, on the other hand, tended to choose the possible pictures to continue both types of story. Although this tendency makes a certain amount of sense for the Realistic story, it is somewhat puzzling in the case of the Fantastical story. There are already a good number of impossible events taking place in this story, so why should children have trouble putting additional impossible events into this context? One possibility was that they simply didn't see the impossible events in the Fantastical story as being impossible. This seemed unlikely, since we chose the impossible events to make up the Fantastical story based on previous studies in which children have judged precisely these types of events as "make-believe." Nevertheless, we explored this option by using video clips rather than picture books to present the story, reasoning that children may be better able to perceive the fantastical nature of the story if it was presented in a more visually salient way. Results from the video study confirmed those from the storybook study: Children preferred to include possible, not impossible, events in the videos when given the choice of how to continue the story.

A different possibility for this response tendency could be that children dislike the impossible events and want to avoid choosing them as a general principle, not because of anything in particular about the stories. To test this, we recruited separate groups of children to look just at the possible and impossible choice pictures from both the storybook and video studies. In the absence of any story context, we asked children to choose which of the two pictures they liked better. Children in these control conditions were split evenly between their choices of the possible and the impossible pictures. Importantly, children's level of choosing the impossible pictures in this task (about 50%) was significantly different from their level of choosing the impossible pictures in the course of the "complete the story" task (about 30%). This indicates that children do not have a general tendency to avoid the impossible pictures, hence that their tendency to choose the possible pictures in the "complete the story" task genuinely reflects something about the way that they view story worlds *per se*.

Even given this reassurance, it is still possible that children misunderstand some aspect of our test question. Consider that we are asking them to do a somewhat difficult task: They need to listen to a story, abstract away from the concrete features of the story to figure out what kind of world we are presenting (what might be called its genre), and then figure out which of the two choice options we are presenting fit most naturally within that abstract category. This is likely to be a difficult task for four-year-olds regardless of their beliefs about different kinds of stories. Can they perform this task at all, leaving aside the question of story worlds? To determine whether they can, we created a simplified set of impossible events and presented these to children in three different conditions. Children in the Story condition were told that the events formed a story, as in the previous study. Children in the Desire condition were told that they were all events that the experimenter particularly liked. Children in the Word condition were told that all of the events were "blickish" or another nonce word with an adjectival form. In all cases, children were asked to choose which of two additional pictures belonged in the story, or was one that the experimenter liked, or was also "blickish:" an impossible event or a possible event.

We designed the Desire and Word conditions to determine whether children could form an abstract category of the type that they needed to in order to solve the "complete the story" task. If children can learn a new word that described this category, for example, this would show that they possessed the prerequisite abilities to match impossible pictures to Fantastical stories, hence that their tendency not to do so in the "complete the story" task really reflects some aspect of how they think about stories and not any general cognitive limitation.

This is precisely what we found. Children in the Story condition tended to pick the possible event at test, as in our previous studies, but children in the Word condition tended to pick the impossible event. Children in the Desire condition were split evenly between the two events, possibly because they assumed that the experimenter's preferences would match their own preferences for a roughly equal number of impossible and possible events.

The important message from all of these studies is that children, unlike adults, would prefer stories to contain possible, non-rule-violating events, even when the story context could potentially permit events that are impossible. This does not seem to be due to a general preference for or against impossible events, nor is it due to a failure to understand the nature of the genre-matching task. Rather, at least in preschool, children seem to prefer to make the stories that they hear match reality as closely as possible.

Why should this be the case? One likely possibility is that this is a simple matter of immaturity: Children can interact with imagined worlds from early ages, but simply lack the creativity or motivation to venture too far from reality in these interactions. On this view, what happens over the course of development involves children becoming more willing or able to consider unrealistic events in their imagined scenarios – contrary to the popular view, which holds that young children are wildly imaginative and creative and lose this ability as they get older.

In a recent paper[20], we proposed a somewhat more refined version of this hypothesis, which speculates that the reason that children stick close to reality in their imagined endeavors is because they are still learning about how reality works. Because they are unsure about many aspects of the structure of reality, they prefer to rely on what they know. When they become secure enough in their real-world knowledge, they can begin to imaginatively explore possibilities in which this knowledge is violated. This view predicts, somewhat para- doxically, that it is those domains of knowledge that children hold more strongly and understand more deeply that are more likely to be counterfactualized in the context of a fantastical fictional story.

To test this hypothesis, we contrasted events from two domains: physics, which children understand very well from a very early age, and biology, a full understanding of which is still developing in the preschool years. As in previous studies, we created sets of possible and impossible events. In this case, the impossible events were impossible because they violated some principle either of physics (e.g., a character walks through a wall) or of biology (e.g., a character never needs to sleep). The possible events presented the realistic ana- logues to these events (e.g., a character walks through a door and needs to sleep when he's tired). Rather than creating stories and asking children to complete them, in this study we simply pre- sented these pairs of possible and impossible events to preschoolers without prior context and asked them to choose which picture they would like to put in their story. There were six such choices, three in the physics domain and three in the biology domain.

We found, as in previous studies, that children's choices were pri- marily of possible rather than impossible events. This is an especially interesting tendency since this task presented no prior story context to match and no task other than to create a story of their own design. Even with such loose constraints, children still preferred to put realistic as opposed to fantastical events into their stories. But an examination of those events for which children did choose the impossible member of the pair confirms our hypothesis: Children were more likely to pick impossible physical events than impossible

[20]   D. M. Sobel & D. S. Weisberg, 'Tell me a story: How children's de- veloping domain knowledge affects their story construction,' *Journal of Cognition and Development* (in press).

biological events. This suggests that children's overall attraction towards realistic events in stories is at least partially a result of their developing understanding of the real world. The more they know about some aspect of reality, the more comfortable they feel leaving it behind to explore alternative structures. This implies that our world-construction abilities develop in tandem with our knowledge of reality: The more we know, the more we can imagine.

The results of this series of studies have some interesting implications for the phenomenon of *imaginative resistance*, which occurs because there are some real-world facts that we can never leave behind when we construct imagined scenarios, either because we are unwilling or unable to do so[21]. Many theories of imaginative resistance have suggested that it occurs primarily for those facts that are central to the structure of reality or to our conceptions thereof, such as logical or moral facts. The results of the adult study I reviewed earlier[22] support this argument, since those subjects were more likely to retain mathematical facts even in the face of a fantastical fictional story. But the current developmental results paint a different picture. Four-year-old children were more willing to consider violations of physics-based events than violations of biology-based events, since their understanding of the latter is still tenuous at this age. This suggests that imaginative resistance may occur not only for those events that we see as structurally central to the real world, but also for those events about which we feel some kind of uncertainty.

The fact that imaginative resistance occurs for two contrasting categories of facts in turn suggests that there may be two different mechanisms driving this phenomenon. When we experience imaginative resistance to facts that we see as central to reality, this may occur because of a genuine inability to imagine a world in which these facts are different. But when we experience imaginative resistance to facts about which we are uncertain, this may occur because of reluctance to step too far outside of the boundaries of our current, and weak, knowledge. In turn, this analysis suggests that the "cure"

---

[21] See T. S. Gendler, 'The puzzle of imaginative resistance,' *Journal of Philosophy*, **97** (2000), 285–299; T. S. Gender, 'Imaginative resistance revisited' and J. Weinberg & A. Meskin, 'Puzzling over the imagination: Philosophical problems, architectural solutions,' in S. Nichols (ed.), *The architecture of the imagination: New essays on pretense, possibility and fiction* (Oxford: Oxford University Press, 2006).
[22] D. S. Weisberg & J. Goodstein, 'What belongs in a fictional world?' op. cit.

Deena Skolnick Weisberg

for imaginative resistance should differ across these two cases. The former type may never subside or be overcome, whereas the latter should disappear with an increase in knowledge in that domain.

However, we should be careful not to take this last point too far, since increased knowledge can impose its own limits on our imaginative abilities. A series of studies have shown that adults tend to get stuck on the structure of reality even when they are trying to exercise their imaginative capacities[23]. For example, adults who were asked to draw alien creatures that were wildly different from Earth animals tended to preserve many of the key features of the real animals, such as bilateral symmetry[24]. So the idea that more knowledge leads to less imaginative resistance and more imaginative freedom is the start of the story, but not the whole story, and more work is needed to map this developmental trajectory in detail.

How do we think about improbable events?

The research discussed thus far has looked at issues of black-and-white distinctions, such as the difference between fiction and reality, or between events that are entirely ordinary and events that are impossible because they break some natural law. But there are also cases that involve somewhat more shades of gray, such as events that may be unfamiliar to children but not necessarily impossible. This category of *improbable* events provides an interesting arena in which we can use the "complete the story" procedure to probe children's understanding of the nuances of the reality/fantasy distinction.

Previous work suggests that young children have a poor understanding of improbable events[25]. As reviewed earlier, four-year-

---

[23]   S. Brédart, T. B. Ward & P. Marczewski, 'Structured imagination of novel creatures' faces,' *American Journal of Psychology*, **111** (1998), 607–625; T. B. Ward, 'Structured imagination: The role of category structure in exemplar generation,' *Cognitive Psychology*, **27** (1994), 1–40; T. B. Ward & C. M. Sifonis, 'Task demands and generative thinking: What changes and what remains the same?' *Journal of Creative Behavior*, **31** (1997), 245–259.

[24]   T. B. Ward, 'Structured imagination: The role of category structure in exemplar generation,' op. cit.

[25]   A. Shtulman, 'The development of possibility judgment within and across domains,' *Cognitive Development*, **24** (2009), 293–309; A. Shtulman & S. Carey, 'Improbable or impossible? How children reason about the possibility of extraordinary events,' *Child Development*, **78** (2007), 1015–1032.

100

olds can explicitly report that possible events are possible and that impossible events are impossible. However, they tend to mis-categorize improbable events as impossible. That is, children tend to see events that are unfamiliar or unusual as being in the same category as events that can't actually happen. We began our study of this issue by replicating this effect[26]. We created three sets of events: ordinary (e.g., Moe has a pet cat), improbable (e.g., Moe has a pet squirrel), and impossible (e.g., Moe has a pet dragon) and asked children to categorize them. As in previous work, children's judgments were accurate except for the improbable events, which they tended to say were impossible.

But we doubted that children really lack an understanding of this category. We suspected that their difficulty with the categorization task was a difficulty in explicitly reporting on the status of these events, not with understanding that they could potentially happen in reality. To test this hypothesis, we presented these same children with a version of our "complete the story" task. In this case, children saw stories made up entirely of events from the improbable set. Then, one group of children was given the choice to continue this story with another improbable event or an ordinary event. In this condition, children did not show a preference; either event was seen as an appropriate addition to the story. A second group of children was given the choice to continue the story with another improbable event or an impossible event. Here, children significantly preferred the improbable event. This behavior demonstrates that children do not believe that improbable events are impossible; if that were the case, they would have seen the two choice events in this condition as belonging to the same category and would have been unable to distinguish between them. So while an explicit understanding of improbability develops after the age of four years, children at this age can demonstrate their knowledge of the difference between improbable and impossible events within a helpful story-based context.

What role does the imagination play in development?

Thus far, this review has focused on two lines of work examining children's abilities to create and interact with imagined representations. Some aspects of these abilities develop early and remain relatively

[26] D. S. Weisberg & D. M. Sobel, 'Young children discriminate improbable from impossible events in fiction,' *Cognitive Development*, **27** (2012), 90–98.

unchanged over the course of development: Even three-year-olds distinguish real from imagined representations and different imagined representations from each other. But other aspects of these abilities take longer to mature and undergo a good deal of developmental change: Four-year-olds, unlike adults, tend to construct realistic imagined worlds, possibly because they they knowledge of the real world is not yet secure enough to consider different kinds of counterfactuals.

Both of these aspects of children's imaginative capacities play an important role in development. As argued earlier, the imagination allows us not only to interact with fictional stories and pretend games, but also to create causal counterfactuals, future hypotheticals, and scientific thought experiments, among other types of representation. The ability to separate multiple imagined representations is at the heart of using these more "serious" imagined scenarios appropriately. Consider future planning: In order to decide whether to do X or Y, one needs to imaginatively work through the consequences of doing X and the consequences of doing Y. But when making this decision, one must be able to represent these two possible futures as separate from each other, so that the two sets of consequences do not bleed into each other[27].

Many have argued that this is the basic purpose that our imaginative capacities serve: evaluating past and future counterfactuals[28]. These counterfactuals are used in planning, as in the example above, and also in learning, as we evaluate possible ways that the world could be. Our default tendency to be "stuck on reality" when imagining fictional worlds makes a good deal of sense, considered within this framework. In order to learn from an imagined scenario or to use one (or more) in planning, these scenarios must be appropriately similar to reality. This will allow the conclusions that we draw

[27] See D. S. Weisberg & A. Gopnik, 'Pretense, counterfactuals, and Bayesian causal models: Why what is not real really matters,' op. cit.
[28] For example, R. M. J. Byrne, *The rational imagination: How people create alternatives to reality* (Cambridge, MA: MIT Press, 2005); A. Gopnik, *The philosophical baby: What children's minds tell us about truth, love, and the meaning of life* (New York: Farrar, Straus, and Giroux, 2009); C. Hoerl, T. McCormack & S. R. Beck, *Understanding counterfactuals, understanding causation* (Oxford, UK: Oxford University Press, 2011); M. Seligman, P. Railton, R. Baumeister, & C. Sripada, 'Navigating into the future or driven by the past,' *Perspectives on Psychological Science*, **8** (2013), 119–141; D. S. Weisberg, 'The vital importance of imagination' in M. Brockman (ed.), *What's next? Dispatches on the future of science* (New York: Vintage Books, 2009).

within the context of an imagined world to transfer appropriately to the real world. To put the same point the other way around, if our imagined scenarios were too different from reality, we would be easily drawn into imagining unrealistic or unlikely scenarios that would then not be helpful in navigating reality.

This argument provides additional insight into the issue of imaginative resistance. If we accept that imagination is crucial to planning, then a bias to stick closely to reality in our imagined representations is a feature, not a bug, of the planning system. Because engaging with fictional worlds is tied up with our ability to create representations that will be useful in visualizing our own futures, our inability (or unwillingness) to consider extremely far-fetched possibilities keeps the process of making plans appropriately realistic, and hence appropriately useful.

From our examination of the development of these two aspects of imaginative cognition, then, we can already begin to see some of the important features of the adult imaginative system. We have also learned that some of these features, like the ability to distinguish among representations, seem to be basic properties of this system. Others, like the ability or willingness to imagine unrealistic scenarios, develop later, although even this fact gives us some insight into the basic cognitive problems that our imaginative capacities allow us to solve. Taking developmental psychology seriously can thus help to advance the study of some aspects of philosophical study of aesthetics. More broadly, engaging philosophers, psychologists, anthropologists, and others in dialogue about these issues in the best tradition of cognitive science can lead to a deeper understanding of how and why our aesthetic capacities work.

The University of Pennsylvania
deena.weisberg@psych.upenn.edu

The Epistemology of Fiction and the Question of Invariant Norms

JONATHAN GILMORE

I.

A primary dimension of our engagement with fictional works of art – paradigmatically literary, dramatic, and cinematic narratives – is figuring out what is true in such representations, what the facts are in the fictional world. These facts (or states of affairs) include not only those that ground any genuine understanding of a story – say, that it was his own father whom Oedipus killed – but also those that may be missed in even a largely competent reading, say, that Emma Bovary's desires and dissatisfactions are fed by reading romance novels.

How we uncover fictional truth parallels how we decide what is true in the real world. When forming beliefs, as well as revising, transitioning among, and relinquishing beliefs, we rely on standard sources of evidence such as testimony, perception, memory, the results of inductive and deductive inferences, and our affective responses. When all goes well, these sources provide the right sorts of reasons for our beliefs: reasons that justify or serve as warrants for what we believe. Analogous operations supply and justify what we imagine to be true in a given fiction.

Sometimes we rely on the testimony of a narrator who is largely transparent to the text. In these cases we treat what is said as true by stipulation: reading, 'it was a dark and stormy night...,' we don't typically need to look for other confirming evidence to be justified in believing that the description captures how things are in the fiction. In other cases where narrators or those in the text whom we rely on for information seem to be fully-realized individuals, we may discount what they convey to us according to the degree of reliability we attribute to them, as we do with Henry James' Maisie, who sees things with only partial comprehension through a child's eyes. Such discounting is of course what we do as good epistemic agents in response to testimony in real life. We also often infer what is true in a story, when it is not explicitly stated, from what is directly asserted to be true: I conclude that Charles Bovary (not a fully qualified physician but only an *officier de santé*) must have botched the surgery

doi:10.1017/S1358246114000204   © The Royal Institute of Philosophy and the contributors 2014
Royal Institute of Philosophy Supplement **75** 2014

Jonathan Gilmore

he performed on the young groom's clubfoot because the boy's leg develops gangrene. Other things I imagine to be true are not described by a text, nor inferred from those descriptions, but are imported into a fiction from my beliefs about the real world – insofar, that is, as I see the fictional world as similar in relevant respects to our own. Hence, unless otherwise specified, we tend to assume in reading a realistic narrative that the human beings it represents are mortal and that the laws of physics hold.

Furthermore, just as I may be mistaken in my beliefs about the real world, so my imagining what is true in a fiction can be faulty – say, if I thought that the brawny peasant on a donkey that Don Quixote encounters really is the beautiful princess he hallucinates, or that Goneril's and Regan's professions of filial devotion are sincere, or that Ganymede in *As You Like It* really is a man within the story, and not Rosalind in disguise. In either case, the defect may be in the belief or imagining itself (its failure of correspondence) or in the epistemic means by which the belief or imagining is arrived at, such as when they arise out of practices that are not truth-apt, such as 'wishful thinking.'

Philosophers and psychologists have worked out a substantial picture of the kinds of normative constraints that are constitutive of epistemic rationality when applied to beliefs – what normative constraints govern a person's formation, maintenance, transitions among, and relinquishing of her beliefs. My question is whether such norms governing our beliefs about what is true in the real world apply *invariantly* to our imaginings of what is true in fictions.[1] Taking P to be a proposition expressing some fact, is it rational to imagine P is true in a given fictional world if and only if it would rational to believe P is true for the same kinds of reasons in real life? In short, is make-believing rational in the same sense as believing?

---

[1]   Related questions concern the degree of commonalities in the way beliefs and imaginings are attributed to agents; whether imaginative states bear the same relations (inferential, causal, supervening, etc.) among themselves as belief states do; and what systematic relations exist between imaginative states and belief states. For discussion of these and other comparisons between beliefs and imaginings, see Tamar Gendler, 'On the Relation Between Pretense and Belief' in Matthew Kieran and Dominic McIver Lopes, eds. *Imagination, Philosophy, and the Arts* (Routledge, 2003), p.125–141; and Shaun Nichols, 'Introduction' in Shaun Nichols, ed. *The Architecture of the Imagination* (Oxford: Oxford University Press, 2006), 1–18.

Fiction and the Question of Invariant Norms

Let me describe two opposed answers. On the one side are those who see imagining in response to a fiction as rational according to the same norms that govern whether a belief is rational. The norms of believing and imagining are invariant across the real and fictional divide. We can call this a commitment to invariance or *continuity*. On the other side, proponents of *discontinuity* see the standards of rationality for forming beliefs about the real world as in tension with, if not collectively inconsistent with, the standards that govern imaginings of what is true in a fictional world.[2]

On the side of continuity is the intuition that our epistemic behavior in relation to the contents of fictions is very much like that in relation to states of affairs in the real world – indeed, it isn't clear how authors could expect us to understand their fictions correctly, to import what needs to be imported, to infer what needs to be inferred, for the fiction to make sense, were they not able to rely on our rational processes for discovery of facts about the world being taken 'offline' and directed to the stories they create.

The discontinuity view, however, relies on the intuition that imagining exhibits a freedom that seems to distinguish it from many other representational states of the mind. It seems, for instance, that I can successfully imagine *at will* that almost any facts hold, but this cannot be said, both conceptually and practically, of remembering, desiring, perceiving, or believing, which seem more greatly constrained by the

---

[2]   Whether or not a given theory of fiction-directed imagining commits to or denies invariance tends to be only implicit. Some of the more salient expressions of continuity can be found in: Ruth M. J. Byrne, *The Rational Imagination: How People Create Alternatives to Reality* (Cambridge, MA: MIT Press, 2005); Shaun Nichols and Stephen Stich, 'A Cognitive Theory of Pretense', *Cognition* **74** (2000), 115–147; and Gregory Currie and Ian Ravenscroft, *Recreative Minds: Imagination in Philosophy and Psychology* (Oxford: Oxford University Press, 2003). Discontinuity is a tenet of Romantic theories of the imagination, as in Coleridge's *Biographia Literaria* (1817), and existentialist and phenomenological treatments of fiction, such as, respectively, Jean-Paul Sartre's *What is Literature?* and Maurice Merleau-Ponty's 'Indirect Language and the Voices of Silence.' Among contemporary theorists, Kendall Walton endorses what appears to be a qualified thesis of discontinuity in stressing the absence of any "simple set of principles" governing the generation of fictional truths (*Mimesis as Make-believe: on the Foundations of the Representational Arts* [Cambridge, MA: Harvard University Press, 1990], 185). My aim in this paper, however, is not to offer critical exegesis of the views of theorists of fictions but to expose a significant conflict between two positions in which they cannot avoid taking a side.

circumstances I find myself in, and the other memories, desires, perceptions and beliefs that I already have and will not relinquish.

No doubt, much recent work in cognitive psychology, neuroscience, and philosophy of the imagination supports the idea that
there are several forms of *descriptive* continuity to be observed
across the stances of believing and imagining.[3] The psychological mechanisms that process believing that P appear to operate in ways parallel to, and employ much of the same cognitive architecture, as those
that process pretending or imagining that P. However, my question is
about the *norms* associated with those propositional attitudes:
whether the criteria governing their epistemic justification hold invariantly across our beliefs about the real world and our imaginings
of what is true in fictional works of art.[4]

In what follows I introduce and assess some considerations in favor
of these two theses of continuity and discontinuity, both of which
have a prima facie plausibility. Ultimately, I defend a version of the
discontinuity thesis: for readers and audiences of fictions, there are
epistemic reasons to attribute facts to a fictional world that would
not count as epistemic reasons to identify analogous facts in the real
world. More generally, the norms in light of which our imaginings
can be epistemically warranted are not, as a whole, consistent with
those in light of which our beliefs are epistemically warranted.

A few caveats are in order:

(1)   There is no doubt that the concept of rationality when applied
        to either beliefs or imaginings requires careful qualification.
        There is no consensus over what theoretical rationality con-
        sists of, hence no easy way to ask whether the norms of
        belief are altogether invariant over believing and imagining.[5]

---

[3]   Representative studies are: Byrne, *The Rational Imagination: How
People Create Alternatives to Reality* (Cambridge, MA: MIT Press, 2005);
Paul L. Harris, *The Work of the Imagination* (Oxford: Blackwell
Publishing, 2000); Shaun Nichols and Stephen Stich, 'A Cognitive
Theory of Pretense', *Cognition* **74** (2000), 115–147; and Timothy
Schroeder and Carl Matheson, 'Imagination and Emotion' in *The
Architecture of the Imagination*, Shaun Nichols, ed. (Oxford: Oxford
University Press, 2006), 19–40.

[4]   For the debate between theories of continuity and discontinuity over
the norms governing our emotional responses to fictions and the actual
world, see Jonathan Gilmore, 'Aptness of Emotions for Fictions and
Imaginings', *Pacific Philosophical Quarterly* **92**.4 (2011), 468–489.

[5]   In this discussion I treat theoretical and epistemic rationality as largely
identical capacities. In other philosophical contexts, however, the two may

In what follows I appeal to the putative invariance of only some of the most familiar and relatively uncontroversial norms identified with theoretical rationality, not to exotic norms that only a perfectly rational person, say an android decision theorist possessed of unlimited working memory, might be guided by. I will also not enter into the debate as to whether such normativity applies in the first instance to beliefs and only derivatively to believers, or to the converse (as in some theories of virtue epistemology). I assume that anything I say about the rational grounds for a belief can be translated into an attribute of someone's epistemic disposition to rely only on such rational grounds.

(2)   Nothing I say here is meant to address the metaphysics of fictional worlds, or more mundanely, what makes something true, part of a story, make-believe, and such, in a fictional world. My only relevant commitment is to the idea that there is criterion of representational correctness in what we imagine when we submit our imaginative activity to the objective constraints of a work of fiction, allowing that most fictions underdetermine what we may imagine of them consistent with correct comprehension.

(3)   Finally, I am not addressing norms that govern the correctness or aptness of beliefs or imaginings, *all things considered*, but only those that govern their intentional, or more specifically, *representational* correctness and the putatively justifying means by which such correctness is achieved. There may be practical, prudential, aesthetic, moral and other norms in virtue of which one has a reason to believe or imagine something, or, more specifically, to put oneself in a position in which one will *come to* believe or imagine it. Sometimes an instrumental reason (e.g., it would be too distressing) might trump an epistemic reason to believe something or to imagine it to be true. But even if practical, moral, aesthetic, and other kinds of reasons can trump epistemic reasons, they do not silence epistemic reasons, in the sense of making them wholly inapplicable. My concern is only with the

---

be distinguished, particularly in how the former but not the latter requires that one be sensitive to certain kinds of instrumental reasons pertaining to the achievement of one's cognitive goals. See Thomas Kelly, 'Epistemic Rationality as Instrumental Rationality: a Critique', *Philosophy and Phenomenological Research* **66**.3 (2003), 612–640.

invariance or otherwise of epistemic norms governing how our beliefs and imaginings present their contents – as, respectively, true of the world, or true of a fiction. Do the same standards of epistemic rationality apply to beliefs and fiction-guided imaginings? Not: Do the same standards of rationality, *in toto*, apply to the two domains?[6]

II.

A continuity proponent might suggest that our abiding by the same rational standards for belief formation and transition is what creators of works of fiction rely on to let us know what is true in a fiction.[7] If the astronaut crew crash-lands on a primitive planet ruled by apes but then comes upon the charred fragments of the Statue of Liberty, audiences can be expected to infer that the strange planet is actually Earth (!) in a post-apocalyptic future. If we are directed to imagine that a fictional world is much like our own, we are entitled to assume that a character in the fiction who is in London in the morning and New York later the same day has traveled there by air.[8] If our epistemic norms were not continuous, such identifications of the facts in a fiction would not be so predictable.

[6]   There is a narrow sense in which pragmatic factors may plausibly be counted as providing epistemic reasons relevant to acquiring a belief, as when the degree of importance associated with being correct in some claim affects what one counts as a sufficient level of evidence to believe it. Whether or not such pragmatic reasons count in epistemic justification need not be addressed here as my question is only whether the kinds of reasons, whatever they may be, that justify beliefs apply invariantly to the justification of imaginings.

[7]   Defenders of the descriptive continuity of believing and imagining or pretending stress what Nichols calls 'inferential orderliness': that individuals working out what is true in a given pretense often make inferences that mirror those that they would employ if the pretense were in fact real. See Shaun Nichols, 'Introduction', in Shaun Nichols, ed. *The Architecture of the Imagination* (Oxford: Oxford University Press, 2006), 1–18.

[8]   Currie and Ravenscroft write: 'It is this capacity of imaginings to mirror the inferential patterns of belief that makes fictional storytelling possible. ...If imaginings were not inferentially commensurate with beliefs, we could not draw on our beliefs to fill out what the story tells us.' Gregory Currie and Ian Ravenscroft, *Recreative Minds: Imagination in Philosophy and Psychology* (Oxford: Oxford University Press, 2003), 13–14. Such preservation of inference in imagining is also demonstrated in studies of child

Of course, one norm that a commitment to invariance should not require the observance of is that a person imagine something to be true only when she has good grounds to believe it to be true. But once we index the *grounds for imagining* some fictional or make-believe fact to the *fictional* world that the imagining is about, we can say that the same constraints that govern the epistemic behavior of any agent with respect to his beliefs govern his epistemic behavior with respect to his fiction-directed imagining. His beliefs present certain facts as holding in the real world and his imaginings present certain facts as holding in a fictional one.

It certainly seems part of the phenomenology of our engagement with fictions that we perform many of the same epistemic operations in imagining what is true in a fiction as we do in coming to believe what is true outside of it. We infer via deduction and induction from what is explicitly described as being the case to other facts of the fiction that are not so described. Through our affective and emotional reactions we imaginatively assign values to things represented in fictions just as we impute values to things in real life. We try to monitor the consistency among our imaginings in response to a fiction just as we monitor such consistency among our beliefs, sometimes giving up what we initially held to be true as a story unfolds. We think it is no more theoretically reasonable to base one's imaginings in response to a fiction on how we desire events to transpire than we do in connection with our beliefs. That I want Anna Karenina to survive, is, I recognize as a reader, no epistemic reason to justify imagining that in Tolstoy's narrative she somehow continues to live. There are, of course, stories that seek to satisfy such desires, as in 'fan fictions' that continue and sometimes revise a narrative without the sanction of the original creator. And there are interesting cases such as when the pseudonymous Alonso Fernández de Avellaneda determined that Don Quixote was in fact more pious than Cervantes posited, and wrote a narrative featuring the character after Cervantes composed the first part of his novel, but before he had finished the second. However these imaginings are not epistemically justified by reasons internal to the original fictions, although they may be justified on aesthetic, moral, or other terms. Indeed, writers sometimes try to redeem characters from others' novels, say, because they see those characters or actual people like them as

---

psychology; see, e.g., Alan Leslie, 'Pretending and Believing: Issues in the Theory of ToMM', *Cognition* **50** (1987), 211–38.

Jonathan Gilmore

deserving of different attributes or experiences than those with which they were originally endowed.[9]

It should also be noted that audiences for fictions regularly discuss fictional characters and events *as if* they were real, debating the fine points of what a protagonist's motivations are on the basis of her behavior. This is evidence that we cite when we are called upon to justify what we imagine to be true in those fictions – as when we debate what really happened at the end of the film *Inception* (was it still a dream?). That is, we appeal to reasons in an inferentially norm-governed way that is continuous with how we appropriately justify what we believe to be true in real life.

Finally, in discovering truths about the actual world we rely on various forms of counterfactual imagining akin to our imagining what is true in a fiction. These include thought experiments, predicting the future, simulating another person's point of view, apportioning legal responsibility for some event, and appealing to scientific models featuring, e.g., frictionless planes. The epistemic value of these imaginings is sometimes controversial, whether as a source of useful moral intuitions or as a guide to metaphysical possibility. However, a proponent of continuity might contend that the very possibility of counterfactual imagining serving as a source of knowledge about the real world depends on our abiding by the same rational constraints in imagining as we do in forming beliefs. Of course, some might embrace that point, not as an intuitive support for continuity, but as a *reductio* showing that some of the products of such imagining, e.g., intuitions drawn from fictions involving trolley problems or dopplegängers exiting from teletransporters, are not a good source of knowledge about morals and metaphysics in this world where the circumstances the fictions prescribe us to imagine don't typically arise.[10]

Still, one might object to the continuity view that there is an essential dimension of the process by which we discover what to imagine as true in a fiction that has no obvious analog in the process by which we form beliefs about the real world. That is where we take an *external* approach to the fiction as an ordinary artifact in our world and

[9] As in Jean Rhys' *Wild Sargasso Sea* (1966), an alternative imagining of the life and mind of the 'madwoman in the attic' of Charlotte Bronte's *Jane Eyre* before her arranged marriage to Rochester and relocation from the Caribbean to England.

[10] That we form intuitions from thought experiments according to the same principles by which we discover truth in fiction is defended in Jonathan Ichikawa and Benjamin Jarvis, 'Thought-Experiment Intuitions and Truth in Fiction', *Philosophical Studies* **142** (2009): 221–246.

appeal to its style, tradition, function, genre, author, technique, and so on, in forming beliefs about its content – what is true from the *internal* perspective.[11] In adopting such an external stance on a work of fiction we refer to properties it has as a vehicle of representation but not (directly) to its represented content. By contrast, in adopting an internal stance, we refer to that content as if it were real or were a story being recounted by a real narrator. Othello's speech is rough from the internal stance ('rude am I in my speech') but eloquent from the external, in the poetic language Shakespeare uses. Mark Antony's funeral oration is eloquent from both the internal perspective – although he claims not to be an orator – *and* the external, in the phrasing Shakespeare employs. External features of a narrative do not lie within the scope of the operator 'it is fictional that' or 'it is part of the content that,' however, they can cause us to form propositional attitudes – beliefs, imaginings, emotions, desires – toward what is. For example, P.G. Wodehouse's novels often feature an earl or lord raising an older child in the absence of her mother, who has died before the period of the story begins. We assume that the characters don't dwell much over that loss (even though it would be natural to import that assumption from real life) because we know that would be foreign to Wodehouse's comic aims. Similarly, we are usually correct in inferring that the party who appears guilty of the murder in the first few pages of a traditional mystery story is not genuinely the villain, for paradigm mystery novels don't give up the game that early. Finally, a viewer of the film *Clueless* about a group of American high-school kids can make reliable assumptions about the significance of various turns in the plot if he's familiar with its acknowledged model, Austen's *Emma*.

However, those appeals to what is true *of*, but not *in*, a work of fiction do not count against continuity. In principle, if we had access to such an external source of understanding our world – say, through reliable beliefs about Providence, Fate, or Karma – we would use it to infer what is true in our world. No such more-than-human-knowledge is available, but in principle it would serve as a

---

[11]   For discussions of internal and external stances on a fiction, see Peter Lamarque, *Fictional Points of View* (Ithaca, NY: Cornell University Press, 1996), chapters 2 and 8; and, Gregory Currie, 'Two Ways of Looking at a Narrative.' In *Narratives and Narrators: a Philosophy of Stories* (Oxford and New York: Oxford University Press, 2010), 49–64. An analogous distinction is noted by Kendall Walton, 'How Remote are Fictional Worlds from the Real World?' *Journal of Aesthetics and Art Criticism* **37** (1978–9), 21.

source of beliefs about what is true in our world as much as external features of a story serve as a source of what to imagine as true about its world. This scenario, of course, is sometimes explored thematically within works of art, as in *The Truman Show* – about a character whose life is orchestrated for the sake of a television series – and *The Comforters*, a short novel by Muriel Spark in which Caroline discovers that she is only a character in a fiction (she continually hears typing on a keyboard) and resolves to frustrate her author's plans.

III.

Let me now turn to the discontinuity view, which also seems prima facie plausible. This is the view, recall, that the rational norms that govern the formation of imaginings with respect to what is true in a fiction can be inconsistent with the rational norms that govern the formation of our beliefs. Sometimes, as in Shelley's Romantic primer, *Defense of Poetry* (1821), this is construed as the denial that reason has any role in the activities of the imagination.[12] In other formulations, imagination is reason-governed but perhaps – this is the question – not subject to the same norms of reasoning as believing. I want to first address, and suggest we reject, the most familiar point appealed to in favor of the thesis of discontinuity – one that pertains to the unconstrained contents of fictions. In its place, I introduce a defense of discontinuity that I think better survives philosophical scrutiny.

The most familiar point made in favor of discontinuity is that it is a highly salient feature of our engagement with fictions that they call for us to imagine things as true that are not, and sometimes could not be, true in our world. Fictional worlds can present fantasies as reality, featuring radical departures from standard laws of physics and states of affairs that are internally inconsistent. And while our real world, like all possible worlds, exhibits logical closure – any genuine proposition is either true of our world or false of our world – fictional worlds are typically incomplete: some propositions, such as that Emma Bovary has blue eyes, are neither true nor false in the world of Flaubert's novel, there being nothing in the narrative that gives us a reason to accept or deny that claim. If fictions call on us to imagine such fantastical states of affairs, so different,

---

[12] In *English Essays: From Sir Philip Sidney to Macaulay. With Introductions and Notes,* edited by Charles W. Eliot (New York: P.F. Collier and Son, 1909).

physically and metaphysically, from the actual world, they must rely on our acceptance of epistemic norms that govern imagining that are distinct from those that govern believing.

But that observation based on the contents of fictions does not succeed as a challenge to continuity. For a proponent of continuity can plausibly propose that what is embedded in those fictions is a kind of metaphysical or physical principle in light of which it would be rational to infer or make-believe the truth of those other fantastical parts of the fiction. If we accept that it is true in the state of affairs of Kafka's *Metamorphosis* that human beings *can* wake up as insects, or as other creatures, then we don't in any straightforward way depart from ordinary rational judgment if we imagine on the basis of the narrator's description that Gregor Samsa *has* indeed woken up as a bug. This is just as when Alice concludes from matters being so queer in general in Wonderland – she's been shrunk and is swimming in a pool of her own tears – that it isn't that odd that the mouse she encounters is able to speak French. The question is whether we would be rational in coming to imagine such fantastical states of affairs without there being such a principle of generation internal to the fiction that serves to license such an imagining.[13]

I suggest that if we were to encounter a fictional world in which such fantastic things occur but where there is no implicit (fictionally true) physical or metaphysical principle that licenses such departures from ordinary reality, we would be just as warranted in assuming that we are reading a story recounted by a *deluded narrator* – one who only imagines all that she or he describes to be true – as we would be in assuming that, e.g., French-speaking mice really do exist in the fictional world. But in most cases there is very little pressure or apparent motivation to assume the presence of a narrator so out of touch with that fictional world. Instead, we assume that the facts of the fictional world really are as they are described because we can readily assume that it is a fact in the fiction that such bizarre, non-naturalistic events can occur – the nature of that world permits it. This experience, of course, should be contrasted with cases in which in a story presents reasons that motivate us to wonder about the narrator's reliability, as in Nabokov's *Pale Fire*, where we try to piece together what is true about the events leading to the death of the poet John Shade

---

[13]   On principles of generation, see Kendall Walton, *Mimesis as Make-believe: on the Foundations of the Representational Arts* (Cambridge, MA: Harvard University Press, 1990), 138–40.

Jonathan Gilmore

through an obviously delusional commentary on the source and meanings of his accompanying poem.

I suggest that a better argument for discontinuity can be found not in the sundry contents of fictions but in some of the myriad ways they succeed in eliciting our imagining of what is true. My proposal is that certain kinds of experiences generated by a fiction do serve as grounds for the imagination of certain associated facts holding in the fiction when those experiences are reliable indicators of those facts. More formally, when an experience E in reading a fiction is a reliable indicator that P is the case in the fiction, E is a (pro tanto) reason for imagining that P. At a general level, this structure of justification holds as well in relation to beliefs: an experience E can serve as a reason for a belief that P if E is a reliable indicator that P.[14] However, at a lower level of description, a fiction can provide an experience that justifies imagining something being true in the fiction while analogous experiences in the actual world may not justify an analogous belief.

It is true that in *Oliver Twist* Fagin is filthy and physically grotesque, as we learn from the attention paid by the narrator to his greasy clothes and matted hair. Yet, we imagine him as morally corrupt as well via the text's exploitation of our well-studied irrational tendency to conflate such feelings of mere physical disgust with justified moral opprobrium. No doubt, other facts internal to the fiction also explain and serve as reasons for this imagining just as they would in an analogous case of belief – such as that he exploits children. But those facts do not exhaust the pro tanto reasons warranting that moral judgment.[15] For in engaging with such a work, we implicitly accept a norm under which such physical disgust is a reliable indicator of such moral facts. No such reliable relation, hence no norm sanctioning an epistemic reliance on it, holds in the actual world. A feeling of disgust prompted by someone's filth in the real world would not offer a reason for judging him immoral. This suggests that we can have some imaginings on account of – warranted by – being caused to have other imaginings where an analogous justificatory relation

[14] I appeal here to a "reliabilist" notion of epistemic justification that does not preclude other grounds of justification. For a defense of an epistemic reliabilism as an exclusive account of justification, see Alvin Goldman, 'What Is Justified Belief?' In Alvin Goldman, *Liaisons: Philosophy Meets the Cognitive and Social Sciences* (Cambridge, MA: MIT Press, 1992).
[15] See Simone Schnall, Jonathan Haidt, Gerald L. Clore, and Alexander H. Jordan, 'Disgust as Embodied Moral Judgment', *Personality and Social Psychology Bulletin* (2008), 1096–1109.

between one set of facts and another would not hold outside of our engagement with the fiction.

There are other kinds of cases in which works of art exploit automatic or subdoxastic tendencies to cause us to imagine as true what we would not have reason in analogous contexts to believe in real life. From these arise two claims. First, such phenomena serve as evidence of a descriptive discontinuity in what can serve as the bases of imaginings and epistemically-rational beliefs. Second, more controversially, these cases reflect normative discontinuity as well. They show how the causes of what we imagine to be true in a fiction can be epistemic reasons for those imaginings even if they would not be such for analogous beliefs about the actual world.

For example, in some genres of art we are induced through physical descriptions of characters – their beauty or ugliness, stereotypical racial or ethnic features of appearance, deportment, size, and so on – to conclude (correctly in relation to the story) that they have certain virtues or vices of character and certain kinds of capacities. Ugliness is often employed to provoke a judgment of nefariousness even though, of course, that would not be a proper inference between such a perception and belief. Many studies of human beauty – through what is sometimes termed the 'Halo Effect' – show that it can elicit not only an attribution of moral goodness but also intelligence: a psychological explanation of the historical idea of psyche and body mirroring each-other in 'beauty of soul.'[16] We are often solicited to construe the literal qualities of the media of some types of visual works of art as literal or figurative properties of whatever content the works depict, evoking a judgment about a represented person or state of affairs that is not grounded in the properties of that person or situation considered independently of the medium of representation. A film may cause us to think of the lives it depicts as happy through presenting them in warm tones and soft focus or a state of affairs as menacing through the use of cold blues and greys.[17] The names of characters, such as Roger Chillingworth,

[16] One representative study is Karen Dion, Ellen Berscheid, and Elaine Walster, 'What is Beautiful is Good', *Journal of Personality and Social Psychology* **3** (1972): 285–290; See also, Richard Nisbett and Timothy D. Wilson, 'The halo effect: Evidence for unconscious alteration of judgments', *Journal of Personality and Social Psychology* **35** (1987), 250–256. On the idea of 'beauty of soul' see Robert E. Norton, *The Beautiful Soul: Aesthetic Morality in the Eighteenth Century* (Ithaca, NY: Cornell University Press, 1995).

[17] Compare the metaphorical transfer exhibited in recent experiments that address the processing of tactile information: in one, volunteers asked

the cerebral husband of Hester Prynne in *The Scarlet Letter* and Gradgrind in *Hard Times,* induce us to attribute qualities to those characters that the mere possession of a name, in real life, would not indicate.

Furthermore, we often exhibit highly irrational forms of in-group/out-group bias in favoring even arbitrarily individuated communities in which we are primed to recognize our membership, but that bias is easily exploited in having us favor and judge as merited or objectively valuable the ends of the characters in a fiction with whom we are made intimate – say through having us simulate their perspective – even if independent of the fiction we wouldn't believe that those are good ends to have.[18] We value, for example, the elegant thief's finely calibrated heist even if means a loss to others with whom we don't identify. Indeed, the devices employed to prime our identification with a character can lead us to appraise the facts in the story as that fictional individual does even if a description of such facts outside of a fiction would be unlikely to garner that evaluation.[19] We worry with Tony Soprano as he frets over threats to his mob dominion and we feel a thrill implicitly approving of the ends of the hired killer in the film version of *Day of the Jackal* as he ingeniously pursues his mission to assassinate the fictional Charles de Gaulle. It is controversial to claim that all affective responses entail concomitant judgments about their objects; but in these cases our emotions do seem to evince certain context-conditioned judgments about the evaluative dimensions of their objects: e.g., "loss of control over his criminal organization would be a bad thing," or "succeeding in the assassination is the right goal to pursue."

Our tendency to see actual events as having a narrative-like structure that goes beyond mere causal and explanatory connectedness can be relied on by authors to supply the kind of closure and unity

---

to assess the quality of candidates for an alleged job tended to rate those applicants whose resumes were attached to heavier clipboards as being, themselves, more serious (i.e., 'weighty'). Joshua M. Ackerman, Christopher C. Nocera, and John A. Bargh, 'Incidental Haptic Sensations Influence Social Judgments and Decisions', *Science* **328**.5986 (2010): 1712–1715.

[18] See the suggestion that mere (arbitrary) categorization of individuals serving as research subjects generated in-group bias in S.Otten, and G. B. Moskowitz, 'Evidence for Implicit Evaluative In-group Bias: Affect-biased Spontaneous Trait Inference in a Minimal Group Paradigm', *Journal of Experimental Social Psychology* **36** (2000), 77–89.

[19] See Morton Ann Gernsbacher, et al, 'Do readers mentally represent characters' emotional states?' *Cognition & Emotion* **6**.2, (1992): 89–111.

among fictional events that traditional plots require. It could only be figuratively true of a person's life, or of a romance, that it had an organically structured and internally related beginning, climax, and denouement, but it can be literally true in a fictional world that such is the case. As both prosecutors and con artists know, embedding facts and explanations within an aesthetically satisfying narrative is more convincing than merely stating the facts and explanations outright. A successful narrative can gloss over major explanatory and causal gaps in what we are to imagine as true, without thereby having any less claim on us to evoke that imagining. The narrator of Proust's novel tells us, from a first-person perspective, of his life and emergence as a writer. But certain sequences, particularly those in the sections recounting the relationship between Swann and Odette, could not have been witnessed by the young Marcel, yet are recounted – and we as readers go along imagining those facts – as if he were there. The seamlessness of the narrative gives us reasons to imagine certain states of affairs as obtaining in the fiction even though other facts in the fiction would make those states of affairs impossible.

In his remarks about the nature of moral demands, Nietzsche portrayed our psychological need to attribute a meaning to suffering as resulting in unjustified beliefs about its redemptive significance: that it is a test of character, a divine punishment, a curse.[20] But works of fiction regularly rely on that tendency to endow objects and events with a significance that is then treated as objectively and independently possessed by them. In, for example, *It's a Wonderful Life,* the character played by Jimmy Stewart undergoes various travails that, satisfyingly, come to appear to have existed *for the sake of* his eventual enlightenment.

We also readily accede to a biased understanding – the fundamental attribution error or correspondence bias – of people's motivations, in seeing their actions as explained by stable character traits and deep psychological dispositions or motivations, rather than much more powerfully explanatory contextual or situational factors.[21] This

---

[20] One of the themes of his 'On the Genealogy of Morals', in *'On the Genealogy of Morality' and Other Writings,* edited by Keith Ansell-Pearson, translated by Carol Diethe (Cambridge: Cambridge University Press, 2006).
[21] On the explanatory limits to relying on a notion of character see John M. Doris, *Lack of Character: Personality and Moral Behavior,* (New York: Cambridge University Press, 2002); and Timothy D. Wilson, *Strangers to Ourselves: Discovering the Adaptive Unconscious* (Cambridge: Belknap Press, 2002).

tendency distorts our beliefs about why individuals act as they do, but it is often relied on by traditional fictional narratives, (perhaps it is essential to certain genres) in systematically eliciting from us insight into why characters in the fiction behave as they do.

I've appealed to the ways in general that fictions draw on our automatic and subdoxastic tendencies, including biases and heuristics, to elicit our imaginings of what is true in those fictions. A more specific account of such devices might show how particular kinds of biases may be indexed to the successful functioning of, respectively, particular categories or genres of fictions. For example, there is the bias of the 'hot hand' in which we unjustifiably tend to believe that gamblers or ball players can enjoy streaks, that they can be 'on a roll,' or 'in the zone' where these aren't merely short runs in a random process.[22] This may be the result of a confirmation bias, but whatever the psychological explanation, it seems tailor made for every film about an underdog team trying to make it to the championships.

There are studies of what has been called the 'Rhyme-as-Reason Effect' in which statements that rhyme are taken to be more truthful or insightful than those that don't even when the meaning is the same.[23] This may be an instance of a more general phenomenon in which a statement's truth is unwittingly evaluated on aesthetic terms.[24] In any case, that seems a cognitive bias made for pop, rock and hip-hop songs where in the midst of absorption we exhibit cognitive, affective, and behavioral cues that suggest we imaginatively endorse, say, a singer's genre-typical promise that love is eternal and unconditional or that violence and mayhem are the only answer to society's ills, even though we would not endorse such claims if we subjected them to scrutiny as candidates for belief. One might worry whether, in being largely constituted by an emotional response, such imaginative endorsement of the lyrics of such songs exhibits any cognitive content. However, if the operative emotions

---

[22]   Amos Tversky and Daniel Kahneman, 'Belief in the law of small numbers', *Psychological Bulletin* **76**.2 (1971), 105–110.

[23]   Compare Nietzsche's remark: '[E]ven the wisest of us occasionally becomes a fool for rhythm, if only insofar as he *feels* a thought to be *truer* when it has a metric form and presents itself with a divine hop, skip, and jump.' *The Gay Science,* edited by Bernard Williams, translated by Josefine Nauckhoff (Cambridge: Cambridge University Press, 2001), 85–6.

[24]   See Matthew S. McGlone and Jessica Tofighbakhsh, 'The Keats Heuristic: Rhyme as Reason in Aphorism Interpretation', *Poetics* **26**.4 (1999), 235–244.

impute descriptive or evaluative facts to their objects, as I suggest they do, they should count as instantiating judgments.

In many of these cases we implicitly ascribe the facts to a fictional world that would rationalize our irrational responses. But this rationalizing, if adopted in relation to our beliefs, would be only of a spurious sort. For in the cases I've described we do not discover genuine evidence of what we imagine to be true, but, rather, are caused to impute that evidence to a fiction and treat it as existing there independent of our imagining. In this respect, our tendency to interpret what we perceive in a way that preserves our rationality – treating, e.g., our physically-caused "moral" disgust for a character as a correct recognition of vices that would genuinely warrant moral disgust – exemplifies the widely studied phenomenon of cognitive dissonance: people are systematically motivated to reduce the dissonance among their cognitions, even when doing so isn't rationally warranted by their sources. Employing spurious rationalization aimed at reducing cognitive dissonance is not a truth-conducive manner of forming beliefs. However, when provoked by a work of fiction, such rationalizing can be a reliable truth-in-fiction-conducive cognitive process.

Artists may exploit not only our tendencies to think in these ways to make certain things true in their fictions but also to create unexpected or ironic discoveries, such as that a character has qualities that run counter to what our automatic responses would impute to him.

It runs counter, for example, to our implicit assumptions about evil to find that Milton's Satan is attractive and charismatic – he is described in topoi more fitting of a heroic figure like Achilles or Aeneas – and has none of the appearance of a foul fiend. Yet, Satan is diminished as an object of fascination as Milton's epic comes to enlighten us of his real nature. Compare the obverse phenomenon in Alexander Nehamas' account of how the initial visual repulsiveness of John Merrick, the title character in *The Elephant Man* (1980), is diminished as we come to empathize with him. His appearance is enhanced as we come to better recognize his dignity.[25]

The epistemic errors and departures from rationality exemplified in the activation of these tendencies are importantly, for my purposes, *systematic*. If we were not systematically biased or irrational in certain ways in forming our beliefs, creators of works of art could not *predictably* exploit such tendencies and rely on them to direct our imagining

[25] Alexander Nehamas, *Only a Promise of Happiness: the Place of Beauty in a World of Art* (Princeton, NJ: Princeton University Press, 2007), 59.

of what is true in a work. Our imagining from such tendencies would not be truth-in-fiction tracking. An author wouldn't know that – or wouldn't write in such a way that reflects an implicit awareness that – she could elicit the desired response, the desired emotion or imagining, unless it was likely that her readers would have such biases. Furthermore, while many of the cases I describe illustrate how a work can prime us to attribute certain truths to the fiction, such priming is not just an *a*rational causing to which the application of epistemic norms would be irrelevant, i.e., a category mistake. Rather, like the exploitation of various irrational tendencies, such priming employed by fictions can be systematically directed at particular ends. Specifically, unlike the cases in psychology experiments in which a subject may be differentially primed to adopt one of a plurality of different perspectives on some essentially ambiguous state of affairs, the priming performed by a fiction is usually systemically directed at the discovery of what is true in it, what sorts of things it is *correct* to imagine.[26]

IV.

One way for a defender of continuity to respond to the examples arrayed above would be to say that while they illustrate how the epistemic norms that govern our beliefs don't always govern our imaginings in accord with a fiction, this only shows that such imaginings are often epistemically unjustified or irrational. Authors exploit some of our irrational tendencies to cause us to imagine certain things to be true in a fiction that we would not, on the basis of like causes in real life, be justified in believing. There is no discontinuity in epistemic norms if the illustrations above confirm only that we are by and large epistemically rational in what we believe but epistemically irrational in some of what we imagine.

The problem with this way of describing such cases is that we need to preserve a distinction between instances in which our responses to a fiction are epistemically rational and others in which they are, indeed, irrational. In some cases, that is, fictions are designed to exploit our subdoxastic tendencies to reliably cause us to recognize what is true in a story. What we imagine is the output of a reliable process by

[26] See John A. Bargh and Tanya L. Chartrand, 'Studying the mind in the middle: A Practical Guide to Priming and Automaticity Research' in Harry T. Reis, ed., *Handbook of research methods in social and personality psychology* (New York: Cambridge University Press, 2000), 253–285.

which we discover what is true in the fiction. In other cases, those tendencies lead us to misunderstand a story, to attribute facts to it that do not hold, as when because of one's own irrational racial prejudices one fails to recognize that it is true in a story that a character has certain virtues. If a defender of continuity holds that all (otherwise unsupported) imaginings we form due to the activation of such tendencies are epistemically irrational, we lose the ability to identify those *distinctively* irrational responses to a fiction that do not result from a systematic means of discovering what is true in it.

Another approach for a defender of continuity might be to say that the examples above do not show that we are epistemically irrational in what we imagine in responding to a fictions; rather, they demonstrate how, we are epistemically rational in inferring what is true in a fiction from recognizing how the fiction is designed to affect us. One might suggest, for example, that in the illustrations above, we rely on external factors of the work to imagine what is fictionally true in the same epistemically warranted way in which we form ordinary beliefs: I come to infer that something is true in a fiction from my recognition that the author or artist has designed it in such a way as to make my discovery of that truth possible. But not all such elicitations to imagine function this way. For there are two kinds of cases here: one that poses no threat to continuity is represented by the case, where characters are named so as to give us reason to believe something about their qualities. There, our imagining that the character has that quality follows from an ordinary rational process of relying on the stipulation of the author or testimony of the reliable narrator. The nouveau-riche Veneerings, in Dicken's story *Our Mutual Friend,* really do live a life of superficial gloss, Daffy Duck really is a daffy duck, and Thwackum, the tutor in Fielding's *Tom Jones,* does have a penchant for the cane. In the second kind of case, however, the names of characters would not give us reason to believe something about their qualities, but, instead, are designed to cause us to attribute those qualities to those characters, through, e.g., activating stereotypes or implicit associations. The fiction presents a character or state of affairs as having certain features and our response to those features causes us to correctly imagine the presence of other features too.

Finally, a defender of continuity might say: if it's true in the fiction that Fagin is morally corrupt, the beautiful person is intelligent and honest, the mobster's ends are merited, and so on, then that justifies imagining such things as true. *Whatever* the means might happen to be that such fictional truths are conveyed to us, they are fictional truths and therefore we are justified in imagining them as such, just as we are justified in believing whatever is true. But that does not employ an adequate concept of justification. A belief that P is not justified on the basis of 'P' being true if having the belief does not come about in the right way. It must not be, e.g., an accident, a knock on the head, or a deviant causal chain that explains why one believes that P if that belief is to be justified. Speaking of a fiction from the internal perspective, one does not have direct access to any non-stipulated facts; the only internal evidence one has for imagining what is true within a fiction is what else one imagines to be true in the fiction. The important point is that rational norms governing beliefs do not speak directly to their contents in isolation, but rather to the reasons in favor of the formation or retirement of those beliefs, and to their relations – such as their consistency-while they are held.

V.

Although in making the case for discontinuity I've referred to the various tendencies exploited by fictions as irrational dispositions and the like, it is a mistake to assume that they are always defects, or flaws, or evidence of improper functioning in our reasoning. There may have been evolutionary trade-offs that produced these forms of cognition and behavior so as to allow other beneficial forms. They may, say, reflect evolutionary history not being able to pass over a fitness valley required to attain a more optimal state. And they may reflect asymmetries in the cost of making an error in judgment and the benefit of getting it right ('better safe than sorry' is a low-cost/high-benefit policy when deciding whether a snake in the wild is dangerous).

My interest is in how the suboptimal aspect of these tendencies means we *try* to correct for them when we can – when it would be irrational not to – in theoretical reasoning with our beliefs. But we do not recognize an epistemic norm calling for us to engage in such correction in response to fictions, when, that is, such ways of thinking are exploited by the fiction in order to reveal what in the fiction is true.

That our epistemic norms for believing and imagining are discontinuous stems, I think, from how the kinds of reasons we countenance as justifications for our cognitive representations depend on the *functions* of the practices in which those representations are formed.

Thus, as we have seen, beliefs are typically directed at accurately representing things as they are.[27] Accordingly, the only reasons that

---

[27] Exceptions may be found in the sort of motivated believing and reasoning involved in thinking of oneself as a better athlete than one is in order

count in favor of a belief in its representational dimension are evidential reasons, those that speak to its truth and to the reliable means by which that truth is obtained.

Analogously, in some cases one's imaginative activity has an epistemic or practical role analogous to that of belief and perception, where the function is to aid in discovering some truth about the actual world, as when we need to plan for the future. That purpose is better realized if one's imaginings are based on reasons that speak to the objective qualities of, and relations among, what they represent.

Many fiction-directed imaginings, however, are generated in activities with ends – such as pleasure, entertainment, and absorption – in virtue of which they can be epistemically warranted on grounds that would not count as justifications for analogous beliefs. One may decide that a character in a film is trustworthy because she has a, so-to-speak, honest face (notice the familiarity of that expression). Even if that judgment is not justified by an inference from any facts imagined to hold in the fiction, it may be still be justified if it is part of the design of the work that it induces audiences to see that character as having that virtue.

It should be clear that in speaking of the rational norms governing fiction-directed imagining my aim has not been to address the canonical philosophical question of whether fictional works of literature are a good source of insight or understanding vis-à-vis the real world. However, I do think that my defense of discontinuity poses certain problems for those who attempt to treat our responses to fictional scenarios as a source of evidence for how we respond to like situations in real life.

I will describe only one such problem here, which concerns the widespread practice in the psychological study of cognition to use fictional narratives and films to ascertain the nature of such things as memory, the emotions, inferences, and perceptions.[28] The problem is that if individuals in those studies have internalized different

---

to perform better than one would in light of a wholly accurate appraisal, or in the various paradoxes of rationality in which one is motivated to adopt an attitude of belief toward what one does not believe. However, it is plausibly a conceptual constraint on the identification of a given attitude toward some content as constituting a belief that it is governed in some sense by a norm of truth. Cf. Nishi Shah and David Velleman, 'Doxastic Deliberation', *Philosophical Review*, **114**:4, 2005, 497–534

[28] See, as an example, James Gross and Robert W. Levenson, 'Emotion Elicitation Using Films', *Cognition and Emotion* **9** (1995), 87–108. For a favorable discussion of this method see Keith Oatley, et al., 'The Psychology of Fiction: Present and Future,' in I. Jaén and J. Simon, eds.,

Jonathan Gilmore

criteria of warrant or justification – different norms – for their imagining what is true in the fiction and their believing what is true outside of it, their responses to the scenarios may differ according to whether they construe the events as real, or as merely the content of a fictional artistic representation.

A subject, for example, may allow herself to be affected by formal and stylistic aspects of a description – and not put the brakes on her automatic and usually distorting responses – when she approaches it as a fictional work of art but may try limit those effects on her responses insofar as she believes the description is intended to be a representation of the real world. It's been shown that people often do this: unwittingly adjust their truth-governed mental representations to take account of the effects of distorting forces if they've been primed to be aware of those effects. Individuals, for example, who were asked about their current level of happiness gave less negative responses when they were primed to be aware of the day's bad weather (and its presumed effect, without any explicit connection being made, on that judgment).[29]

Of course, if we do generally respond to fictions in a way that gives free rein to our biases and automatic subdoxastic tendencies, this does not mean that, in all cases, we ought to. I denied earlier that reasons that speak to the moral, aesthetic, or instrumental aspects of an imagining can serve as warrants for the *representational correctness* of that imagining. But, of course, non-epistemic reasons may be built into a theory of the proper ends as a whole that we should have in engaging with fictions. Perhaps we should not allow ourselves to have our irrational tendencies exploited by a fiction when, for example, it is designed to trigger our highly fallible in-group biases and implicit associations in shaping our judgments about a character with stereotypical racial or ethnic characteristics. Likewise, we may have reasons of self-respect not to succumb to the overly sentimental or sure-fire causes of imagining relied on by kitsch. However, it is the insidious power of art that our better judgment doesn't always constrain what we may be elicited to imagine.

Columbia University
jsg8@columbia.edu

Cognitive Literary Studies (Austin, TX: University of Texas Press, 2012), 235–249.
[29] Norbert Schwarz and Gerald L. Clore, 'Mood, misattribution, and judgments of well-being: Informative and directive functions of affective states', *Journal of Personality and Social Psychology* **45**.3 (1983), 513.

Explanations: Aesthetic and Scientific*

SHEN-YI LIAO

In recent years, aesthetics – like many other philosophical areas – has gradually replaced conceptual analysis projects with theory construction projects. For example, in a presidential speech of the American Society for Aesthetics, Kendall Walton advocates for the theory-construction methodology, which does not primarily aim to capture the meaning of aesthetic terms in ordinary English.[1] Instead of trying to define what beauty or art is, philosophers have shifted their focus to explaining aesthetic phenomena that arise from our interactions with narratives and artworks.[2] We are experiencing a shift from what Jonathan Weinberg and Aaron Meskin call the 'traditional paradox-and-analysis model' to a new paradigm, the 'phenomenon-and-explanation model'.[3] The methodology of the new paradigm

* For helpful comments throughout the development of this article, I thank Sarah Buss, Steve Campbell, Gregory Currie, Stacie Friend, Eduardo Garcìa-Ramìrez, Gordon Graham, Jim Hamilton, Lina Jansson, Matthew Kieran, Ian McCready-Flora, Aaron Meskin, Margaret Moore, David Plunkett, Sara Protasi, Jon Robson, Murray Smith, Kendall Walton, William York, Lei Zhong, reviewers for this volume, and participants of the 2012 Philosophical Aesthetics and the Sciences of Art conference. Additionally, I thank Emily Coates, Nancy Dalva, and Sara Protasi for giving me a wealth of postmodern dance examples.

[1] Kendall Walton, 'Aesthetics—What? Why? and Wherefore?', *The Journal of Aesthetics and Art Criticism*, **65** (2007): 147–161.

[2] Which phenomena count as aesthetic? This question is difficult to answer because there are no widely-accepted objective criteria for delineating different kinds of phenomena. As a working definition, take aesthetic phenomena to be the ones that hold interest for aestheticians and are described in aesthetic vocabulary. This working definition takes its cue from the special sciences: for example, sociological phenomena could be understood as those phenomena that hold interest for sociologists and are described in sociological vocabulary.

[3] Jonathan M. Weinberg and Aaron Meskin, 'Puzzling over the Imagination: Philosophical Problems, Architectural Solutions,' in Shaun Nichols, ed., *The Architecture of the Imagination* (Oxford: Oxford University Press, 2006), 175–202, 177.

doi:10.1017/S135824611400023X   ©The Royal Institute of Philosophy and the contributors 2014

explicitly takes its cue from the sciences: look for observable data, propose theories that aim to explain the data, adjudicate competing theories, and repeat.

Despite this shift, there is surprisingly little work on aesthetic explanations. Perhaps the current dearth of writings on this topic can be attributed to the dominance of the traditional paradox-and-analysis model in aesthetics. However, as the phenomenon-and-explanation model becomes more prominent in aesthetics, it becomes increasingly important to investigate the nature of aesthetic explanations.

Given that the methodology of the phenomenon-and-explanation model explicitly takes its cue from the sciences, this paper starts the investigation by looking to recent developments in philosophy of science. In recent decades, philosophers of science are increasingly turning away from conceptions of laws and explanations that are devised in metaphysicians' armchairs to conceptions of laws and explanations that are developed with attention to actual scientific practices, especially practices in the special sciences. One prominent picture that emerged is a pragmatist and pluralist view of scientific explanations.

Taking the methodological similarities between the new paradigm of aesthetics and the sciences as the starting point, I advocate a pragmatist and pluralist view of aesthetic explanations. To bring concreteness to this discussion, I focus on the case of *genre explanations*: explanations of aesthetic phenomena that centrally cite a work's genre classification. Even though some philosophers have given genre explanations of aesthetic phenomena, others have categorically dismissed genre explanations, calling them unhelpful at best and meaningless at worst. Of the opponents of genre explanations, Gregory Currie most clearly states the theoretical grounds for categorically dismissing genre explanations.[4] However, I argue that these theoretical grounds do not stand up to scrutiny once we incorporate the central insights from recent works on scientific explanations. On a pragmatist and pluralist view of aesthetic explanations, there is room for genre explanations. In fact, the reasons for accepting genre explanations alongside other kinds of aesthetic explanations are also reasons for accepting a pragmatist and pluralist view of aesthetic explanations.

§1 introduces genre explanations and Currie's arguments against them. §2 draws on one aspect of Currie's arguments to develop the *robustness challenge* for genre explanations: given that the

[4]   Gregory Currie, 'Genre', in his *Arts and Minds* (Oxford: Oxford University Press, 2004), 43–62.

generalizations underlying genre explanations appear to admit of many exceptions, they seem incapable of supporting as wide a range of counterfactuals as law-like generalizations in other domains can. §3 looks to recent works on *ceteris paribus* laws and counterfactual robustness to respond to the robustness challenge. §4 draws on another aspect of Currie's arguments to develop the *informativeness challenge* for genre explanations: given that genre classifications are metaphysically grounded in lower-level features of works, genre explanations seem incapable of being more informative than, or even as informative as, the aesthetic explanations that only cite those lower-level features. §5 looks to recent works on levels of explanation to respond to the informativeness challenge. To conclude, §6 uses the case study of genre explanations to say what it means to be a pragmatist and a pluralist about aesthetic explanations.

1. Genre Explanations

As introduced earlier, genre explanations are explanations of aesthetic phenomena that centrally cite a work's genre classification. In this section, I give further characterizations of genre explanations as a kind, first with simple but illustrative examples and second with references to genre explanations that have been given for specific aesthetic phenomena. I then review Currie's arguments against genre explanations as a kind.

1.1. Lab Specimens

Consider first a case in which the genre of a dance performance explains the appropriate audience response. Suppose you are seeing a dance performance, performed by ordinary people wearing ordinary clothes and doing ordinary things like walking, standing, and sitting down. That's it.

If this is a performance of modern dance, then the appropriate response is probably a mishmash of boredom, confusion, and perhaps even annoyance. There is no recognizable technique. There is no awareness of rhythm and tempo. There is no narrative, and not even any movement that can arouse some emotions. Everything is so ordinary.

But if this is a performance of postmodern dance – indeed, I am (rather minimally) describing Steve Paxton's *Satisfyin' Lover* (1967) – then the appropriate response is quite different. How

129

curious! How interesting! As a member of the Judson Dance Theater, Paxton and his contemporaries – Yvonne Rainer, Elaine Summers, etc. – consciously rejected the aesthetics of modern dance and sought to legitimize ordinary movements as dance. Ordinary movements, even when performed by ordinary people, can have aesthetic interest for the viewers – in itself, without embodying any narrative or overtly arousing any emotion. Far from boredom or annoyance, the appropriate response to this performance includes puzzled curiosity and cognitive interest.

A promising explanation of the appropriate response to Paxton's *Satisfyin' Lover* appeals to its classification as a postmodern dance performance. Specifically, this explanation appeals to the generalization *ordinary movements in postmodern dance warrant puzzled curiosity and cognitive interest*. There may be more to *completely* explaining the appropriate audience response to this piece. However, for my purpose, it is enough that genre *partially* explains the appropriate response to this dance performance.

Consider next a case in which the genre of a film explains the appropriate audience response. Suppose you are watching a gory scene in a film, in which a character is being decapitated in gruesome details.

If this scene is a part of a straight-up horror film, then the appropriate response is to scream. Horror films elicit fear in their audiences. As part of a horror film, a gory decapitation scene is scream-worthy. But if this scene is a part of a horror comedy film, then an appropriate response is to laugh. Horror comedies elicit amusement in their audiences. As part of a horror comedy, a gory decapitation scene is laughter-worthy.[5]

Again, a promising explanation of the appropriate response to a gory decapitation scene in, say, *Evil Dead 2* appeals to its classification as a horror comedy. Specifically, this explanation appeals to the generalization *decapitation scenes in horror comedies warrant laughter*.

---

[5]   It is possible that a gory decapitation scene in a horror comedy is also scream-worthy. Indeed, if Noël Carroll is correct that there exists an intimate connection between horror and humor, then the gory decapitation scene could well be laughter-worthy *because* it is scream-worthy. For my purpose, it is enough that a gory decapitation scene would not be laughter-worthy in a straight-up horror film, regardless of whether it would also scream-worthy in a horror comedy film. See Noël Carroll, 'Horror and Humor', *The Journal of Aesthetics and Art Criticism*, **57** (1999): 145–160. I thank Aaron Meskin for reminding me of the possible connection between horror and humor.

1.2. Wild Beasts

More complicated genre explanations can be found in the philosophical aesthetics corpus. Philosophers have appealed to genre to explain the following aesthetic phenomena: *comedic force of jokes*[6], *ethical criticism of art*[7], *imaginative resistance*[8], *criticism and evaluation*[9], *perceived realism in fictions*[10], and *moral persuasion*[11]. Moreover, style – a close relative, if not a subset, of genre – is also invoked in explaining *interpretation of pictorial art*[12] and *understanding of theatrical performance*[13]. In this paper, I will use the two simple examples of genre explanations provided earlier to indicate and illustrate what can be said about these more complicated genre explanations.

[6]　See Ted Cohen, 'Jokes', in Eva Schaper, ed., *Pleasure, Preference, and Value: Studies in Philosophical Aesthetics* (Cambridge: Cambridge University Press, 1987), 120–136.

[7]　See Alessandro Giovannelli, 'The Ethical Criticism of Art: A New Mapping of the Territory', *Philosophia*, **35** (2007): 117–127; and Jonathan Gilmore, 'A Functional View of Artistic Evaluation', *Philosophical Studies*, **155** (2011): 289–305.

[8]　See Jonathan M. Weinberg, 'Configuring the Cognitive Imagination', in Kathleen Stock and Katherine Thomson-Jones, eds., *New Waves in Aesthetics* (Basingstoke: Palgrave Macmillan, 2008), 203–223; Bence Nanay, 'Imaginative Resistance and Conversational Implicature', *The Philosophical Quarterly*, **60** (2010): 586–600; and Shen-yi Liao, *On Morals, Fictions, and Genres*, PhD thesis, University of Michigan, Ann Arbor (2011).

[9]　See Noël Carroll, *On Criticism* (Oxford: Routledge, 2009).

[10]　See Allan Hazlett and Christy Mag Uidhir, 'Unrealistic Fictions', *American Philosophical Quarterly*, **48** (2011): 33–46.

[11]　See Shen-yi Liao, 'Moral Persuasion and the Diversity of Fictions', *Pacific Philosophical Quarterly*, **94** (2013): 269–289; and Shen-yi Liao and Sara Protasi, 'The Fictional Character of Pornography', in Hans Maes, ed., *Pornographic Art and the Aesthetics of Pornography* (Basingstoke: Palgrave Macmillan, 2013), 100–118.

[12]　See Jenefer M. Robinson, 'Style and Significance in Art History and Art Criticism', *The Journal of Aesthetics and Art Criticism*, **40** (1981): 5–14; and Richard Wollheim, 'Pictorial Style: Two Views', in Berel Lang, ed., *The Concept of Style* (Ithaca, NY: Cornell University Press, 1987), 183–202. Note that Robinson and Wollheim think that only individual style categories, e.g. Picasso's style, are explanatory, but not general style categories, e.g. cubism. I thank Aaron Meskin for the clarification.

[13]　See James R. Hamilton, *The Art of Theater* (Oxford: Blackwell, 2007).

Shen-yi Liao

A clarification is in order: my use of the term 'genre' broadly corresponds to what Kendall Walton calls 'category of art'.[14] A **genre** is a special grouping of fictions that is recognized by a community as such.[15] On this inclusive definition of 'genre', aesthetic explanations that appeal to style, period, etc. all count as genre explanations.

Nothing substantive hangs on this terminological choice. My following defense of genre explanations applies, *mutatis mutandis*, to any other aesthetic explanation that centrally cites a work's classification, such as its style or its period. Hence, even if one adopts a less inclusive definition of 'genre', genre explanations still stand as exemplars of a broader kind of aesthetic explanation.

1.3. Opponents

Since there has been little work so far on the nature of aesthetic explanation as such, genre explanations have been rarely criticized as a kind. Instead, criticisms of genre explanations typically come as arguments against some specific genre explanation of some specific aesthetic phenomena. It is not possible to address such specific criticisms without getting deep into the first-order debate. So, regrettably, I will set them aside.

However, there are theoretical commonalities to the specific criticisms. These theoretical commonalities are most clearly brought out by Gregory Currie, who stands out for focusing on the theoretical grounds for rejecting genre explanations as a kind. Currie argues that

[14] Kendall Walton, 'Categories of Art', *The Philosophical Review*, **79** (1970): 334–367. There are two minor differences. First, I set aside the question of whether a work is art. Second, while Walton is concerned with only perceptually-distinguishable categories, I am including non-perceptually-distinguishable categories also. Alternative conceptions of genre are developed in Currie, *op. cit.*, note 4; Brian Laetz and Dominic McIver Lopes, 'Genre', in Paisley Livingston and Carl Plantinga, eds., *The Routledge Companion to Philosophy and Film* (Oxford: Routledge, 2008), 152–161; and Catherine Abell, 'Comics and Genre', in Aaron Meskin and Roy T. Cook, eds., *The Art of Comics: A Philosophical Approach* (Oxford: Blackwell, 2012), 68–84. As far as I can tell, what I say about genre explanations is compatible with these alternative conceptions of genre. I thank two reviewers for pressing me to clarify my usage of the term.

[15] Context plays a role in specifying who the community includes. Which groupings are special for a given community is an empirical matter, and why they are special may require us to look to, say, sociology or literary theory for a non-philosophical explanation.

we should categorically reject genre explanations because they are neither informative nor robust. I will briefly review Currie's arguments to bring out two theoretical challenges that, in my view, drive the criticisms of genre explanations. I will then focus on these theoretical challenges for the core of the paper.

To begin, Currie says that genre explanations are not as *informative* as individualistic explanations, or explanations that appeal to metaphysically fundamental features of a specific work:[16]

> Suppose we want to explain the effect of the work on the audience, and cite its being a tragedy. The objector will say that what really matters for explaining the effect of the work is the specific way it is (together with, perhaps, similarities between these specific ways and specific ways possessed by other specific works the people in the audience are familiar with). On this view, the work's being a tragedy does not explain anything left unexplained by the individualistic explanation. Indeed, the individualistic explanation explains more; different tragedies affect their audiences in different ways, and the individualistic explanation cites details capable of accounting for these differences. We need not rest content noting that the effect was 'generally of the kind we expect from a tragedy'.[17]

Furthermore, while some explanations that relatively lack informativeness make up for the vice through other virtues, genre explanations do not. Specifically, Currie says genre explanations also lack the explanatory virtue of robustness: genre explanations are not as *robust* as sociological explanations:

> In interesting cases, explanation by appeal to genre does not provide the sort of information about counterfactual states of affairs that explanation by appeal to *industrialization* does ['industrialization' is short for the generalization *the popularity of organized religions declines when the population shifts due to industrialization*]. *Hamlet* has the effects we associate with a Shakespearean tragedy, but its having them is due to highly specific and contingent features that its being a tragedy tells us nothing about; it could fail utterly to have these effects and still be a tragedy. While *industrialization* is counterfactually robust, *being a tragedy* is counterfactually fragile, or relatively so.

---

[16] §4 clarifies the terms 'individualistic explanations' and 'metaphysically fundamental features'.
[17] Currie, *op. cit.*, note 4, 56.

...Why is *Hamlet* so intellectually and emotionally affecting? An informative answer may cite the fact that it is a tragedy, but no informative answer will be robust under changes to any of a vast range of details about the play: a small word change here or there would have altered the effect significantly.[18]

Genre explanations fail to be robust because, not only do they admit of some exceptions, they are in fact shot through with numerous exceptions. Given their relative lack of informativeness and robustness, Currie concludes that genre explanations ought to be of no interest to aestheticians.

2. The Robustness Challenge

We start with the theoretical criticism that genre explanations, as a kind, are relatively fragile. We can illustrate this criticism by returning to the two simple examples. Aren't there many boring and annoying postmodern dance pieces? Indeed, in Claudia La Rocco's review of a recent Judson Dance Theater retrospective, *The New York Times*'s dance critic knocked Carolee Schneemann's *Lateral Splay* (1963) as 'an amusing but slight exercise in task-based choreography'.[19] In performances of such pieces, ordinary movements warrant neither puzzled curiosity nor cognitive interest. Similarly, aren't there many unfunny horror comedies, such as all the films in the *Scary Movie* franchise? In such films, a gory decapitation scene does not warrant laughter. Worryingly, genre explanations appear to lose their explanatory force easily.

The **robustness challenge** indirectly questions the explanatory worth of genre: it points to the lack of counterfactual robustness to indicate that genre explanations are not genuine explanations. Among the distinctive roles that laws and law-like generalizations perform in science are *supporting robust counterfactuals* and *grounding genuine explanations*.[20] Counterfactual robustness thus goes hand in hand with genuine explanatoriness. Purported explanations that are not counterfactually robust are therefore unlikely to be genuinely

[18] Currie, *op. cit.*, note 4, 56–57.
[19] Claudia La Rocco, 'Modernism Celebrates Its Incubator', *The New York Times*, November 1st, 2010. Available online at http://www.nytimes.com/2010/11/01/arts/dance/01judson.html.
[20] Marc Lange, 'Who's Afraid of *Ceteris-Paribus* Laws? Or: How I Learned to Stop Worrying and Love Them', *Erkenntnis*, **57** (2002): 407–423, 412.

explanatory because they are unlikely to be grounded in laws or law-like generalizations.

This challenge to genre explanations is driven by the **no-exception intuition**: genuine explanations must involve exceptionless laws or law-like generalizations. Since the generalizations that genre explanations cite are apparently shot through with exceptions, they can neither support robust counterfactuals nor ground genuine explanations. As Currie reminds us, just think of cases where two works of the same genre produce significantly different effects on audiences, or cases where small changes to a work make a genre generalization that previously applied to no longer do so. Such cases suggest that genre generalizations are not counterfactually robust. In turn, this lack of counterfactual robustness suggests that genre explanations are not genuinely explanatory. To answer the robustness challenge, we must show that genre generalizations can support robust counterfactuals despite the numerous apparent exceptions to them.

3. Genre Laws and Counterfactual Robustness

The no-exception intuition behind the robustness challenge is misguided. It fails to acknowledge the important role that *ceteris paribus* laws, or cp-laws, play in actual scientific practices, especially practices in the special sciences. Although cp-laws are apparently shot through with exceptions, they nevertheless support a wide range of counterfactuals. Special scientific cp-laws can support genuine explanations in the special sciences, despite the numerous exceptions that they apparently admit of. I argue that genre laws are best understood as cp-laws. As is the case with other cp-laws, they are counterfactually robust despite the apparent exceptions that they admit of. In this section, I clarify the nature of cp-laws and then consider how they help in responding to the robustness challenge.

3.1. Ceteris Paribus Laws

We start by seeing what *ceteris paribus* clauses do. Consider the generalization *fish eggs develop into fish*. This generalization is apparently shot through with exceptions: some fish eggs get ennucleated with sheep DNA and become sheep, some fish eggs get eaten and become nutrients for a turtle, and some fish eggs get irradiated and turn into strange and dysfunctional piles of flesh.[21] Yet, despite these apparent exceptions, this generalization seems true. That is because we do not implicitly understand the generalization to be making the evidently-false universal claim that *all* fish eggs turn into fish. Instead, we tacitly understand the generalization to mean that *ceteris paribus*, fish eggs turn into fish; the apparent exceptions are not genuine counterexamples to the generalization because they are already excluded by the *ceteris paribus* clause.[22]

Although it would be practically, if not theoretically, impossible to list every one of the infinite number of trajectories a fish egg might take that the *ceteris paribus* clause excludes, this generalization has a determinate meaning. Importantly, meanings of generalizations like this do not rest on the statistical typicality of the respective standard cases. The number of fish eggs that do not turn into fish is likely to be greater than the number of fish eggs that do. Instead, meanings of generalizations like this ultimately depend on our tacit understanding of what would constitute genuine counterexamples and what would be mere apparent exceptions – even if such tacit understanding is rarely, if ever, fully articulated. We only understand what the generalization *fish eggs develop into fish* means because we tacitly understand which trajectories of fish eggs are *relevantly like* the apparent exceptions listed earlier, and so should be excluded by the *ceteris paribus* clause.

This reliance on our tacit understanding of the *ceteris paribus* clause may seem rather unsatisfying at first. Can we not explicate the infinite number of cases that are relevantly like the apparent exceptions listed earlier? Even if we can in theory, as Marc Lange points out, our capacity for making such an explicit list would still be itself derived from our tacit understanding of what would constitute genuine counterexamples to this generalization and what would be mere apparent exceptions:

> But in what sense would such an expression really *be* fully explicit? It would derive its content in just the way that the original qualifier did: by virtue of our implicit background understanding of

[21] I borrow this generalization and the apparent exceptions from Mark Lance and Margaret Olivia Little, 'Defeasibility and the Normative Grasp of Context', *Erkenntnis*, **61** (2004): 435–455.

[22] Ordinary language synonyms of *ceteris paribus* include – among many others – 'in the absence of disturbing factors', 'defeasibly', 'in the standard condition', 'as a rule', and 'subject to provisos'. For other ordinary language synonyms of *ceteris paribus*, see Lange, *op. cit.*, note 20, and Lance and Little, *op. cit.*, note 21.

what would count as compelling reasons for (or against) the correctness of applying it to a given case.[23]

The meaning provided by such an explicit list cannot be anything over and above the meaning provided by our tacit understanding of the *ceteris paribus* clause because the former is dependent on the latter.

Coming to a shared understanding of a *ceteris paribus* clause is understandably difficult. We would have to come to agreements on what the canonical examples of exceptions are, how we can compare a novel case to the canonical examples, and whether a given novel case counts as a genuine counterexample to the generalization or a mere apparent exception excluded by the *ceteris paribus* clause. However, trying to come to agreements on these matters is simply the standard mode of operation in actual scientific practices, especially in the special sciences.[24] Our tacit understanding of particular *ceteris paribus* clauses is central to scientific investigations.

Call a *non-accidental* generalization that contains a *ceteris paribus* clause a *ceteris paribus* **law**, or **cp-law** for short.[25] There is a *pragmatic* dimension to the *ceteris paribus* clause: it '[restricts] the law's application to certain purposes'.[26] Cp-laws only do the works that laws are

[23] Lange, *op. cit.*, note 20, 409.

[24] See Lange, *op. cit.*, note 20, and citations therein; *contra* John Earman and John Roberts, '*Ceteris Paribus*, There is No Problem of Provisos', *Synthese*, **118** (1999): 439–478. It is unclear how substantial their disagreement is. Earman and Roberts think that the existence of a *ceteris paribus* clause functions as an indicator of a 'near-law' – a work in progress – rather than a genuine law. However, they are also perfectly willing to grant that the near-laws play an important role in the actual practices of the special sciences, and fulfill many of the roles that genuine laws do in fundamental physics, such as supporting counterfactuals and grounding explanations.

[25] The difficulties with distinguishing non-accidental or law-like generalizations from others are well known. Different accounts of cp-laws give different conditions for separating law-like *ceteris paribus* generalizations from accidental *ceteris paribus* generalizations. For a survey, see Alexander Reutlinger, Gerhard Schurz, and Andreas Hüttemann, '*Ceteris paribus* Laws', In Edward N. Zalta, ed., *Stanford Encyclopedia of Philosophy*. (Stanford: Center for the Study of Language and Information, Stanford University, Spring 2011 edition).

[26] Lange, *op. cit.*, note 20, 412. Lange cites John Stuart Mill as an early proponent for the aim-dependence of *ceteris paribus* clauses. Other contemporary developments of cp-laws similarly make room for their aim-dependence; see, for example, Jonathan Cohen and Craig Callender, 'A Better Best System Account of Lawhood', *Philosophical Studies*, **145** (2009): 1–34.

Shen-yi Liao

thought to do, such as supporting counterfactuals and grounding explanations, in suitable contexts – namely, contexts where the disturbing factors that the *ceteris paribus* clause excludes are irrelevant. Whether a particular cp-law can ground an explanation partly depends on the question that we are asking, or what we are trying to explain.

The range of counterfactuals that cp-laws support is neither *identical to* nor *narrower than* the range of counterfactuals that other laws, such as the fundamental laws of physics, support.[27] We can see this point via an example.[28] Suppose that *the popularity of organized religions declines when the population shifts due to industrialization* is a sociological law. Then it supports the counterfactual *if the population were to shift due to industrialization, then the popularity of organized religions would decline*. First, there are scenarios where fundamental laws of physics hold but our example sociological law does not. For example, suppose that the fundamental laws of physics are the same as they actually are but that human beings are psychologically incapable of following organized religions. Then population shifts due to industrialization would have no effect on the popularity of organized religions. Second, there are scenarios where fundamental laws of physics do not hold but our example sociological law does. For example, suppose that some fundamental parameter of physics is just slightly different from the way it actually is, but without any downstream effects on human sociological behavior. Then the population shifts due to industrialization would still have the same exact effect on the popularity of organized religions.

Whether our example sociological law is a genuine (cp-)law is an open question, depending on whether it supports a stable range of counterfactuals in conjunction with other sociological laws. The goal here is only to show that cp-laws of autonomous social sciences can support robust counterfactuals that range over distinct sets of scenarios, none of which is wholly contained in any other. Hence,

[27] Philosophers do not unanimously agree on what it means to say that a range of possible scenarios is narrower than another range of possible scenarios. Given that all ranges are likely to contain an infinite number of scenarios, we cannot compare the size of ranges simply by counting. While *wholly contained in* is not an uncontroversial definition of *narrower than*, it is the most clear and workable definition available. At any rate, this is the sense of 'narrower than' that I will use throughout this article.
[28] I borrow this example, though for a different purpose, from Frank Jackson and Philip Pettit, 'In Defense of Explanatory Ecumenicalism', *Economics and Philosophy*, **8** (1992): 1–21.

138

this sociological law cannot be said to be less robust than, say, fundamental physics – contrary to what the no-exception intuition suggests.

3.2. Response to the Robustness Challenge

Now, let us return to the robustness challenge. Counterfactual robustness functions as an indicator of genuine explanations. To answer this challenge, we must show that genre laws can support robust counterfactuals despite the numerous apparent exceptions to them. Conceiving of genre laws as cp-laws allows us to do so.

To develop a strategy for responding to the robustness challenge, we start with the postmodern dance case from §1. Consider the generalization *ordinary movements in postmodern dance warrant puzzled curiosity and cognitive interest*. As is the case with *fish eggs develop into fish*, we should not construe this genre generalization as an evidently-false universal claim, that *all* ordinary movements in postmodern dance warrant puzzled curiosity and cognitive interest. Instead, we should understand this genre generalization to mean that *ceteris paribus*, ordinary movements in postmodern dance warrant puzzled curiosity and cognitive interest. As explained earlier, this genre generalization is meaningful as long as we have an implicit understanding of what the *ceteris paribus* clause excludes, even if we can never fully articulate this understanding.

Suppose now that *ordinary movements in postmodern dance warrant puzzled curiosity and cognitive interest* is a genre law. (Whether it is in fact non-accidentally true is an open question; the point here is only to illustrate the response strategy.) As the litter of unsuccessful postmodern dance pieces shows, an ordinary movement in a postmodern dance piece could fail to warrant puzzled curiosity and cognitive interest due to the presence of a number of disturbing factors: lack of innovation from the choreographer, poor execution by the dancers, etc. This genre law therefore admits of numerous – in fact, an infinite number of – apparent exceptions. Despite apparent exceptions like these, this genre law still holds because our implicit understanding of the *ceteris paribus* clause allows for the rejection of the numerous apparent exceptions as genuine counterexamples, given the presence of a disturbing factor with each apparent exception.

This genre law is also counterfactually robust. The counterfactual it supports, *if an ordinary movement were in a postmodern dance, then it would warrant puzzled curiosity and cognitive interest*, ranges over a wide variety of scenarios, including scenarios where fundamental laws of physics fail to hold. For example, suppose that some fundamental parameter of physics is just slightly different from the way it actually is, but without any downstream effects on human aesthetic behavior. Then an ordinary movement in a postmodern dance would still warrant puzzled curiosity and cognitive interest. The range of this genre counterfactual is thus no narrower than the range of counterfactuals associated with the fundamental laws of physics. For analogous reasons, the range of this genre counterfactual is also no narrower than the range of counterfactuals associated with sociological laws, biological laws, or indeed any other special science laws. Therefore, this genre law is no less robust than the laws in other domains.

We now have a strategy for responding to the robustness challenge: understanding the generalizations that genre explanations appeal to as cp-laws. Before moving on, let me emphasize two points concerning the foregoing discussions.

First, I am not assuming that the notion of cp-laws, or indeed the notion of *ceteris paribus*, is unproblematic. Rather, the centrality of cp-laws to the special sciences shows that whatever problems cp-laws have, they are everyone's problems. The no-exception intuition is misguided because it is insufficiently attentive to actual scientific practices, especially practices in the special sciences. Once we reject the no-exception intuition, as we must, we can see that there is nothing uniquely problematic about the appeal to cp-laws in aesthetic explanations.

Second, I am not claiming that all generalizations that cite genre are genre laws. Rather, whether a generalization that cites genre is a genre law, or even whether there are any genre laws at all, is an open question. We can only answer this question by performing tasks typical of actual scientific practices: coming to an agreement on what the canonical examples of exceptions are, how we can compare a novel case to the canonical examples, and whether a given novel case counts as a genuine counterexample to the generalization or a mere apparent exception excluded by the *ceteris paribus* clause. In responding to the robustness challenge, I am only explaining why genre explanations, as a kind, cannot be ruled out as good aesthetic explanations simply because they appeal to generalizations that cite genre. The *a priori* and categorical rejection of genre explanations for their alleged counterfactual fragility is not justified. Ultimately, assessing whether a particular genre explanation counts as a good aesthetic explanation demands that we investigate the phenomenon that it purports to explain. In slogan form: evaluating the worth of a specific genre explanation requires doing aesthetics, not meta-aesthetics.

3.3. Weaker Motivations?

One might wonder whether the robustness challenge can be motivated via weaker, more plausible intuitions.[29] For one, it could be that while explanations can admit of some exceptions, genre explanations admit of *too many* exceptions. For another, it could be that, unlike scientific explanations, we have *no tacit understanding* of which exceptions count as genuine and which exceptions count as merely apparent when it comes to genre explanations.

Take the too-many-exceptions thought first. The difficulty with this thought is that it demands a quantitative comparison of exceptions. However, given combinatorialism about possibilities, the number of exceptions is typically either zero or (countably) infinite. For example, in the postmodern dance case, the *ceteris paribus* clause excludes an infinite number of ways that an ordinary movement in a postmodern dance can fail to warrant puzzled curiosity and cognitive interest due to the presence of a disturbing factor. For another example, in the fish egg case, the *ceteris paribus* clause excludes an infinite number of trajectories that a fish egg might take which do not result in a fish due to the presence of a disturbing factor. Since exceptions multiply infinitely, once a *ceteris paribus* clause excludes one apparent exception, it typically excludes an infinite number of them. Therefore, it is difficult to make sense of the not-too-many-exceptions complaint without reducing it to the no-exceptions complaint.

Take the no-tacit-understanding thought second. Let us grant that, with some purported genre explanations, we may not have an adequate tacit understanding of which exceptions count as genuine and which exceptions count as merely apparent. However, that is consistent with acknowledging that other purported genre explanations, such as the postmodern dance one given earlier, we do have an adequate tacit understanding of the *ceteris paribus* clause. As emphasized earlier, specific genre explanations still need to be assessed on a case-by-case basis, through engagement with the relevant first-order debate. Even though the no-tacit-understanding thought may motivate the rejection of some specific genre explanations, it cannot motivate the robustness challenge to genre explanations as a kind.

---

[29] I thank Aaron Meskin for pressing this objection.

Shen-yi Liao

4. The Informativeness Challenge

We now turn to the theoretical criticism that genre explanations, as a kind, are relatively uninformative. We can illustrate this criticism by returning to the two simple examples again. Why can't the appropriate response to *Satisfyin' Lover* be explained by, say, Paxton's intentions in creating the choreography? Since Paxton's intention behind this piece is one factor that *makes* this piece a postmodern dance, it seems that an explanation that appeals to it must be as explanatory as, if not more explanatory than, an explanation that appeals to the genre of postmodern dance. Similarly, why can't the appropriate response to *Evil Dead 2* be explained by, say, the specific ways in which it is similar to other specific horror comedies (e.g. the music cues used)? Since these specific resemblances are factors that *make* the movie a horror comedy, it seems that an explanation that appeals to the specific resemblances must be as explanatory as, if not more explanatory than, an explanation that appeals to the genre of horror comedy. Worryingly, genre explanations appear to be less informative than other aesthetic explanations – specifically those that appeal to the bases of genre classification.

The **informativeness challenge** directly questions the explanatory worth of genre: it alleges that genre explanations lack an essential feature of genuine explanations because they are relatively uninformative. It is driven by the **smaller-grain intuition**: explanations at lower levels give more information than explanations at higher levels.

All metaphysical accounts of genre acknowledge that a work's appropriate classification in a genre depends on some other features of the work, even if these accounts do not always agree on what the relevant features are. Call the potential bases for genre classification *lower-level features*. In contrast, genre is a *higher-level feature* because a work's appropriate classification in a genre depends on its lower-level features. Since genre is not *metaphysically* fundamental, it is tempting to think that it is not *explanatorily* fundamental either. Following Currie, we can contrast genre explanations with *individualistic explanations*, which denote in this context explanations that cite metaphysically fundamental features.[30] Individualistic

[30] The terminology is somewhat obscure. The phrase 'individualistic explanation' comes from methodological individualism in the social sciences. According to methodological individualism, since individuals' preferences and actions are metaphysically prior to, say, groups' preferences and actions, because the former constitute the latter, lower-level

142

explanations tell us more about the specifics of a work, especially how it differs from works that are similar in other respects, such as other works in the same genre. To answer the informativeness challenge, we must say what information genre explanations can provide that individualistic explanations cannot.

5. Genre Explanations and Informativeness

The smaller-grain intuition behind the informativeness challenge is misguided. Explanations at different levels provide different kinds of information, suitable for different interests and aims. Although physics is ontologically more fundamental than the social sciences, physical explanations are not always preferable because they can fail to provide information that higher-level social scientific explanations provide. Similarly, I argue, although genre classification depends on lower-level features, individualistic explanations need not be always preferable because they can fail to provide information that genre explanations provide. In this section, I present explanatory pluralism, the view that explanations at different levels can be valuable for different interests and aims, and then consider how it helps in responding to the informativeness challenge.

5.1. Explanatory Pluralism

Explanatory pluralism says that explanations at different levels are valuable for different interests and aims. On the version developed by Angela Potochnik, this is because explanations at different levels illuminate different *patterns of dependence* – typically in the sciences, patterns of causal relationships – that hold in different circumstances.[31]

---

explanations of social or economic phenomena that cite individuals' preferences and actions are uniformly preferable to higher-level explanations of social of economic phenomena that cite groups' preferences and actions.

[31] Angela Potochnik, 'Explanatory Independence and Epistemic Interdependence: A Case Study of the Optimality Approach', *British Journal for the Philosophy of Science*, **61** (2010): 213–233, and 'Levels of Explanation Reconceived', *Philosophy of Science*, **77** (2010): 59–72. Jackson and Pettit, *op. cit.*, note 28, develop a different version of explanatory pluralism, on which explanations at different levels are valuable because they exhibit different explanatory virtues that are preferable for different interests and aims. While lower-level explanations exhibit the virtue

Shen-yi Liao

To illustrate, consider Potochnik's example:

> Population genetics and evolutionary ecology provide competing
> explanations of why many traits evolve. Genetic [lower-level] ex-
> planations show how the distribution of genotypes related to the
> trait changed generation by generation, whereas phenotypic
> [higher-level] explanations show how the environment selective-
> ly advantaged the trait in question. [...] The two explanations cite
> different properties, at different levels of organization, to explain
> the same event.[32]

Genetic and phenotypic explanations illuminate different patterns of
dependence. A genetic explanation of a trait's evolutionary development can withstand variances in the environmental source of fitness.
A phenotypic explanation of a trait's evolutionary development can
withstand variances in the genetic details. The two patterns of
dependence do not perfectly overlap; they hold in different ranges
of circumstances.

Patterns of dependence illuminated by lower- and higher-level explanations do not overlap when properties cited in higher-level explanations do not supervene on just the properties cited in lower-level
explanation:

> Yet phenotypes do not supervene on genes or genotypes but on a
> *complex combination of properties* including many other properties
> of the organism, properties of the environment, and sometimes
> even properties of other organisms. The lower-level properties
> under investigation – genes – are not proper candidates for the
> supervenience bases of phenotypes.[33]

It is because phenotypes do not supervene on just genotypes that
there can be variances in phenotypes that are due only to variances
in its other supervenience bases, such as properties of the environment. Genetic explanations cannot capture these phenotypic variances. Moreover, there can also be variances in genotypes that are
not reflected by variances in phenotypes, perhaps due to the

---

of specificity, higher-level explanations exhibit the virtue of generality.
However, Potochnik persuasively argues that Jackson and Pettit's account
is problematic because it mistakenly assumes that the properties cited in
higher-level explanations standardly supervene on just the properties cited
in lower-level explanations.

[32]   Potochnik, 'Levels of Explanation Reconceived', 64.
[33]   Potochnik, *op. cit.*, note 32, 63; my emphasis.

constancy in the phenotypes' other supervenience bases. Phenotypic explanations cannot capture these genotypic variances.

Different interests and aims call for different patterns of dependence. If we want to know how organisms of different species in the same environment can share the same trait, then a phenotypic explanation is more informative. If we want to know how organisms of the same species in different environments can share the same trait, then a genetic explanation is more informative. Given that the patterns of dependence that these explanations illuminate hold in different circumstances, neither explanation is more general than the other. (The present point about generality thus echoes the point about counterfactual robustness in §3.) Therefore, neither explanation can always be said to be more informative than the other because each has a range of applicability different from the other's.

Explanatory pluralism's sensitivity to interests and aims does not deny that lower-level properties are more fundamental than higher-level properties in some sense. After all, phenotypes do partly depend on genes. What explanatory pluralism denies is that this kind of fundamentality implies, or is equivalent to, *explanatory* fundamentality. Since lower- and higher-level explanations can give us different information about distinctive patterns of dependence, neither kind of information ought to be uniformly preferred over the other, contrary to what the smaller-grain intuition suggests.[34]

5.2. Response to the Informativeness Challenge

Now, let us return to the informativeness challenge. To answer this challenge, we must show that genre explanations can provide information that individualistic explanations cannot. Explanatory pluralism shows us how.

To develop a strategy for responding to the informativeness challenge, we start with the horror comedy case from §1. There are (at least) two aesthetic explanations that one can give for why laughter is the appropriate response to a decapitation scene in *Evil Dead 2*.

---

[34] Theoretically, there can be a lower-level explanation that captures every single dependence relationship. Such an explanation would indeed be explanatorily fundamental, but it would also be much more detailed – specifying, say, various modal relationships – than any lower-level explanation that has actually been given. To be precise, then, my claim is that no *actual* lower-level explanation – aesthetic or otherwise – is explanatorily fundamental. I thank Lina Jansson for discussion on this point.

First, one can give a genre (higher-level) explanation that appeals to the generalization that decapitation scenes in horror comedies warrant laughter. (We are supposing that *decapitation scenes in horror comedies warrant laughter* is a genre law.) Second, one can give an individualistic (lower-level) explanation that appeals to 'the specific way [the work] is (together with, perhaps, similarities between these specific ways and specific ways possessed by other specific works the people in the audience are familiar with)'.[35]

What is the relationship between the properties cited in the higher-level aesthetic explanation – genre classifications – and the properties cited in the lower-level aesthetic explanation – specific resemblances to other horror comedies? Although there are disagreements about the details, philosophers agree that genre classifications, like phenotypes, supervene on a *complex combination of properties*. For example, Kendall Walton says that a work's appropriate classification in a genre depends on its relevant resemblances to other works in that genre, authorial intention, critical judgment, and that genre's propensity for increasing aesthetic pleasure.[36] In other words, *Evil Dead 2*'s appropriate classification as a horror comedy is due to a complex combination of factors that includes its specific resemblances to other horror comedies. The relationship between the properties cited in the two aesthetic explanations above parallels the relationship between the properties cited in phenotypic and genetic explanations.

Since genre classifications do not supervene on just specific resemblances, there can be variances in genre classifications that are only due to variances in its other supervenience bases, such as authorial intention. An individualistic explanation that cites only specific resemblances cannot capture these genre classification variances. Therefore, in this case, the genre explanation illuminates a pattern of dependence that differs from the ones that the individualistic explanation illuminates.

Consider again why we should laugh at a decapitation scene in *Evil Dead 2*. The genre explanation holds in circumstances where the individualistic explanation does not. It tells us why we should also laugh at a decapitation scene in, say, *Shaun of the Dead* even though that movie does not contain the same specific resemblances to other horror comedies as *Evil Dead 2*. Furthermore, it tells us why we should still laugh at a decapitation scene in *Evil Dead 2* even if some of the specific works that it is similar to never existed. These

---

[35]   Currie, *op. cit.*, note 4, 56.
[36]   Walton, *op. cit.*, note 14.

limitations of the individualistic explanation show that the genre explanation can be preferable for *some* interests and aims.

We now have a strategy for responding to the informativeness challenge: recognizing that genre explanations can illuminate patterns of dependence that individualistic explanations cannot. Importantly, we can acknowledge that genre classifications depend on lower-level properties, such as specific resemblances, while denying that explanations that cite lower-level properties are explanatorily fundamental. Explanatory pluralism situates genre explanations alongside other aesthetic explanations, including individualistic explanations. Aesthetic explanations at different levels are complementary in the same way that scientific explanations at different levels are. Rather than insisting that one kind of aesthetic explanation is uniformly superior to another, we should use whichever kind of aesthetic explanation best suits our aims and interests in a given context.

Our response to the informativeness challenge shows that whether a genre explanation is a good aesthetic explanation depends on whether it can provide information about a phenomenon that an individualistic explanation of the same phenomenon cannot. Genre explanations cannot be ruled out as good aesthetic explanations simply because they are higher-level explanations. So, the *a priori* and categorical rejection of genre explanations on dependence fundamentality grounds is not justified. To reiterate the earlier slogan: evaluating the worth of a specific genre explanation requires doing aesthetics, not meta-aesthetics.

6. Concluding Remarks

6.1. Specifics

With the resources developed in previous sections, we now return to Currie's arguments against genre explanations, presented in §1. Currie makes two implicit assumptions in his arguments. First, Currie assumes that it is unproblematic to switch the comparison class for genre explanations between the two objections. Genre explanations are initially compared to lower-level aesthetic explanations and then compared to higher-level sociological explanations. Second, Currie assumes that it makes sense to talk about a unique best kind of explanation irrespective of the questions that are asked. Although he only mentions one particular question one could ask, about why *Hamlet* is so intellectually and emotionally affecting, he draws the categorical conclusion that genre generally does not

Shen-yi Liao

figure in 'explanations that have *any* artistic or aesthetic interest'.[37] Both assumptions turn out to be problematic.

As §5 argues, there is a pragmatic dimension to explanations. Whether an explanation is suitable depends on contextual factors such as the question asked and the aims and interests of the questioner. In answering questions about aesthetic phenomena, sociological explanations are simply irrelevant. Hence, even if Currie were right that genre explanations are relatively less robust than higher-level sociological explanations, in answering questions about aesthetic phenomena, higher-order sociological explanations are simply not in the salient comparison class. Only comparisons to individualistic aesthetic explanations, and not comparisons to higher-level sociological explanations, are relevant for assessing the robustness of genre explanations.

However, as §3 argues, Currie is also wrong in assuming that genre explanations are relatively less robust than higher-level sociological explanations. Both kinds of explanations are counterfactually robust despite the exceptions that they apparently admit of. The range of counterfactuals that genre laws support is no narrower than the range of counterfactuals that sociological laws support. Specifically, there are scenarios where a genre law holds but a sociological law does not. Suppose that the psychology of human beings is the same as it actually is, except that human beings are incapable of following organized religions. Then, in this scenario, it would still be true that decapitation scenes in horror comedies warrant laughter but false that the popularity of organized religions declines when the population shifts due to industrialization. Given that each discipline is autonomous, each discipline's laws support counterfactuals that range over a distinct set of scenarios.

6.2. Generalities

Both challenges to genre explanations come from misguided armchair intuitions. We can correct these armchair intuitions by paying attention to central insights from recent works on scientific explanations. The no-exception intuition behind the robustness challenge loses its force once we recognize the centrality of *ceteris paribus* laws in actual scientific practice. The smaller-grain intuition behind the informativeness challenge loses its force once we recognize the need for explanatory pluralism in the special sciences. These insights also

[37] Currie, *op. cit.*, note 4, 57; my emphasis.

148

allow us to transform the specific responses to Currie's arguments into general lessons for better understanding aesthetic explanations.

First, we should be *pragmatists*. What allows for a satisfying response to a given question depends on contextual factors, such as the aims and interests of a research program. There is a pragmatic dimension to which explanation counts as best. In assessing the worth of an explanation, what matters is how it measures up to other competing explanations in the same research program.

Second, we should be *pluralists*. Aesthetic explanations at different levels, like scientific explanations at different levels, illuminate different patterns of dependence. The pragmatic dimension of explanations suggests that explanations at different levels are good for answering questions with different aims and interests. We should not uniformly prefer explanations at one level to explanations at another.

Nanyang Technological University
liao.shen.yi@gmail.com

Against Nature? or, Confessions of a Darwinian Modernist

MURRAY SMITH

> Taste is, after all, a matter of will, of moral and social decision. To take a famous example from the modernist tradition in literature, we are assured that Joyce's *Ulysses* is a difficult masterpiece, and we try to read it, determined, perhaps, to prove our cultural superiority by our appreciation. After the initial repugnance for much of the book experienced by a great many readers, most of us succeed in the end in deriving great pleasure from all of it. Similarly, in the history of music from Bach to the present, by repeated listening we have learned to love the music that has at first puzzled and even repelled us.
>
> Charles Rosen, 'Who's Afraid of the Avant-Garde?'[1]

> The dominant theories of art and criticism in the twentieth century grew out of a militant denial of human nature. One legacy is ugly, baffling, and insulting art. The other is pretentious and unintelligible scholarship.
>
> Steven Pinker, *The Blank Slate*[2]

Introduction: Klangfarbenmelodie and cognitive constraints

A few years ago I gave a paper on the aesthetics of 'noise,' that is, on the ways in which non-musical sounds can be given aesthetic shape and structure, and thereby form the basis of significant aesthetic experience. Along the way I made reference to Arnold Schoenberg's musical theory, in particular his notion of *Klangfarbenmelodie*, literally 'sound colour melody,' or musical form based on timbre or tonal colour rather than on melody, harmony or rhythm. Schoenberg articulated his ideas about *Klangfarbenmelodie* in the final section of his *Harmonielehre* (1911). 'Pitch is nothing else but tone colour

---

[1] Charles Rosen, 'Who's Afraid of the Avant-Garde?' *The New York Review of Books* **45**:8 (14 May 1998), 21.
[2] Steven Pinker, *The Blank Slate: The Modern Denial of Human Nature* (London: Penguin, 2002), 416.

doi:10.1017/S1358246114000174 ©The Royal Institute of Philosophy and the contributors 2014
Royal Institute of Philosophy Supplement **75** 2014

151

Murray Smith

measured in one direction,' wrote Schoenberg. 'Now, if it is possible to create patterns out of tone colours that are differentiated according to pitch, patterns we call 'melodies'...then it must also be possible to make such progressions out of the tone colours of the other dimension, out of that which we simply call "tone colour."'[3] In other words, traditional melodies work by abstracting and structuring the dominant pitch characterizing a musical sound, while 'sound colour melodies' work, Schoenberg argues, by structuring the combined set of pitches contained in a given musical sound (the overtones as well as the dominant pitch). Schoenberg is emphatic that, although a neglected and underdeveloped possibility within Western classical music, 'sound colour melody' is a perfectly legitimate and viable form of musical expression; indeed for Schoenberg it is a musical form with enormous potential.

Schoenberg's ideas on *Klangfarbenmelodie* were also explored by his pupil Anton Webern, and further developed in the 1950s by Stockhausen, among others, who attempted to systematize the treatment of timbre through the application of serialist principles; and still later, combining composition with the psychology of music, by Fred Lerdahl.[4] Parallel with these developments in the worlds of music and music theory, we see the same principles surfacing in a particular strand of avant-garde filmmaking, especially from the 1960s onwards.[5] In certain films, in place of conventional soundtrack elements – dialogue, sound effects, and music, integrated with the moving image to create a unified storyworld – we find abstract, textured soundtracks, eschewing or subordinating both reference (to a fictional diegesis, or to the world itself) and traditional musical form (scores based on conventional uses of melody, harmony and rhythm). William Raban's *Sundial* (1992), for example, creates a playful montage based on the sights and sounds of East London around the original Canary Wharf tower (figure 1). The sounds of traffic, trains, voices, jackhammers and other urban sonic detritus are abstracted and structured into patterns of similarity and contrast, sometimes flowing, at other times staccato, in their development. We

[3] Arnold Schoenberg, *Theory of Harmony* (Berkeley: University of California Press, 2010), trans. Roy E. Carter, 421–2.
[4] See Section 5 of Paul Mathews (ed.), *Orchestration: An Anthology of Writings* (London: Routledge, 2006); Fred Lerdahl, 'Timbral hierarchies,' *Contemporary Music Review* 2:1 (1987), 135–60.
[5] In this essay I follow Rosen and many others in treating the terms 'modernism' and 'avant-garde' as synonyms – though in certain contexts, they are not completely interchangeable concepts.

152

Figure 1. Sundial (William Raban, 1992).

never lose sight of the fact that we are looking at a miniature portrait of a corner of London; but it is equally plain that the film aspires to a kind of musicality, one born in part out of the *Klangfarbenmelodie* woven into the soundtrack.

All of this, it turned out, was a mistake.

Or if it wasn't a mistake, the line of thought I presented on *Klangfarbenmelodie* and the aesthetics of noise certainly hit a lively nerve with some members of the audience. I was told, in no uncertain terms, that Schoenberg's theory and his proposal for 'timbre melody' flew in the face of everything we knew about the nature of musical form and our perception of sound. In reviving Schoenberg's ideas, and suggesting that they were in some measure embodied in *Sundial*, I was 'spitting in the wind' – of our natural predispositions. We simply don't possess, so the objection went, an auditory system capable of perceiving the subtle but systematic patterns of timbral variation and form that I argued were present in *Sundial*; these patterns are 'cognitively opaque,' to use Lerdahl's phrase.[6] *Sundial* is

---

[6] Lerdahl's phrase, but a charge he levels not against *Klangfarbenmelodie*, but rather against Schoenberg's twelve-tone method of composition: Fred Lerdahl, 'Cognitive Constraints on Compositional Systems,' *Contemporary Music Review* 6:2 (1992), 97. In 'Timbral

153

a representational work, triggering our recognitional capacities, and as such it invites us to perceive and interpret its sounds referentially, that is, in terms of depicted locations, objects, and events. Our perceptual apparatus compels us to interpret the sounds of the film ecologically, as sounds affording information about the space depicted. And even if it does succeed in creating a kind of quasi-musical, abstract structure overlaid upon its depictive content, it is far from clear that this musical structure takes or indeed can take the form of a *Klangfarbenmelodie*.

Or so my detractors claimed. What this episode points to most directly is the question – again drawing on Lerdahl's terminology – of the 'cognitive constraints' at play in cognition in general, and in the making and apprehension of artworks in particular. Are there perceptual and cognitive limits to what perceivers of artworks can appreciate? If so, what are they, and to what degree is it possible for us to predict and specify what and where those limits may lie? Behind this problem lies a broader question, concerning the extent to which philosophically naturalistic approaches to the arts, especially those which appeal to evolutionary theory, are compatible with the kind of creative freedom that has been central to the ethos and the practice of avant-garde art. And this is a question whose descriptive, explanatory, and normative strands are tightly interwoven. In the remainder of this essay, I begin by exploring the question of 'cognitive constraints' in a little more detail, by examining practices of point-of-viewing editing and the depiction of emotion in film, before focussing on this framing issue.

Cognitive-evolutionary explanations of artistic practices

As often as not I find myself on the other side of such animated exchanges about the grounding of artistic forms and techniques in our natural psychological capacities. There are now well-established cognitive-evolutionary explanations for many basic cinematic techniques, including point-of-view editing, reverse-shot editing, the norms of pictorial composition, and sound perspective. Noël

---

hierarchies,' op. cit., Lerdahl does make reference to arbitrarily constructed timbral syntaxes which are 'rigorous but opaque to musical understanding,' 137. But in this essay Lerdahl is making the case that a musically apprehensible timbral system, working with rather than against or in disregard of the natural constraints of human audio perception, is possible.

Carroll, for example, has persuasively argued that point-of-view editing works by mimicking 'deictic gazing,' that is, the perceptual behaviour of following the glance of an agent to its target (from the Ancient Greek δεῖξις, a display, demonstration, or reference).[7] In a real situation, you glance over my shoulder in mid-conversation, and I am prompted to follow your gaze in order to discover just what is of such momentous interest. Watching a movie, I see character A looking off-screen right; the next shot shows character B, and I infer that B is the object of A's gaze. A sequence in *The Bourne Identity* (Doug Liman, 2002) shows the technique in action (figures 2.1–2.8). Pursued by police, Jason Bourne (Matt Damon) seeks refuge in the US Embassy in Zurich. He joins a line of American citizens awaiting service. The space of the embassy is now mapped out by a series of point-of-view edits, alternating shots of Bourne glancing off-screen with shots of other characters and objects occupying different zones of the embassy space.

Each shot on the right is immediately preceded by the paired shot on the left. According to Carroll, the reason we so readily infer that the figures in the right hand series of shots are the objects of Bourne's gaze, as it is depicted in the left hand series, is that this way of stitching shots together exploits the basic 'biological inheritance'[8] of deictic gazing. Viewers of sequences exemplifying the practice of point-of-view editing, like this one, are able to readily map the elements of the real world behaviour onto the equivalent filmic elements: my perception of my interlocutor's glance is mapped onto the shot of the character looking off-screen, while my act of following the glance of my interlocutor is mapped onto the 'answering' shot in the film sequence, the shot that shows us the second character. Point-of-view editing, as a conventional

[7] Noël Carroll, 'Towards a Theory of Point-of-View Editing: Communication, Emotion, and the Movies,' *Poetics Today* **14**:1 (Spring 1993), 123–41. Carroll does not use the phrase 'deictic gazing,' but the expression is widely used to refer to this behavior, as it is by Per Persson in his development of Carroll's argument in *Understanding Cinema: A Psychological Theory of Moving Imagery* (Cambridge: Cambridge University Press, 2003), chapter 2. Note that Carroll's definition of 'point-of-view' is broad, encompassing all cases where an edited sequence shows the object of an agent's glance, but not requiring (as do some accounts of point-of-view) that the object is shown from the vantage point of the looking agent (as it is in the sequence from *The Bourne Identity* analysed here).
[8] The phrase is Carroll's: ibid, 139.

Figures 2.1 – 2.8. Point-of-view editing in *The Bourne Identity* (Doug Liman, Universal Pictures, 2002).

practice, thus builds upon and exploits the ordinary behaviour of deictic gazing.

Shot/reverse-shot editing, as represented by this pair of shots (figures 3.1–3.2) from *Trainspotting* (Danny Boyle, 1996), is based on an elaboration of this principle. We see Begbie (Robert Carlyle) looking and blowing smoke off-screen left; this shot is directly 'answered' by the shot of Renton (Ewan McGregor) looking off-screen right, returning Begbie's gaze while receiving the smoke blown into his face. The directions of the glances of the two characters thus knit together just as they would if we were encountering a real confrontation of this type in an actual space. Shot/reverse-shot editing is thus a special case of point-of-view editing in which the reciprocal gazing of two characters is represented mimetically, tapping into our

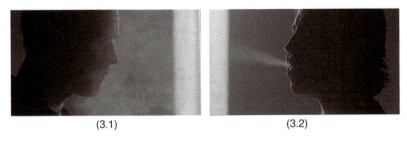

(3.1)   (3.2)

Figures 3.1 – 3.2. Shot/reverse-shot editing in *Trainspotting* (Danny Boyle, PolyGram Filmed Entertainment, 1996).

evolved propensity to track and follow the glances of others to their objects.

Note that there are two layers to such an explanation of an artistic practice. Most immediately, a representational practice – here point-of-view or shot/reverse-shot editing – is explained by reference to a real-world perceptual behaviour on which the representational practice piggy-backs. The second (often implicit) layer of explanation concerns the perceptual behaviour itself. So in this case, deictic gazing is held up as a product of evolution (it is a 'biological inherit-ance'). It is important to see that these two layers of explanation are detachable, however. A non-transitive relation obtains across the three elements: the fact that certain evolutionary considerations explain deictic gazing does not mean that those same considerations explain point-of-view editing. We cannot get from evolutionary pressures to film practices in one explanatorily homogeneous step. A representational practice might be mimetic – imitative of some ordinary perceptual behaviour – but the mimicked behaviour might be culturally specific, and not in that sense apt to be directly explained in evolutionary terms. And, as will become plain in this paper, representational practices can be non- or anti-mimetic, in the sense that they may *evoke* or refer to a perceptual routine (biologically basic or culturally specific) while *not* seeking to *mimic* or feed off of that routine (in the way that, on Carroll's argument, the practice of point-of-view editing feeds off of deictic gazing). This last point is particularly complex and will certainly need further unpacking. At this stage, the important thing to grasp is that a full-blooded cognitive-evolutionary explanation conjoins these two layers (even if they are detachable): as in the point-of-view example, the claim is that a representational practice mimics a perceptual behaviour that is plausibly regarded as a product of biological evolution.

Murray Smith

Importantly, then, there is no claim here that point-of-view editing is itself a product of evolution, as Carroll himself firmly underlines.[9] In a parallel context, Jesse Prinz notes that while '[s]carcity [according to certain evolutionary psychologists] may trigger a biological disposition for belligerence...[it] does not cause us to invent canons, peace treaties, or agriculture. These specific tools for coping with scarcity depend on insight and toil, rather than innate knowledge.'[10] In Carroll's and Prinz' examples alike, we can tease out four distinct elements: an ecologically-given *problem* (the need for food and other material resources; the need for information about the environment and our conspecifics' relationship with it); a suite of *capacities and behaviours* which have evolved in response to those problems (belligerence, deictic gazing); and a variety of cultural *inventions* – including technologies – which build upon these capacities in order to expand and enhance the *solutions* available (canons, peace treaties, agriculture; cinema, point-of-view editing). And we can lay out the relationship between these four elements, and the two layers of cognitive-evolutionary explanations discussed above, in the following way (figure 4):

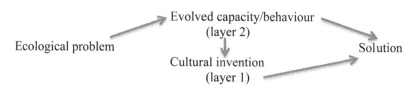

Figure 4. Layers of explanation.

Layer 2 (deictic gazing) precedes layer 1 (point-of-view editing) historically, of course, even though layer 1 occupies the frontal position, so to speak, in the explanation at stake (and is numbered

---

[9] 'I do not assert that the emergence of point-of-view editing was mandated by human nature. There is, for example, no reason to reject the possibility that point-of-view editing might never have been discovered. Rather, my claim is that, given certain of our biological propensities, point-of-view editing, once discovered, was an extremely viable and compelling means of visual communication in general and of emotional communication in particular.' Ibid, 138.
[10] Jesse Prinz, 'Culture and Cognitive Science,' *The Stanford Encyclopedia of Philosophy* (Winter 2011 Edition), Edward N. Zalta (ed.), http://plato.stanford.edu/archives/win2011/entries/culture-cogsci/, section 2.4, 'Bio-cultural Interaction.'

as such). The impulse behind naturalistic explanations of the arts and human behaviour more generally is to capture all four of these elements, not to fold everything into the box labelled 'biology.'

Such cognitive-evolutionary arguments, even when carefully qualified in this way, are not always well received. Some audiences are bothered not only by what they see as the 'reduction' of culture to nature – an issue to which we will return – but by what they believe to be the implications of these arguments for experimental forms of cinema like *Sundial*, that is, the cinematic equivalents of the sort of modernist musical innovations proposed by Schoenberg; artworks based on practices which don't seem to exploit our natural propensities, and in some cases seem to cut deliberately against them. They suspect that some sort of naturalistic sleight of hand is in the offing; is an 'ought' being smuggled in via an 'is,' they query?

As further examples of experimental practice where the kind of explanation offered by Carroll in relation to point-of-view editing seems unlikely, consider the two unusual forms of editing that James Peterson identifies as constituents of the 'radicalized rhetoric' of American avant-garde filmmaking. Peterson labels the first of these two types of editing *radical metonymy*. In ordinary metonymy, a complex action or sequence of events is represented by a single salient detail; an entire trip might be represented by a single shot of a character seated on an airplane, for example. In radical metonymy, however, we are required to infer an event on the basis of a marginal detail rather than a central and salient feature. In Fritz Lang's *M* (1931), for example, in order to understand the story, we have to infer that the little girl Elsie (Inge Landgut) has been murdered by virtue of the sight of her balloon – which we have seen the child murderer buy her – drifting free and becoming entangled in telephone wires (figure 5). The balloon stands in metonymically for Elsie (and perhaps there is a hint of metaphor in the way that the telephone lines trap the balloon). An ordinary use of metonymy here might involve a shot of a single limb of the dead girl, or the sound of her cries heard off-screen: parts of the action which more directly represent the whole action (the murder).

In such cases, Peterson notes, 'the inference we make is more difficult and less certain' than in the case of ordinary metonymy; moreover, although in the example from *M* the murder is confirmed in the following scene, in avant-garde films the inferred event will often remain a more tentative hypothesis. In the world of avant-garde film, 'we must be prepared to make bold inferences and live

159

Murray Smith

Figure 5. Radical metonymy in *M* (Fritz Lang, 20th Century Fox, 1931).

without confirmation.'[11] Peterson tellingly notes that critic and film-maker Jonas Mekas, who was to become one of the staunchest advocates of avant-garde cinema, was at first 'puzzled and irritated' by such filmmaking, an instance of Rosen's typical 'first reaction' of perceivers of modernist works.[12]

Peterson discusses such radical metonymy alongside the second constituent of the radical rhetoric of the avant-garde, *radical metaphor*, the comprehension of which requires us to discern the target of the metaphor through the source of the metaphor alone. In Stan Brakhage's *Reflections on Black* (1955), for example, Peterson argues that a shot of a coffee pot boiling over is most reasonably interpreted as a metaphor for male orgasm.[13] As in the case of radical metonymy in *M*, the larger context of the film allows us to make this metaphorical

---

[11] James Peterson, *Dreams of Chaos, Visions of Order: Understanding the American Avant-garde Cinema* (Detroit: Wayne State University Press, 1994), 43.

[12] Peterson, ibid, 1. Mekas' transformation from enemy to ally of the avant-garde is evident in his *Movie Journal: The Rise of the New American Cinema, 1959–71* (New York: Collier Books, 1972).

[13] Peterson, ibid, 44.

160

inference. But this interpretation is nevertheless 'retarded' – in the Russian Formalist sense of 'made difficult' for the sake of artistic interest – by virtue of the fact that we are only shown the coffee pot, not the coffee pot (the source of the metaphor) and the male figure experiencing the orgasm (the target). What radical metonymy and radical metaphor share, and what makes them 'radical' variants of ordinary metonymy and metaphor respectively, is their highly-elliptical nature. The metonymic parts and metaphorical sources in these rhetorical figures are only indirectly and tenuously connected with their targets. Perhaps we can envisage a cognitive-evolutionary explanation for ordinary metonymy and metaphor; perhaps these aspects of our cognition are basic biological endowments that form the basis for certain representational practices. It is difficult to see how such an explanation could extend to the radical variants of metonymy and metaphor, however, as this would require identifying an ecological function – a function in ordinary rather than artistic contexts – apt to be selected, for such elliptical and indirect representation.

Generalizing from such techniques, we might wonder about the stylistic practices associated with Soviet montage, Yasujirō Ozu, Robert Bresson, Jean-Luc Godard, and other radical innovators in the cinema. Can a cognitive-evolutionary approach illuminate the broadly modernist explorations that we find in the work of such filmmakers? One well-trodden path leads from this question to the kind of stand-off I have staged through the two quotations at the head of this essay. On the one hand, we have Charles Rosen's view that artistic appreciation ('taste') is 'a matter of will, of moral and social decision,' implying an infinite or at least indefinite range of artistic possibilities, the appreciation of many of which will require sustained engagement and effort with works that we may initially find incomprehensible or 'repugnant.' Ranged against this perspective we have Steven Pinker's view that the type of position represented by Rosen involves a 'militant denial of human nature' resulting in 'baffling' art – art that cannot be genuinely appreciated; that is, appreciated without self-deception or some secondary, non-artistic rationale. Rosen himself astutely acknowledges the pursuit of social status and 'cultural superiority' through art appreciation, a phenomenon famously explored by Thorstein Veblen, and in our time by Pierre Bourdieu.[14]

[14] Thorstein Veblen, *The Theory of the Leisure Class: An Economic Study of Institutions* (Oxford: Oxford University Press, 2009). Pierre Bourdieu, *Distinction: A Social Critique of the Judgement of Taste* (London: Routledge, 1984), trans. Richard Nice.

Murray Smith

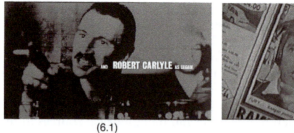

(6.1)   (6.2)

Figure 6.1 – 6.2. Sneering in reality and in *Trainspotting* (Danny Boyle, PolyGram Filmed Entertainment, 1996).

Emotional expression in film

The extent to which (some) artistic practices can be explained on a cognitive-evolutionary basis comes more sharply into focus if we juxtapose two ways in which the *facial expression of emotion* has been treated by filmmakers. On one end of the spectrum, there are filmmakers who treat such expression more-or-less naturalistically – in the sense that they adopt the familiar patterns of such expression in the everyday world, with only relatively minor modifications and expressive heightenings. Consider as an example the sneer exhibited by Begbie in *Trainspotting*, seen here in the film's concluding freeze frame credit sequence (figure 6.1). Set alongside a still from Kevin Keegan's infamous live television rant against fellow football manager Alex Ferguson (figure 6.2)[15] – like *Trainspotting*, from 1996 – and the similarities in both the component parts of the expression and its overall form are evident.

This comparison illustrates the strong continuities between the generally unrehearsed expressions captured by documentary footage, and the kind of facial expressions we see in fiction films committed to naturalistic performance styles. And here again we see the two layers of cognitive-evolutionary explanations of representational practices I noted above: the form of the practice in question (facial expression of emotion as performed and depicted) is held to mirror a facet of actual behaviour (facial expression of emotion), and that behaviour is held to be a product of evolution (a widely-held perspective with regard to at least 'basic' emotional expressions). Note,

---

[15] Recently voted the Most Memorable Moment of Managerial Madness: http://metro.co.uk/2011/04/21/kevin-keegans-love-it-newcastle-rant-at-sir-alex-ferguson-voted-most-memorable-moment-652654/

however, that – as in the case of point-of-view editing – this does not imply that the representational practice is itself directly explained as a product of evolution; no-one is arguing that close-ups of emoting faces or 'scenes of empathy' are direct products of evolution.[16] Instead, the evolutionary element enters the explanation in the second or 'lower' (and often implicit) layer of explanation. The practice of using shots depicting legible, basic emotional expressions is an artistic invention that represents through mimesis the evolved behaviour of expressing and communicating emotions facially.

In contrast to this practice and at the other end of the spectrum, there are modernist directors who use the human visage in quite 'unnatural,' or at least, unfamiliar ways. The films of Robert Bresson provide an excellent example, challenging us as they do with a style of acting which almost wholly eschews facial expression, substituting a ritualized emphasis on objects and gestures. In one sequence from Bresson's *L'Argent* (1983), the protagonist Yvon (Christian Patey) is accused of attempting to avoid paying his bill in a restaurant. His indignation is given expression through a series of stylized movements – standing up, grasping the shirt of the restaurant waiter and pushing him away – and capped by a cut to a shot of Yvon's hand extended in the shape of a fan, sustained for several seconds (figure 7).

This striking and rather abstract shot replaces the prototypical shot of the 'climax' of a facial expression – that is, the moment when it is fully developed – of the type that we see in *Trainspotting*, and indeed in the vast majority of popular narrative films worldwide.[17]

So the treatment of facial expression in film ranges from the mimesis of familiar everyday expressions, towards exaggeration of

[16]   On the 'scene of empathy,' see Carl Plantinga, 'The Scene of Empathy and the Human Face on Film,' in Carl Plantinga and Greg M. Smith (eds.), *Passionate Views: Film, Cognition, and Emotion* (Baltimore: the Johns Hopkins University Press, 1999). The role of facial expressions of basic emotions in conveying emotional states in film also enters into Carroll's argument in 'Towards a Theory of Point-of-View Editing,' op.cit.

[17]   Another ubiquitous, realist practice involves the representation of each individual character in a narrative film with an individual performer. This too has been subject to occasional challenge by modernist innovation, as in Luis Buñuel's use of two performers to play a single character in *That Obscure Object of Desire* (1977). For further discussion, see my *Engaging Characters: Fiction, Emotion, and the Cinema* (Oxford: Clarendon Press, 1995), 125–32. Here again the question arises as to whether the ease or difficulty of comprehension in the two cases arises from evolved predispositions, or enculturation, or some blend of the two.

Figure 7. Stylized performance in *L'Argent* (Robert Bresson, MK2 Diffusion, 1983).

such expressions in one direction, and suppression and displacement of them in the other. Doubtless there are many further possibilities not captured by this analysis. Now, one might think that our grasp of this array of possibilities is aided by the recognition that main-stream narrative films adopt, to a very considerable degree, the modes of facial expression that are operative in real life, expressions that are largely the product of evolution. Again, though, there are those in aesthetics, film studies, and the humanities more generally, who are allergic to evolutionary psychological explanations of any aspect of any type of film or cultural object, taking issue even with the present modest proposal. The stance here is culturalist and social-ly constructivist: human existence is understood to be cultural 'all the way down,' in the sense that human behaviour is held to be so variable that (it is argued) our underlying biology plays no substantial role in shaping the forms of culture. Through much of the twentieth century, the orthodox view of emotional expression in anthropology was culturalist in this sense: all expression was considered culturally 'constructed' and learned.[18] The anthropologist David Schneider de-clared biology to be irrelevant to anthropology, and in more recent times the philosopher John Dupré has defended what Kim

[18]   See the Afterword in Paul Ekman's edition of Charles Darwin, *The Expression of the Emotions in Man and Animals* 3rd Edition (London: HarperCollins, 1999). Ekman places particular emphasis on the work of Ray Birdwhistell, *Kinesics and Context* (Philadelphia: University of Pennsylvania Press, 1970).

Sterelny aptly labels a 'post-biological' perspective on human behaviour.[19] 'Literary Darwinism' is the most recent lightning rod for dispute around the question of the relevance of our evolved biology to culture, with many critics dismissing the insights claimed by the literary Darwinists as either trivial or mistaken.

Semiotic arguments concerning the putative 'naturalization' of cultural and ideological practices – the distorting and illegitimate treatment of culturally-specific behaviours and practices as biologically-given universals – are orthodox in contemporary literary and film theory; the classic text is Roland Barthes' *Mythologies* (1957). But the anxiety predates the emergence of semiotics. Writing in 1911 of the traditional system of harmony as it had developed up to the nineteenth century, Schoenberg complained that this 'system would arrogate to itself the status of a natural system, whereas it will scarcely do as a system of presentation.'[20] For Schoenberg, a 'system of presentation' is something like a 'cultural tradition' – a set of possibilities that have been 'built up' over time, but only a set of possibilities, not an exhaustive mining of every option within the natural spectrum of possibilities. Schoenberg's position (in his theory and practice) accords well with the theory of 'radical innovation' in the arts advanced by Patrick Hogan (a theory in turn heavily influenced by the work of cognitive psychologist Howard Gardner).[21] According to Hogan, radical innovation involves reclaiming a set of possibilities which have not been selected or systematized ('built up') within a certain culture, but which can then be made the basis of a new system. Childhood practices, as well as the aesthetic practices of other cultures, might both function as sources of inspiration and initial models for the new aesthetic system. Taking Picasso as one example, Hogan writes that 'African, Iberian, and other traditions [of art]...suggest to him his own forgotten practices and they offer him preliminary systematizations of those practices. He then takes

[19] On Schneider, see Adam Kuper, *Culture: The Anthropologists' Account* (Cambridge: Harvard University Press, 1999), 122, 125. John Dupré, *Humans and Other Animals* (Oxford: Clarendon Press, 2002); reviewed by Kim Sterelny, 'Po-Bo Man?' *Studies in the History and Philosophy of Biological and Biomedical Sciences*, **35**:4 (December 2004), 729–741.
[20] Schoenberg, op. cit., 321.
[21] Patrick Hogan, *Cognitive Science, Literature, and the Arts: A Guide for Humanists* (New York: Routledge, 2003); Howard Gardner, *Art, Mind, and Brain: A Cognitive Approach to Creativity* (New York: Basic Books, 1982).

up these practices and systemizations for his own purposes and shapes them for a different audience.'[22]

The critical point here is that 'a system of presentation' involves the selective development of certain natural affordances; it depends upon choice, dialogue, and co-ordination among many individuals, often over many generations. It is at least as much a matter of invention as of discovery. By contrast, a 'natural system' on Schoenberg's view is one mandated by physics and physiology, allowing little or no scope for choice and selective development, and is a matter of discovery. And Schoenberg insists that 'a system of presentation' should not be confused with 'a natural system,' though our assimilation of the principles of a 'system of presentation' make it very easy to mistake one for the other. If we are immersed from an early age in the principles of tonal harmony – whether through formal education or informal exposure – that system will become our musical reality, and be experienced as the natural musical order of things. Assuming that it is correct to think of tonality as a 'system of presentation' in Schoenberg's sense, it will take considerable effort to experience it as such, rather than as a 'natural system.'

Art, Freedom, and Naturalistic Explanation

All of the above points to a dilemma facing those studying art and aesthetics from an evolutionary perspective: how to reconcile the mutability of art, and its strong association with human freedom, with an approach that by definition seeks to ground and explain art in naturalistic terms? This is a familiar enough dilemma, echoing as it does one of the antinomies (the Third) that Kant regarded as a fundamental and ineradicable part of ordinary human thought. Human beings appear, on the one hand, as part of the fabric of the physical, causal world, and we take their behaviour to be determined as such; on the other hand, we appear to ourselves and one another as rational agents, possessing and exercising free will. The association of art with human freedom is particularly strong in the Romantic tradition: for the Romantic theorist, art is the pre-eminent vehicle for individual expression, and individual expression is valued in part according to its unique and idiosyncratic character. Joris-Karl Huysmans' novel *À rebours* (1884) – 'against the grain,' or as it is usually translated, 'against nature' – is a classic example from this tradition, depicting a character who asserts his freedom through the pursuit of eccentric artistic tastes

---

[22] Hogan, op. cit., 79.

and quests. And not coincidentally, *À rebours* is widely regarded as an important precursor or early example of avant-garde culture, because of its emphasis on strident artistic non-conformity and the overturning of established practice. The values of such works grate with naturalistic approaches that seek to identify and explain pattern and regularity in the world of art – and so the dilemma emerges.

Stated in the starkest, Manichean terms, the argument here is between a kind of sociobiology which sees culture as being 'on the leash' of nature, and a form of social constructionism which assumes total plasticity in the domain of the human mind and culture, the (in)famous 'blank slate.'[23] The quotation from Rosen that I began with seems to assume something like total plasticity. If '[t]aste is...a matter of will, of moral and social decision,' it would appear to operate within few constraints; certainly Rosen's essay does not pause to acknowledge any constraints. No matter how sympathetic one might be to Rosen's desire to defend 'difficult' art, the assertion in the first sentence of the quoted passage comes across as little more than a declaration of hope by a sentimental avant-gardist. It is, however, in the very starkness of the opposition we find between Rosen's position and the sociobiological stance exemplified by Pinker, that we begin to see the possibility of a resolution to the dilemma. Neither of these extreme positions are very plausible, and more refined and moderate conceptions of the relationship between nature and culture will begin to open up some elbow room – to enable us to see, that is, how a naturalistic approach to art can accommodate a measure of freedom of action, of choice within constraints, and an acknowledgement of the unpredictability of the future course of art.

So how, and to what extent, does a naturalistic, evolutionary account of art allow for modernism? Before working through this question in detail, two broad preliminary points are worth emphasizing. First, an appeal to evolutionary theory does not entail the claim that evolutionary factors entirely *determine* cultural phenomena – as we have seen in the analysis of cognitive-evolutionary explanations

---

[23]   The leash metaphor was first deployed by Edward O. Wilson: '[G]enes hold culture on a leash. The leash is very long, but inevitably values will be constrained in accordance with their effects on the human gene pool. The brain is a product of evolution. Human behavior—like the deepest capacities for emotional response which drive and guide it—is the circuitous technique by which human genetic material has been and will be kept intact.' Edward O. Wilson, *On Human Nature* (Cambridge: Harvard University Press, 1978), 167.

of point-of-view editing and facial expression of emotion in film. Thus an appeal to evolutionary theory does not necessarily imply that the theory will furnish a *comprehensive* explanation of all facets of the phenomenon in question. In other words, an appeal to evolutionary theory should not be confused with a commitment to 'adaptationism,' that is, the view of the mind as wholly or largely the product of natural and (for some theorists) sexual selection.[24] David Bordwell has suggested that evolutionary considerations should be treated 'as *one* constraint on theorizing about the psychology of film;'[25] while Stephen Jay Gould argued that 'biological potentiality' was as important a concept and phenomenon as biological determinism. With this concept, Gould meant to emphasize the range of directions evolution might take from any given point in the history of an environment, depending on the mutations which happened to arise, changes in the environment, and so forth. Other perspectives beyond evolutionary ones may be necessary to explain why a particular direction in evolutionary history was indeed realized, and thus to complete an explanation of which evolutionary theory forms a part. In order to investigate the relevance of evolutionary theory to some domain, we need only hypothesize that there is an evolutionary *dimension* to this domain; we do not need to commit to the idea that it can be comprehensively described and explained in evolutionary terms.[26]

A second preliminary point worth stressing is that the environments described, explained and envisaged by evolutionary biology centrally feature both 'innovation' (in the form of genetic mutation) and 'diversity' (in the form of the diversity of species that come to occupy different niches within the environment). So even in what is usually regarded as the 'home' territory of evolutionary theory (ie. biology), we can see how it accommodates two phenomena that are important in any theory of art, that is, *change* and *diversity* (variability through time and across space, as it were). The fact that the features of snakes, spiders and sea cucumbers – not to mention

---

[24] On this point, see Paul Bloom, *How Pleasure Works: The New Science of Why We Like What We Like* (London: The Bodley Head, 2010), xiii. Bloom adds, on the same page: '*Evolved* also does not mean "stupid" or "simple."'

[25] David Bordwell, Foreword, in Joseph D. Anderson and Barbara Fisher Anderson (eds.), *Moving Image Theory: Ecological Considerations* (Carbondale: Southern Illinois University Press, 2005), xi, my emphasis.

[26] Stephen Jay Gould, 'Biological Potentiality versus Biological Determinism,' in *Ever Since Darwin* (Harmondsworth: Pelican, 1980) 251–9.

humans – are all explained by the theory of evolution hardly makes us overlook the very significant differences among such species. So any worry that evolutionary theory seeks to reduce the diversity of phenomena in a given domain (biological, cultural, and so forth) to some sort of false homogeneity seems misplaced. Identifying shared underlying principles should be no more of a worry here than it is with respect to any other form of *theory* – as theorization is an activity that by definition seeks general principles. The semiotician, or the expressive theorist of art, is just as interested in discovering general principles that apply to a wide range of cases as the evolutionary theorist. None of them are guilty of 'reduction' in this sense. (Of course there may be worries about other forms of 'reductiveness' lurking – reduction to a single principle or kind of explanation, for example; but we can at least head off concerns about 'blindness to difference and variation,' as one form of reduction, at the outset.)

Thus far I have been running together naturalism, cognitivism, and evolutionary theory, as well as (for the most part) talking of evolutionary theory in the singular. It is time to make some distinctions. Evolutionary theory as I am using the term encompasses not only evolutionary biology, but evolutionary psychology, as well as evolutionary epistemology and the study of cultural evolution (which includes, but is by no means exhausted by, the somewhat disreputable field of 'memetics'). What binds all of these semi-discrete fields and research programmes together is a commitment to a post-Darwinian conception of evolution; all of them hold that change occurs through a process of variation, replication, and selective retention across time. The locus of replication, the rate and dynamics of evolutionary change – these and many other factors both vary and are the object of debate across these sub-fields; but all orient themselves towards the conceptual framework introduced by Darwin. From our point of view, evolutionary psychology and the study of cultural evolution are the most relevant research domains, and I will organize the remainder of this essay by considering each of them in turn. What role might evolutionary psychology on the one hand, and research on cultural evolution on the other, contribute to a naturalized aesthetics in general, and an understanding of modernism in particular?

Cultural Evolution and Memetics

Among the theories of cultural evolution that have been advanced, memetics is the best-known but most controversial variant. The label for this nascent field of study is derived from the concept of the 'meme' (short for 'mimeme'), posited by Richard Dawkins as the cultural equivalent of the 'gene' – that is to say, a cultural 'unit of replication' which acts as the vehicle of 'cultural transmission' just as the gene acts as the unit of biological transmission. Dawkins lists 'tunes, ideas, catch-phrases, clothes fashions, ways of making pots or of building arches' as examples of memes.[27] On Dawkins' theory, we can conceive of all of these items as packets of information, sets of instructions for the creation of cultural representations and artifacts. Daniel Dennett, who has elaborated Dawkins' proposal in the greatest detail, adds that memes are 'distinct memorable units,' and that memetic 'units are the smallest elements that replicate themselves with reliability and fecundity.'[28] The process of cultural transmission is constituted by the copying of these packets of information from one agent to another – that is, through a process of *mimesis* or imitation of one agent by one or more other agents. Just as mutations (and thus variation) occur in the biological domain through errors in the copying of DNA from one generation to the next, so the process of copying-through-imitation throws up errors and variation. And, crucially, the spread of memes is not to be explained in intentional terms, that is, in terms of what individual agents and groups of agents seek to achieve through their actions. The proposal, rather, is that memes will be reproduced selectively according to their 'fitness' within the cultural environment that they exist. Memetics invites us to see the world of cultural entities in terms of a blind process of selective replication, rather than as a field of intended individual and collective actions.

This very direct analogy between biological and cultural evolution has provoked heated debate, and there are certainly many difficulties for the proponents of memetics to overcome. Dawkins' list looks like a quite heterogeneous heap of items, ranging from very abstract (ideas) to very concrete (building techniques) entities. While the direction of genetic transmission is downward through the generations, memes spread laterally (through social groups well beyond the bounds of the biological family) and may be transmitted 'upwards' as well as downwards in generational terms (your children may have learned nursery rhymes from you, but a few years later you may find yourself

[27] Richard Dawkins, *The Selfish Gene* (Oxford: Oxford University Press, 1976), 206.
[28] Daniel C. Dennett, *Darwin's Dangerous Idea: Evolution and the Meanings of Life* (Harmondsworth: Penguin, 1995), 344.

humming songs that they have brought into the family home). My aim here, however, is neither to shoot down nor to defend memetics, but rather to emphasize a point already touched upon briefly above, namely, that the theory of memetics involves a radical rethink of what we regard as the proper domain of evolution. Evolution has been traditionally conceived as a *biological* theory. Biology is its 'home' territory. Memetics, by contrast, implies that evolution describes a more general principle and process of development, which explains and can be applied to many domains, including the biological and cultural. So long as there are entities that are replicated, variation among these entities, and a selective process of replication based on the differential fitness of the variations to the environment in which they exist, we can talk *without analogy* of evolution. From this perspective, sometimes referred to as 'Universal Darwinism,' it is a mistake to think of talk of the 'evolution of culture' as merely metaphorical.

What contribution, then, might memetics make to our understanding of culture, and of modernism in particular? I want to suggest that memetics might provide a description of the ordinary cultural backdrop – and the process by which this backdrop gets established and sustained – against which modernism occurs. An important assumption here, then, is that modernism is a kind of 'counter-tradition' that latches onto familiar conventions in order to modify them radically or reject them altogether. The idea of an artistic or other cultural practice that might act 'against nature' is an instance of just this sort of revolutionary stance. Because modernism has this strongly 'dialectical' character, we need an understanding of the cultural backdrop against which modernism reacts. How does the memetic perspective aid us in this task?

As I have already noted above, Hogan emphasizes that the development of artistic practices works in part through a process of cultural *selection* and *systematization*. Certain practices are selected by cultures from among the array of possibilities that emerges in the development of the child; these are then systematized into a more elaborate set of conventions and associated techniques. In this way, the practices that are transmitted and sustained across generations come to constitute a *cultural environment* that exerts selective pressure on which conventions will continue to be replicated. Techniques and practices which either duplicate existing practices, or which fit comfortably alongside them, are much more likely to be selected and transmitted. There is thus a self-perpetuating dimension to this process. This dynamic accords with what social psychology tells us about the strong tendency towards conformity within social groups: people tend to copy whatever is most prevalent in their society.[29]

On the face of it, the spread and stabilization of a cultural practice across a social group, and its evolution – that is, its replication-with-variation-and-selective-retention – through time, look rather similar to a phenomenon at the centre of research in the humanities, and one that I have referred to several times in the course of the argument so far: the *tradition*. When we speak of a tradition we refer to a set of assumptions and practices shared by a large community, sustained over generations. The realist novel, classical Hollywood filmmaking, and popular songwriting are all artistic traditions in this sense. But the word 'tradition' implies something more: it implies that the practice has coalesced and been sustained by a process of guided judgement. Practitioners and critics reflect on the works produced within the tradition, innovating within its parameters and offering judgements on the value of individual works within the tradition, or even the value of the tradition as a whole. Huysmans wrote *À rebours* partly out of disillusionment with the tradition of the naturalistic novel that he had, up to that point, worked within. In the preface to the 1903 reprint of the novel, Huysmans wrote:

> Naturalism was then at its height; but that school, which was supposed to perform the unforgettable service of showing real personages in their precise surroundings, was doomed to repeat itself endlessly, to mark time on the same spot. It could barely tolerate, in theory at any rate, the exceptional; it therefore limited itself to the delineation of everyday existence, forced itself, under the pretext of making its characters lifelike, to create beings as similar as possible to the general average of people.[30]

Huysmans' reflections here testify to his conscious awareness of the tradition in which he is writing, one that he eventually comes to challenge; a process quite distinct from the blind process of selective retention theorised by memetics and other accounts of cultural evolution.

[29] Prinz, 'Culture and Cognitive Science,' op. cit., section 2.3, 'Biases in Cultural Transmission.' Note that caution must be exercised around the word 'selection' here: Hogan uses the term to refer to intentional choices made by individuals and groups, while authentic arguments regarding cultural evolution use the term to refer to a 'blind' process of retention. As I note below, however, these two phenomena – intentional and evolutionary selection – are not mutually exclusive.
[30] Joris-Karl Huysmans, *Against Nature* (Sawtry: Dedalus, 2008), trans. and ed. Brendan King, 237.

Given these differences between memetics and the humanistic study of cultural tradition, it does not seem that they are redundant with one another. But to the extent that they share an *explanandum* – the emergence and maintenance of networks of shared, integrated cultural practices – we might ask: are they, as *explanans*, in direct competition with one another? Are they mutually exclusive? This too seems doubtful. Looking at cultural dynamics from a memetic perspective, we make the supra-individual dimensions of culture highly salient, and we specify the nature of transmission in a particular way. Practices get replicated or 'reproduced' because the cultural environment selects for them, not (only) because of more mysterious or at least elusive factors, like the charismatic power of individual practitioners. In effect, memetics is one way of approaching the 'problem of the unintended social repercussions of intentional human actions,' in E. H. Gombrich's words.[31] So there is no intent to deny the significance of human intention to culture; rather the point is to insist that there is *more* to culture and its development than the intentions of agents. The co-presence of evolutionary and intentional processes within the sphere of culture is no more mysterious than the co-presence of casual and intentional factors. When, for example, we describe Josef Von Sternberg's ability to create a certain kind of pattern of light and shadow, we assume that he's doing this on the basis of the physical laws governing light, not in place of them. Likewise there is no contradiction between intentional and memetic processes. The underlying thought here, then, is that far from being either redundant or mutually exclusive with the humanistic study of cultural tradition, memetics is complementary to it.

The presence of both *arms races* (where intense competition within an environment gives rise to 'extravagant exaggeration,' as embodied by the peacock's tail) and *convergent evolution* (where identical adaptive features emerge in similar, though separate, environments) within the cultural sphere gives further support to the hypothesis that evolutionary dynamics are found in culture (if not specifically to the memetic version of this hypothesis). Examples of cultural arms races might include the progressive increases in the height of Gothic spires in the late medieval period, and of skyscrapers in our own time; similarly Gombrich argues that the 'flamboyant Gothic style' of ornament arose from a competitive dynamic among artists

---

[31] E. H. Gombrich, 'The Logic of Vanity Fair: Alternatives to Historicism in the Study of Fashions, Style and Taste,' *Ideals and Idols: Essays on Values in History and in Art* (London: Phaidon, 1979), 61.

working within that tradition to outdo one another.[32] In the world of filmmaking, the increasing length and complexity of action sequences, culminating in the positively baroque constructions of the contemporary action film, provide another example. In all of these cases, the race seems to continue until it is curbed either by prevailing limitations at the level of engineering (a spire or skyscraper can only go as high as the techniques of the day allow) or by virtue of the exaggerated feature causing the work as a whole to become dysfunctional and maladapted (a Hollywood film cannot be completely subsumed by extended action sequences and still function as a film of that type – it needs, for example, narrative exposition to set up what is at stake in the action sequences).

The world of filmmaking also affords us with examples of convergent cultural evolution. Over the first two decades of cinema, such fundamental techniques as the close-up, the match on action, and staging in depth emerged independently in different national contexts; filmmakers were discovering, more or less simultaneously, the same solutions to the same problems, the overarching problem being: how to use the new technology of film to convey stories clearly and vividly? Of course, influence and interchange among filmmakers working in different national contexts rapidly emerged, but this does not gainsay the reality of convergence on the same solutions and practices by filmmakers working in isolation from one another.

Evolutionary Psychology

So the study of cultural evolution may enrich our understanding of the fabric of culture, complementing the more familiar study of cultural traditions as they are sustained by the reflections, judgements and creative acts of individuals and groups. What of evolutionary psychology – that more familiar branch of evolutionary theory which considers, among other things, the consequences of the evolutionary history of the human mind for modern social and cultural phenomena? What role might it play in explaining modernism, if it is not simply ruling out the project as a whole, as it pretty well does in the hands of Pinker? Evolutionary psychology reveals, I want to suggest, the broad, underlying psychological processes that establish the array of possibilities from which culture selects. It thus establishes the natural parameters for the 'cultural survival' of memes in

---

[32]   E. H. Gombrich, ibid, 65.

general, and the radically innovative memes of modernism in particular. Innovations which simply fly in the face of our perceptual or cognitive predispositions, or exceed our capacities – those which are wholly 'cognitively opaque' – are not likely to be replicated. A symphony composed in pitches entirely outside the range of human hearing – *Smith's Silent Symphony* – will probably not form the basis of a new artistic genre (though it might well survive as a conceptual joke). So there are natural constraints on the kinds of innovation that can be expected to succeed in the long run. Pinker is right about that. Culture is on a leash. Total plasticity of the mind and thus of culture is a fantasy. This is a bullet that, I fear, even the most devout modernist must bite.

That said, there are much trickier cases than *Smith's Silent Symphony*. Consider *Twin Earth Trainspotting*, in which our assumptions about spatial direction are systematically disrupted. In this hypothetical film, with each successive shot, screen direction is reversed – in other words, with each shot the camera is repositioned on the opposite side of the 'axis of action,' the imaginary line running between the two characters. Thus in the two shots here (figures 8.1–8.2), Begbie and Renton are still locking glances, even though both are shown in right profile, and it will be difficult for us to resist the inference that both characters are looking off to the right, rather than at each other. Or imagine *Sneer < > Smile*, a film that takes Bresson's strategies a step further, not merely attenuating and displacing facial expression, but, so to speak, *reversing its polarities* – so that a smile stands for anger and other negative emotions, while joy is expressed by a grimace, and sneering is to be understood as a means of communicating respect and social ease. It seems unlikely that the gravitational force of our evolved assumptions about the meaning of expressions could ever be wholly eradicated, even by *Sneer < > Smile*.

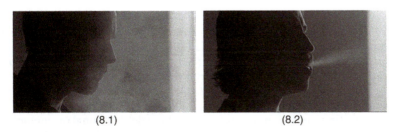

(8.1) (8.2)

Figures 8.1 – 8.2. 'Contranuity' editing in *Twin Earth Trainspotting.*

Murray Smith

This hypothetical example bears some resemblance to the actual case of twelve-tone composition – the radical innovation for which Schoenberg is best known. From the outset, Schoenberg's twelve-tone theory and the works composed on the basis of its principles attracted controversy, with various commentators holding that the harmonic structures created in such works cannot be cognized by listeners. In Lerdahl's terms, dodecaphonic works are 'cognitively opaque' because of the gap between the harmonic structures created by their composers and listeners' (in)ability to apprehend them – between compositional and listening 'grammar.' Diana Raffmann goes so far as to suggest that twelve-tone works may be artistically 'defective' or 'fraudulent' because 'twelve-tone pitch structure is not perceptually real.'[33] Denis Dutton, drawing on the work of music psychologist David Huron to demonstrate the deeply strange, 'reverse musical psychology' of serialism, is similarly sceptical of its perceptual and aesthetic legitimacy.[34] Huron himself is more circumspect, noting that some listeners 'have adapted to the contrarian aesthetic [of modernists like Schoenberg], and have internalized the same contrarian principle as a basis for auditory expectation.'[35] In Lerdahl's terms, these listeners have acquired a listening grammar to match the compositional grammar of the works themselves. In a similar spirit, Lerdahl notes that a listening strategy apt for serial works is 'much harder to learn than is its tonal counterpart,' while elswhere noting his admiration for the 'remarkable work' by Pierre Boulez, *Le Marteau sans Maître* (1954), that forms his primary case study, as well as his general allegiance to the spirit of avant-garde exploration: 'Like the old avant-gardists, I dream of the breath of other plants.'[36]

Perhaps most significantly here, Lerdahl argues that certain principles of tonal harmony together act as an inevitable 'cognitive reference point,' even in more experimental musical contexts, because these experiments necessarily operate within our evolved cognitive constraints. The same is plausibly true of *Sneer* $<$ $>$ *Smile* and

---

[33] Diana Raffman, 'Is Twelve-Tone Music Artistically Defective?' *Midwest Studies in Philosophy* XXVII (2003), 86.
[34] Denis Dutton, *The Art Instinct: Beauty, Pleasure, and Human Evolution* (Oxford: Oxford University Press, 2009), 216.
[35] David Huron, *Sweet Anticipation: Music and the Psychology of Expectation* (Cambridge: MIT Press, 2006), 333.
[36] The first quotation comes from Fred Lerdahl, 'Atonal prolongational structure,' *Contemporary Music Review* 4:1 (1989), 84; the second and third from 'Cognitive Constraints,' op.cit., 97 and 119; both essays originally published in 1989.

Twin Earth Trainspotting: it would be hard to learn and to habituate oneself to a viewing strategy in which the polarities of expression, and of spatial orientation, were systematically reversed, but assuming it is possible, our normal assumptions regarding the valence of expressions and implications of gaze direction would remain in the background, poised for re-activation, and giving sense to the alternative strategies as calculatedly contrarian aesthetic devices.[37] So this is the sense in which an artistic practice may evoke an ordinary behaviour without seeking to mimic it, a possibility we noted above (see page 7). Bresson's treatment of facial expression is the clearest case of such a strategy among the actual examples canvassed here.

So the picture I am painting here is by no means all bad news for Rosen. I have already stressed the fact that an evolutionary perspective allows for, indeed would 'predict' for, variation and diversity. There is no suggestion here that all culture will or should converge into a homogeneous, banal glop. Lerdahl stresses that 'there are innumerable and radically new ways to use and extend' the space available within the constraints of human perception and cognition; '[t]he future is open.'[38] We might add that the complex interaction among modalities of perception, levels of cognition, and types of affective response involved in art makes it hard to predict where the constraints on artistic innovation lie. Thought experiments may be sufficient to establish the principle of cognitive constraints, but actual artistic experiment is usually necessary to find specific boundaries. John Stuart Mill argued that 'experiments of living' were necessary to discover the possible forms of the good life, that the good and the right could not be predicted or known *a priori;* we may similarly hold that artistic 'experiments of living' play an essential role in discovering what is cognitively open to us and valued as art by us.[39] For all these reasons, recognition of cognitive constraints should be contrasted with a stronger 'cognitive closure' thesis: that

[37]   These cases might also be compared with the question of human landscape preferences, as analysed by Stephen Davies: '...whatever the role of culture in channeling and directing our preferences, there is a strong undercurrent of widely shared responses to natural environments.' *The Artful Species: Aesthetics, Art, and Evolution* (Oxford: Oxford University Press, 2012), 99.
[38]   Lerdahl, 'Cognitive Constraints,' op.cit, 119. Compare Bordwell's remarks on the 'openness' of a Gibsonian approach to filmic representation, notwithstanding its concern with the ecological constraints on perception. *Moving Image Theory*, op.cit, xii.
[39]   John Stuart Mill, *On Liberty* (Harmondsworth: Penguin, 1982), chapter 3: 'there should be different experiments of living...the worth of

Murray Smith

the kind of radical innovation in the arts associated with modernism cannot be appreciated because it exceeds our cognitive capacities. The closure thesis is 'atheistic' in spirit; the constraints thesis by contrast represents a kind of naturalized aesthetic agnosticism, much more sceptical about our ability to know in advance what will and what will not work in artistic practice.

In my sketch of memetics, I wrote as if it made sense to talk of a single, unified cultural environment. Large, modern cultures, however, are not complelety unified, but contain within them various 'niches' in which different sorts of cultural activity thrive. Now the types of artistic activity that thrive in these different niches will be various, and one way such activity will vary will depend on the degree of tutelage, formal or informal, imposed or self-motivated, that it requires. Learning to comprehend and appreciate Joycean prose or Brakhagean 'plastic editing' requires both considerable will and formal cultural apprenticeship, in a way that watching a film based on canonical compositional and narrative norms does not. Now, in one sense in which the word 'natural' is used, one might say that this makes the more canonical film more natural than the experimental works – the sense in which something is 'natural' to the extent that it is not the product of human intervention or artifice. But from the perspective I have advanced in this essay, the greater significance of cultural learning in the modernist, experimental cases does not straightforwardly make one of these sorts of culture more or less natural than the other, any more than dolphins are more or less natural than sea anemones. In each case, the phenomena vary in terms of their complexity and the elaborateness with which they exploit their environment, but in a deeper sense they are both part of that environment. And in the human case, cultural practices are integral to the way that the environment is shaped and exploited. It is not as if there is such a thing as a purely natural type of filmmaking, standing completely outside or before cultural influences and intentional activity. But it does not follow that our natural, evolved history and the predispositions and capacities they bestow upon us are irrelevant. All films – all artworks – are products of human artifice, and all human artifice involves the cultural elaboration of natural affordances.

Rosen himself puts his finger on another important point. His talk of 'will' is really shorthand for the way in which our natural capacities

---

different modes of life should be proved practically, when any one thinks fit to try them' (x).

can be developed and 'educated' in particular directions. Indeed, since culture is an evolved aspect of human nature, our natural capacities *must* be realized through cultural expressions, just as much as our cultural practices must draw on our natural capacities. Think of a lullaby, for example. Undoubtedly the concept 'lullaby' is a cultural concept, and close investigation would probably reveal subtle differences between our notion and apparently identical notions in other cultures. But only certain sounds and rhythms will serve our cultural purpose in singing a lullaby – good luck to the relativist parent (if such exists) who sings 'Rock a Bye Baby' in the manner of 'Rock Around the Rock' – because of our natural predisposition to respond to certain sounds and rhythmic patterns in certain ways. A lullaby composed of grating dissonances will probably not be replicated; though those same dissonances might serve another musical purpose very well.

Recall here that in Hogan's framework, systematization is as important as selection, and systematization amounts to the cultural elaboration of a natural possibility. The leash is long; in certain respects the mind possesses great, if not total, plasticity. In the words of Peter Goldie, a great many of our evolved psychological capacities are characterized by considerable *developmental openness* (though such openness comes in degrees, and some psychological capacities are more open than others). For example, while the predisposition to learn language is widely held to be instinctive, the particular language that we speak and the way we speak it will be shaped according to the specific path of our development in a particular cultural environment; Goldie contends that this is true also of much of our emotional development. He argues against what he calls the *avocado pear* conception of the relationship between natural predisposition and cultural elaboration, in which there is a dichotomy between 'a soft outer structure (that which varies culturally), and a hard inner core (that which is biological and universal).' His own model might be likened to a *squwish*[40] – a firm but flexible structure capable of considerable, but not total, reshaping, in which a 'single developed capability' has been 'shaped by the culture and environment in which the individual is placed.'[41] If Goldie is right about the developmental

---

[40] A squwish is an infant's toy, comprised of small wooden beams and elasticated string, forming a polygonal shape. The shape can be pushed, pulled and distorted in various ways – but not utterly transformed.

[41] Peter Goldie, *The Emotions: A Philosophical Exploration* (Oxford: Oxford University Press, 2000), 99, 101. Goldie contrasts his characterization of the 'openness' of emotional development with the relative lack of

openness of such specific cognitive attributes as language and the emotion system, how much more plausible is this idea in relation to something as 'high-level' and synthetic as art? Here, openness is compounded by the range of psychological capacities that art in general, and film in particular, draw upon.[42]

Some Concluding Remarks

Does this, as Arthur Danto claims is characteristic of philosophical interventions, leave everything just where it was before?[43] Are we, in effect, back to the familiar, vague characterization of human behaviour as an admixture of nature and nurture? Well, not quite. For one thing, on the model outlined here, culture is no longer *opposed* to nature, but seen as part of (human) nature. As the blank slate gives way to the squwish, to a conception of the mind as prestructured but developmentally open, so the Hegelian 'alienation' between culture and nature gives way to a view of culture as emergent from, and as an extension of, nature.[44]

I have concentrated in this essay on the possibility of a naturalistic, evolutionary description and explanation of modernist art. But lurking in the background, even more contentiously, is the question of *evaluation*. What bearing, if any, does our evolutionary inheritance have upon our aesthetic *standards*? As we have seen, some would reject this question out of hand, insisting that aesthetics, as an aspect of culture, is entirely independent of biology and our evolutionary history. But even if we take a more moderate position, accepting that our evolved natures will have some bearing on aesthetic and artistic evaluation, it remains to be specified – for we surely do not

---

such openness with respect to instinctual responses like eye blinks. In a broader but kindred move, Dennett stresses the phenotypical plasticity of humans in his *Kinds of Minds: The Origins of Consciousness* (London: Phoenix, 1997), 110.

[42] The perspective here might be contrasted with the lack of openness in Pinker's account of aesthetic perception, which puts an emphasis on aesthetic practices that latch on directly to inflexible, low-level aspects of perception and cognition. Pinker, *The Blank Slate*, op. cit, chapter 20.

[43] Arthur C. Danto, *Connections to the World: The Basic Concepts of Philosophy* (New York: Harper & Row, 1989), xv.

[44] For an elaboration of this line of thought, see my 'The Evolutionary Paradigm: the View from Film Studies,' *Style* **42**:2/3 (Summer/Fall 2008), 277–84.

want to say simply that the more *straightforwardly* a work of art exploits our natural predispositions, the *better* it is. As Lerdahl suggests, '[t]here is no obvious relationship between the comprehensibility of a piece [of music] and its value. Many masterpieces are esoteric, while most ephemeral music is all too comprehensible.'[45] Pinker is tellingly equivocal on this matter. He seems to imply for the most part that artworks should mesh straightforwardly with our adaptive capacities if they are to give us aesthetic pleasure (which he defines rather narrowly); but then he concedes that some modernist works 'offered invigorating intellectual workouts.'[46]

One way of handling the question of value within a cognitive-evolutionary framework is to propose that our perceptual and cognitive make-ups are such that there is a certain 'optimal' level of stimulation which will engage us most fully, or a range within which successful works of art are going to need to operate, if they are not to bore or frustrate us.[47] Even putting this in terms of a range rather than a single point, however, won't take us very far in establishing standards of aesthetic value, since the level of 'challenge' or 'difficulty' presented by a work of art is itself a normative question. That is, different cultural traditions value Rosen's 'puzzlement' to different degrees. A finely-crafted whodunnit is not going to fare very well in the modernist cultural niche, in spite of its many excellent features, to the extent that it lacks the 'difficulties' prized in this tradition. Such a novel is not well-adapted to the modernist cultural niche. Evolutionary psychology – allied with psychology more generally – can limn for us the natural, cognitive constraints on our perception and cognition, and we can describe the developmental dynamics of cultural traditions in the language of evolution. But neither the study of cultural evolution nor evolutionary psychology can decide for us, or explain, how it is that we value particular possibilities, with different levels and types of challenge, within the natural array of possibilities. Traditional humanistic approaches remain important with respect to these questions, and not only these questions: the case being made for evolutionary theory here is that it may complement and enrich familiar humanistic approaches, not that it can or should supplant them.

There can be little doubt that Schoenberg was spitting in the wind – nobody knew this better than he did. But the wind into which he was spitting was not quite as straightforwardly organic as

---

[45]   Lerdahl, 'Cognitive Constraints,' op. cit, 118.
[46]   Pinker, *The Blank Slate*, op. cit., 413.
[47]   Hogan, *Cognitive Science, Literature, and the Arts*, op. cit., 9–10.

the *mistral*, but rather the force of a musical tradition that develops from and progressively refines certain naturally-occurring phenomena. Writing of his compositional work with timbre inspired by Schoenberg's *Klangfarbenmelodie*, Lerdahl urges 'that timbral consonance and dissonance be developed not on some arbitrary foundation but on the sensory experience of timbre. The resulting system can get a running start, so to speak, from perception.'[48] Traditions of this type, developed over many generations, can be very powerful, but they are never all-consuming, as the persistence of variety and innovation in the domain of art testifies. Looking back, I'm confident that my antagonists were far too quick to dismiss the efforts of *Sundial* to explore 'tone colour' and indeed the film's achievements in this regard. Taste – aesthetic responsiveness – may not be entirely a matter of will, but no more is it entirely a matter of uneducated natural predisposition. We need to keep in view, simultaneously, not only the power of traditional 'systems of presentation' and the fact that there are limits to the kinds of aesthetic form we finite and contingent humans are capable of experiencing, but the humility and patience necessary to see such systems of presentation for the naturally-grounded, culturally-elaborated entities that they are. Only then will we be open to artistic 'experiments of living' – to the multitude of viable artistic innovations lying beyond the horizons of these systems and our existing artistic histories.

University of Kent
M.S.Smith@kent.ac.uk

---

[48]   Lerdahl, 'Timbral hierarchies,' op. cit, 143.

Mixed Motivations: Creativity as a Virtue

BERYS GAUT

1. Introduction

The thought that creativity is a kind of virtue is an attractive one. Virtues are valuable traits that are praised and admired, and creativity is a widely celebrated trait in our society. In philosophical ethics, epistemology, and increasingly aesthetics, virtue-theoretical approaches are influential, so an account of creativity as a virtue can draw on well-established theories. Several philosophers, including Linda Zagzebski, Christine Swanton and Matthew Kieran, have argued for the claim that creativity is a virtue, locating this claim within a broader picture of intellectual, ethical and aesthetic virtues respectively.[1] Moreover, a prominent research programme in psychology, led by Teresa Amabile, holds that people have an intrinsic motivation when they are creative, and this seems seamlessly to fit with the view that creativity is a virtue, for it is often held that a requirement for a trait to be a virtue is that the virtuous agent acts from an intrinsic motivation.[2]

I am going to argue that the notion of a virtue is polymorphous, with more and less focal senses, and in some of these senses creativity

---

[1]   Linda Zagzebski, *Virtues of the Mind: An Inquiry into the Nature of Virtue and the Ethical Foundations of Knowledge* (Cambridge: Cambridge University Press, 1996), esp. 123–125 and 182–183; Christine Swanton, *Virtue Ethics: A Pluralistic View* (Oxford: Oxford University Press, 2003), chapter 7; and Matthew Kieran, 'Creativity as a Virtue of Character' in Elliot Samuel Paul and Scott Barry Kaufman (eds.), *The Philosophy of Creativity: New Essays* (New York: Oxford University Press, 2014). All of them hedge their claims, however: Zagzebski (op. cit., 125) thinks that creativity lies somewhere between a virtue, and a natural talent and faculty; Swanton thinks that it is not a separate virtue but an aspect of the profile of the virtues; and Kieran holds that it is only 'exemplary' creativity that is a virtue. Depending on how his qualifications are spelled out, Kieran's view may in fact be close to the one I defend in this paper.
[2]   Teresa M. Amabile, *Creativity in Context: Update to The Social Psychology of Creativity* (Boulder, Co.: Westview Press, 1996).

doi:10.1017/S1358246114000198
Royal Institute of Philosophy Supplement **75** 2014

is indeed a virtue, for creativity is a kind of dispositional excellence, but it is not a virtue in the paradigm sense of that term, what I will call 'fully-fledged' virtue. This is because of the motivational structure of creativity, with its characteristically mixed motivations. The argument will draw on conceptual analysis, consideration of examples, and an assessment of the social psychological research on creativity, particularly that of Amabile.

2. Three concepts of virtue

We can talk of the virtues of things (hammers or poems, for instance) and the virtues of people. Restricting ourselves to the latter, a virtue is a kind of excellence of a person, where purely physical excellences such as being strong or fit, are excluded. There may be other conditions on this broad notion, such as being acquired by habituation, being deep and enduring, and being integrated with other such states in a certain way. For instance, in one of the more influential contemporary formulations, Zagzebski defines a virtue as 'a deep and enduring acquired excellence of a person, involving a characteristic motivation to produce a certain desired end and reliable success in bringing about that end'.[3] For our purpose, which concerns an examination of the relation of virtue to motivation, we can be largely silent about these further conditions.

In a broad sense of the term, a virtue is an excellent state of a person (where excellence is understood as a valuable property rather than necessarily a supremely valuable one); and states come in a wide range, comprising not just traits (dispositions) but also capacities of one sort or another, including skills and abilities, both practical and intellectual.[4] One can have a capacity without having a motivation to exercise it: someone can have the ability to cycle, even though she has not cycled for years. Though to acquire these abilities in real life requires practice, a person could in principle have acquired

---

[3] Zagzebski, op. cit., p. 137. Julia Annas, *Intelligent Virtue* (Oxford: Oxford University Press, 2011), chapter 2, also argues for these features, and holds that there is also an integration requirement on virtue (108).

[4] Some virtue epistemologists, unmoved by the thought that virtues must be acquired, hold that intellectual virtues include faculties such as sight, hearing and memory. See, for instance, Ernest Sosa, 'Knowledge and Intellectual Virtue', *Monist* **68** (1985), 226–245; John Greco, 'Virtues and Vices of Virtue Epistemology', *Canadian Journal of Philosophy* **23** (1993), 413–432.

them without any practice at all (perhaps the cycling fairy endowed her with the ability with a touch of her magic wand). So one could in principle have some excellences, those that are capacities, without having ever exercised them.

Excellences are in this way distinct from what I will call dispositional excellences or excellent traits. These are states that have to be exercised when appropriate conditions present themselves if a person is to possess them. Consider traits such as being reliable, hardworking and nice. These are all valuable states, but for a person to possess them it is not sufficient that she have the capacity to be reliable, hardworking or nice: unreliable, lazy and nasty people presumably have those capacities too. Rather, the requirement is that on suitable occasions a person acts in a reliable, hardworking or nice way. A disposition or a trait of a person requires the exercise of the appropriate capacity, so its possessor must be appropriately motivated.

The nature of that motivation can vary. Someone may for instance be nice because she wants to be nice for its own sake. I will call this kind of motivation an intrinsic one, in a sense that I will clarify shortly. Alternatively, someone may be motivated to be nice out of fear of social sanctions (being disliked, ostracised, etc., if she is not nice) and so have a non-intrinsic, that is, an extrinsic motivation. One may be reliable because one takes being reliable as a fundamental end, or alternatively because one believes that it is the best way to advance one's career. One may be industrious because one thinks that hard work is a good thing, or because it is a mere means to other things one values, such as a good salary and a job. So dispositional excellences can be actualised by either intrinsic or extrinsic motivations.[5]

The third notion of virtue is what I will call a 'fully-fledged' virtue. This is a dispositional excellence that requires an intrinsic motivation, rather than requiring either an intrinsic or an extrinsic one. This notion applies to paradigm moral virtues: for instance, a kind person must be motivated to perform a kind action because it is kind, and not because it is an action that will advance her own interests. This is a standard requirement on the moral virtues in ordinary thought, and many philosophers from Aristotle onwards have endorsed it. In what follows, I will often for the sake of brevity call fully-fledged virtues simply 'virtues'.

[5]   It does not matter for my purposes whether you agree with the particular examples chosen: what matters is that you agree that there are some excellent traits that can be motivated either intrinsically or extrinsically.

Berys Gaut

How should we understand the notion of an intrinsic motivation invoked in the notion of a virtue? A kind person does not do simply what kindness requires: if someone gives money to a street person merely in order to impress his socially conscious girlfriend or to get rid of the loose change weighing in his pocket, he does what a kind person would do, but he does not do it from kindness, and so he is not really kind. I will say that the actions of such a person *conform to* kindness or are in accordance with kindness; but that he does not act *from* kindness, he does not act for the sake of kindness.[6] Saying that someone acts from kindness requires that the person act with the aim of being kind. But having such an aim does not suffice for acting from kindness. If a person acted merely because he thought that kindness in general advanced his interests, that 'kindness is the best policy', he would still not be genuinely kind. As Archbishop Richard Whately famously remarked of another virtue, 'Honesty is the best policy, [but] a man who acts on that motive is not an honest man.'[7] The policy motivation is ruled out if not only a person acts with the aim of being kind, but also he does not have this aim merely because he believes that it is the best means to some further end. I will say that kindness is his *ultimate* end, that is, it is an end that is adopted not merely because it is the means to some further end that he has.

Thus we have the following condition on virtuous motivation, generalising from kindness to other virtues: a virtuous agent must act for the sake of virtue, where acting for the sake of virtue is understood in terms of the agent's aiming at being virtuous and this aim being her ultimate end:

> (V) Necessarily, a virtuous agent (i) aims at being virtuous (takes being virtuous as her end) and (ii) this end is an ultimate one (she does not adopt it merely as a means to some further end).

An agent is intrinsically motivated by virtue just in case she fulfills those two conditions. My claim is that a dispositional excellence is a (fully-fledged) virtue only if the actions that actualise it must be intrinsically motivated in this sense. If the actions that realise the

---

[6] The terminology is based on Kant's distinction between acting in accord with duty and acting from duty; he holds that only the latter confers true moral worth on the action. See Immanuel Kant, *Grounding for the Metaphysics of Morals*, 3rd ed., trans. James W. Ellington (Indianapolis, Ind.: Hackett, 1993), Section I.
[7] Quoted in John Kay, *Obliquity: Why Our Goals Are Best Achieved Indirectly* (London: Profile Books, 2010), 82.

186

disposition need not be intrinsically motivated, the disposition is not a virtue.[8]

Hence we can take the satisfaction of the V-schema as a necessary motivational condition on a state's being a (fully-fledged) virtue. For instance, substituting 'kind' for 'virtuous' in it, makes it come out true: necessarily a kind agent aims at kindness and she does not pursue kindness merely as a means to some further end. But niceness is not a (fully-fledged) virtue: one can be nice even though one performs nice actions out of fear of social sanctions, thus violating the first condition, or merely because one believes that nice people tend to get ahead, thus violating the second condition.

The virtuous agent may, though need not, have an explicit belief that she is acting virtuously and desire to so act, if she is acting for the sake of virtue. She may, for instance, desire to perform kind actions for their own sake and believe that the action she is currently performing is kind. I will call this sort of virtuous agent *highly reflective*. But one can act for the sake of virtue without having any explicit belief or desire concerning virtue; that is, agents other than highly reflective ones can be virtuous. Someone may simply be moved by the plight of a street person to hand him some money, without conceptualising her action as kind: she may just believe that he needs help and feel moved by that belief to help him; or she may simply feel a surge of sympathy towards him; and so on. Beliefs, desires and feelings may be realisers of the state of acting for the sake of virtue without containing explicit reference to the concept of virtue.

We can visualise the relationships between these three concepts of virtue in terms of a 'bull's eye' structure, with a fully-fledged virtue sitting at the centre, dispositional excellences surrounding and including them, and these in turn being surrounded by and included in excellences. If a state is a fully-fledged virtue it follows that it is a dispositional excellence, since the former requires an intrinsic motivation, whereas the latter is satisfied by either an intrinsic or an extrinsic motivation. And if a state is a dispositional excellence, it is also an excellence, since the former requires some motivation, but the latter may be motivated but need not be.

---

[8] Cf. the second condition in Aristotle's definition of virtue: 'for actions expressing virtue ... the agent must also be in the right state when he does them. First, he must know [that he is doing virtuous actions]; second, he must decide on them, and decide on them for themselves; and, third, he must also do them from a firm and unchanging state'; Aristotle, *Nicomachean Ethics*, trans. Terence Irwin (Indianapolis, Ind.: Hackett, 1985), 1105a 29–35 (Book II.4).

Berys Gaut

3. Creativity and concepts of virtue

In which, if any, of these senses is creativity a virtue? We are setting aside putative extra conditions such as being a state acquired by habituation. So to establish that creativity is an excellence, we merely have to establish that it is a valuable psychological quality. That is widely acknowledged: we praise and admire people for their creativity, we seek to foster it in various ways through educational and cultural projects, and so on. We also do not value creativity merely as a means, i.e. for its effects, but also value it as an end: that is, we think that it has final or intrinsic value.

One might challenge the excellence claim: we do not invariably value creativity: the creativity of a torturer and creative testimony in a law court are bad things. There are several points to be made about such examples, but for our purposes we can note that to say that something is a good, even a final good, is not to say that it is an unconditional good, i.e., good under all circumstances. Being intelligent is a final good, but if one is trapped in a boring, stultifying job one might reasonably wish that one were less intelligent, for one would suffer less. Likewise, happiness is a final good, but it may not be good under conditions in which it is at the expense of achievement. So noting that creativity is not an unconditional good does not undermine the excellence claim.

Is creativity a dispositional excellence? Some hold that creativity is a mere capacity or ability. For instance, Margaret Boden defines creativity as 'the ability to come up with ideas or artefacts that are *new, surprising and valuable.*'[9] Thinking of creativity as an ability would make it an excellence but not a dispositional excellence. However, there are reasons to think of it as a trait, i.e., something that must be exercised under appropriate conditions. The poet Arthur Rimbaud gave up poetry by the age of twenty-one, having decided to pursue a life of adventure. He presumably still possessed the ability to produce creative poetry, but he was no longer a creative poet. To be that, he would have had to actualise the ability on appropriate occasions: and he was no longer a poet, let alone a creative one. Or consider someone who possessed the ability to write creative poetry but who had never exercised it at all. We would not say that this person was a creative poet, but that he merely possessed the ability to become one. 'Being creative' is a success-term: one must have actually done something creative in order to qualify and not

---

[9] Margaret A. Boden, *The Creative Mind: Myths and Mechanisms*, 2nd ed. (London: Routledge, 2004), 1.

188

merely have the ability to do something.[10] In this it is like traits such as kindness, niceness, reliability and so on.

So creativity is not just an excellence, it is a dispositional excellence. Is it also a (fully-fledged) virtue? We have seen that a necessary condition for this is that creativity satisfies the V-schema. It would do so if the following were true:

(V$_{CR}$) Necessarily, a creative agent (i) aims at being creative (takes being creative as her end) and (ii) this end is an ultimate one (she does not adopt it merely as a means to some further end).

Does creativity satisfy the first condition? Creativity requires the production of original and valuable items (how the items are produced matters as well). So the creative person must aim at producing original items if the schema is to be satisfied. But there are many examples of people being creative who do not aim at producing anything original. For instance, the anthropological evidence shows that not all societies value originality. Members of the Abelam, a New Guinea tribe, were insistent that their carvings were not original but in the ancestral style, even though they were discernibly very different from those produced a hundred years earlier, and they persisted in this belief even when this was pointed out to them by the anthropologist Anthony Forge. They did so because they were aiming to produce very traditional carvings, not original ones. Serbo-Croatian epic poets claimed that they performed their songs identically each time, even though tape-recording by the folklorist Albert Lord showed that the length of songs could vary by several thousand lines at different times even when performed by the same singer.[11] Members of these cultures value stability of tradition and not originality: when confronted by the claim that they have produced something original, they deny that they have done so, since they do not want to produce anything original. So it is not part of their aim to produce original things and therefore not part of their aim to be creative, even though they do in fact produce creative things. The point here is not that they do not conceptualise their activities as original: the point is that their reactions, when it is pointed out to them that they have produced something original, show that they are not aiming at being original; indeed, their reactions show that they are aiming at being not original.

[10] See also James Grant, 'The Value of Imaginativeness', *Australasian Journal of Philosophy* **90** (2012), 275–289.
[11] Keith R. Sawyer, *Explaining Creativity: The Science of Human Innovation*, 2nd ed. (New York: Oxford University Press, 2012), 275.

These kinds of cases are not uncommon. Many non-Western and early societies regard their art as a form of ritual or magic, so it is important to make art exactly according to the correct, established method. If that is the function of art in their societies, it is important not to be original in any respect that would affect a work's ritual or magical efficacy. But, given the individuality of human beings and because it is very hard to maintain exact historical knowledge in such societies, almost inevitably their artists end up doing something original. And given their aims it is entirely understandable that they deny that their work is original when this is pointed out to them. There are many other examples: for instance, Ancient Egyptian tomb art was a way of making sure that the deceased navigated his way successfully through the afterlife. One did not want a dead pharaoh stranded due to some artist's having done something original; nevertheless, some of these artists ended up doing just that. And there are even some creative artists in Western cultures who disavow the pursuit of originality, but instead regard their work as preserving or reviving a tradition: this may be true of the composer John Tavener, for instance. More generally, an artist can produce work that is unintentionally creative: he comes across some original device in the course of working without having aimed at it. These cases show that it is not a necessary condition on being creative that one aim at being creative.

There is another reason why a creative person does not always have being creative as her aim. For the pursuit of originality can sometimes be self-defeating as a strategy for being creative, since one strives too hard for something new and thereby produces something worthless. Think of the plethora of modernist and contemporary works that strive for novelty in some salient way, but lack any significant value. Kant notes the existence of 'original nonsense', and calls the phenomenon in art 'Mannerism', which he describes as a 'sort of aping, namely that of mere *individuality* (originality) in general, in order to distance oneself as far as possible from imitators, yet without having the talent thereby to be *exemplary* at the same time.'[12] The Mannerist, intent on originality, runs the risk of producing worse work than he otherwise could, and thus of defeating his aims. So there is good reason why creative people do not always aim to be creative.

So creativity fails the first motivational condition on being a fully-fledged virtue. Is the second condition always fulfilled, in those cases

---

[12]   Immanuel Kant, *Critique of the Power of Judgment*, trans. Paul Guyer and Eric Matthews (Cambridge: Cambridge University Press, 2000), 196 (Ak. 318).

where a person does aim at being creative? That is, does a creative person with this aim invariably adopt creativity as her ultimate aim, or is it adopted merely as a means to some further end? We say that a person is not really kind if she aims at kindness merely because she thinks that kindness has instrumental benefits. Would we say the same about someone who aims at being creative but who is motivated by purely instrumental considerations – that is, would we say that she is not *really* creative?

Consider George, a successful, creative graphic designer. When he was younger he used to design for the love of it, and was motivated by the thought that designing creative products is worthwhile in itself. But as middle age has crept over him, he has grown disillusioned, but he still wants the income, lifestyle and fame that his design success wins him. So now he still aims at and produces creative designs, but does so only because they are a means to securing the material and social goods that he wants. He has in short lost his intrinsic motivation; now his motivation is merely instrumental, and so extrinsic. He continues, nevertheless, to be a creative designer. So creativity does not require an intrinsic motivation and hence is not a fully-fledged virtue; rather, it is a dispositional excellence.

Is this counterexample successful? First, one might object that, as we noted, creativity has final or intrinsic value, i.e. it is valuable for its own sake, and since this is so, in order for an agent to be creative she must be motivated to act because of the intrinsic value of creativity and hence she cannot regard it as being of merely instrumental value. George's case is therefore not a coherent possibility: he must be motivated by the belief that creativity is intrinsically valuable and hence take it as an ultimate aim.

However, that argument fails for two reasons. To say that a state is intrinsically valuable does not entail that an agent *believes* that it is intrinsically valuable. Also, it is possible to believe that some state is intrinsically valuable but not to be motivated to actualise it for that reason. So George may either not believe that creativity is intrinsically valuable or if he believes it, it may play no role in his motivations to be creative. It is important not to confuse the claim that a state is intrinsically valuable with the distinct claim that an agent is intrinsically motivated to produce it.

Second, one might object that George is not really creative. To be creative it does not suffice that one produce original and valuable items; it also matters *how* one does this. For instance, producing original and valuable items merely by luck or by mechanical search procedures devoid of all understanding would not count as exercises of creativity.[13] One of the constraints on how items are produced is that the creative agent must exhibit a certain kind of reasons-sensitivity: he takes the actual and potential values of the product he is working on as reasons to fashion it in one way rather than another.[14] Since George is interested only in money and fame, he does not exhibit this kind of reasons-sensitivity.

However, George does exhibit this kind of rationality: he takes the fact that making a design in a certain way would make its design values more original as a reason to make it in that way. Of course, he takes it only as an instrumental reason: design values serve his ends of securing fame and fortune, and he does not take them as intrinsic reasons to produce something. But he does take them as reasons because of their beneficial effects, so he does exhibit sensitivity to reasons directed at the value of the product. And this reasons-sensitivity allows him to take credit for his designs, as would not be the case if they were the product of mere luck or of mechanical search techniques.

Third, it may be objected that George is not fully or properly creative because his activities lack the degree of reliability that we require in a creative person's activities. It is just a contingent fact outside his control that his design activities are socially rewarded; were this to alter, he would give up designing. Kieran, for instance, appeals to considerations of reliability in holding that extrinsically motivated agents do not exhibit what he calls 'exemplary' creativity.[15] Recall that Zagzebski holds that a virtue must be 'deep and enduring' and Aristotle that it is 'a firm and unchanging state'. Sarah Broadie has interpreted Aristotle here to mean, in part, that whereas one could give up a skill voluntarily without its counting against the claim that one possessed that skill, giving up a state voluntarily is incompatible with that state's being a virtue.[16]

However, Aristotle offers the 'firm and unchanging' test as one for fully-fledged virtues such as fairness and courage, so this objection misfires, since it merely strengthens the claim that creativity is not

[13] See my 'Creativity and Imagination' in Berys Gaut and Paisley Livingston (eds.), *The Creation of Art: New Essays in Philosophical Aesthetics* (Cambridge: Cambridge University Press, 2003), 148–73, at 150.
[14] I call this kind of reasons-sensitivity 'product-value rationality'; for an argument for why its possession is required for someone to be creative, see my 'Creativity and Rationality', *Journal of Aesthetics and Art Criticism* **70** (2012), 259–270, at 267–8.
[15] Kieran, op. cit.
[16] Sarah Broadie, *Ethics with Aristotle* (New York: Oxford University Press, 1991), 89.

this kind of virtue. George is creative but his state is not deep and enduring in this sense, for he would voluntarily give it up if social incentives changed.

Moreover, the fact that he might voluntarily give up the state does not impugn its status as one of full or proper creativity. Rimbaud, as noted, voluntarily abandoned poetry by the age of twenty one to pursue a life of active adventure, but that he did so in no way impugns his claim to have been a highly creative poet before then. One can be creative at a spectacularly high level without the state's being deep and enduring. And recall Tynnichus, the poet mentioned in Plato's *Ion*, who produced only one praise-song of any merit: he was creative once, but evidently not reliably so.[17]

It is also important not to confuse reliability with degree of creativity. Creative actions are, by ordinary standards of reliability, often highly unreliable: they involve going beyond established outcomes, procedures or techniques, so are more likely to fail than routine actions. Indeed, Zagzebski thinks of creativity as an unusual kind of virtue in part because it does not involve reliable success in the same sense that holds for normal kinds of virtue.[18] But even when we set reliability at the less demanding success-rate appropriate to creativity, it does not follow that the more creative someone is the more reliable they are in their creativity. An amateur watercolourist may far more reliably produce modestly creative paintings than an extremely creative but very experimental painter, most of whose paintings are failures. Indeed, there is a general reason to think that the more original work will have a higher failure rate, since it goes beyond established outcomes or procedures more than does less original work.

A fourth objection to the George scenario notes that his creativity is less admirable than that of someone, such as his earlier self, whose motivations are intrinsic. We admire people who create out of love of their activity or subject in a way that we do not admire those who are motivated by factors such as fame and money. But someone's creativity is deficient if we have reasons not to admire it: so George's creativity is not full or true creativity. Kieran for instance appeals to reasons for admiration in his defense of creativity as a virtue.[19]

However, we do admire George – he is after all a great designer. And if we admire him less than his younger self, it is not because his motivation is now extrinsic, but rather because of the values he

---

[17]   Plato, *Ion*, 534d5-e1, in *The Collected Dialogues*, eds. Edith Hamilton and Huntington Cairns (Princeton: Princeton University Press, 1961).
[18]   Zagzebski, op. cit., 181–2.
[19]   Kieran, op. cit.

is now pursuing. Consider a creative thief, who finds ways to rob people in original ways. One kind of creative thief robs out of the sheer love of robbery, a second robs the rich to give to the poor; but in so far as we admire them, we admire the first, intrinsically motivated thief less than the second, instrumentally motivated one: a kleptomaniac is less admirable than Robin Hood. An investor who is intrinsically motivated invests for the sheer love of accumulating money, but an extrinsically motivated investor may invest in order to generate a large sum of money to give away to charity. Here too, we admire the extrinsically motivated agent more than the intrinsically motivated one. Likewise, we may find more admirable a father who is motivated to produce a creative toy to cheer up his sick son than someone who produces the toy simply for the love of being creative. So the explanation of our diminished admiration for the later George is because of the values (fame and money, rather than design values) that ultimately motivate him, not because he now has an extrinsic motivation. Having an intrinsic motivation per se does not explain admiration: the nature of the values that ultimately motivate one does. So we should not hold that George's creativity is somehow deficient because of its extrinsic motivation.

Finally, one may object that the George scenario merely shows that there are two types of creativity: intrinsically motivated creativity is a fully-fledged virtue but extrinsically motivated creativity is not. Hence there can be virtuous and non-virtuous creativity, and that is all that the virtue theorist of creativity needs to claim.

But this objection concedes the point to the dispositional excellence view. If there are some exercises of creativity that are instances of fully-fledged virtue and some that are not, then creativity per se cannot be a fully-fledged virtue. There cannot be, for instance, virtuous and non-virtuous exercises of kindness, because kindness is a virtue, so one cannot exercise it non-virtuously. But dispositional excellences can have fully-fledged virtuous exercises (someone is nice because she takes being nice as an ultimate end) and exercises that are not instances of fully-fledged virtues (she is nice out of timidity or from a desire to gain advancement). So creativity is a dispositional excellence, not a fully-fledged virtue.

So we should admit that George is someone who is genuinely creative but has purely extrinsic motivations, and thus does not exhibit a fully-fledged virtue. A variant case would give him both a purely intrinsic motivation and a purely extrinsic one. He would have mixed motivations. Clearly he would be creative in this scenario too. But note the difference to a fully-fledged virtue: if we discovered that someone were fair partly because she thought that it was right to be fair and partly because she thought cultivating a reputation for fairness would help her advance her career as a politician, then in so far as her actions were motivated by the extrinsic motivation, we would say that they were not fair. This is not true of creativity.

Thought-experiments prove conceptual possibility, but one might wonder how psychologically plausible such scenarios are. Though one can of course always dispute what the motivations are in actual cases, the presence of extrinsic motivations in cases of even landmark creativity is plausibly common. James Watson and Francis Crick discovered the structure of the DNA molecule in 1953. According to Watson's account in his book, *The Double Helix*, they were extremely competitive and motivated by the desire for scientific glory, reputation, and to win a Nobel Prize. Their main rival in the race was Linus Pauling, a celebrated biologist who developed some of the methods they used. Watson writes that their goal was 'to imitate Linus Pauling and beat him at his own game.'[20] When they discovered that Pauling had developed his own solution, the triple helix, they were distraught, and when shortly thereafter they discovered he was mistaken, they were jubilant. There is no reason to deny that they also had an intrinsic motivation to produce valuable, original science. Their motivations were mixed, but they were certainly creative and their extrinsic motivations added to the incentives for them to come up with their breakthrough discovery.

This kind of competiveness and focus on reputational and material benefits is certainly not confined to science. Pablo Picasso was famously competitive and this shaped his artistic creativity at many points. The art historian Jack Flam has argued that the professional rivalry between Picasso and Henri Matisse was a driving force in both their careers, leading to the creation of some of their most radical works: *Les Demoiselles d'Avignon* (1907) was in part a response to Matisse's *Blue Nude* (1907).[21]

Inventions are often motivated by extrinsic factors. Paul McCready won the Kremer Prize in 1977 for the first human-powered glider to complete a mile-long flight in a figure of eight. In an interview, McCready explained that he had accumulated a lot of debt at the time and that 'I felt that I didn't have the time to mess with such things, but I had this strong economic motivation to take an interest in man-powered flight, so I charged around trying to figure out a way

[20] James Watson, *The Double Helix: A Personal Account of the Discovery of the Structure of DNA* (London: Penguin, 1999), 46.
[21] Jack Flam, *Matisse and Picasso: The Story of their Rivalry and Friendship* (Boulder, Co.: Westview Press, 2003), 37.

to solve it.'[22] And according to Simon Singh, the major early work on decoding the Germans' Enigma Code was done by Poles, drawing on French intelligence, whereas the French and American intelligence communities gave up on it, since it was so hard. Singh notes that this was because the Poles were more terrified of a German invasion than were the French or Germans.[23] Fear of death is a more powerful motivator than the intrinsic satisfactions of code breaking.

One could multiply examples, but let me give a final pertinent one. The Research Excellence Framework exercise and its predecessor the Research Assessment Exercise have been a major influence on shaping academic resourcing and careers in the UK for more than twenty years. Its criteria for the quality of academic outputs are that they should show rigour, originality and significance; so they should be creative. A good deal of overproduction of run-of-the-mill academic work has resulted from this major extrinsic motivation, but it has also produced a good deal of very creative work. And of course academics are also familiar with the extrinsic incentives provided by promotion decisions, including the rigours of the US tenure decision procedure. It is hard to believe that academics would be anywhere nearly as productive, including productive of creative work, without such incentives. Simple reflection on the everyday conditions of their existence ought to convince academics that creativity can be extrinsically motivated.

4. The psychological evidence

I have argued that creativity is a disposition, as well as an excellence, so it requires some motivation to be present, but this motivation need not be an intrinsic one; hence creativity is not what I have called a fully-fledged virtue. Not only can we coherently imagine cases of creativity that lack intrinsic motivations or that combine extrinsic and intrinsic motivations, but there are also many real examples where the motivations are plausibly mixed or even purely extrinsic. However, the claim that creativity is not a fully-fledged virtue seems to stand in tension with a major research programme in psychology, which argues that intrinsic motivation plays a central role in creativity.

[22] Quoted in Robert J. Sternberg and Todd I. Lubart, *Defying the Crowd: Cultivating Creativity in a Culture of Conformity* (New York: The Free Press, 1995), 242.
[23] Simon Singh, *The Code Book: The Secret History of Codes and Code-Breaking* (London: Fourth Estate, 1999), chapter 4.

One of the earliest studies in this programme was the charming 1973 'magic marker' study, which gave three to five year old nursery children magic markers (felt pens) with which to draw. The fifty-one children who showed an interest in drawing with the markers were divided into three groups. The group who were told that they were drawing in order to obtain a 'Good Player Award' showed significantly lower interest in the task (as witnessed by their shorter periods of playing with the markers in subsequent free play sessions) and lower quality of drawings than the groups who were offered no reward or who were given an unexpected one.[24] So offering an extrinsic reward reduced children's intrinsic interest in the task and lowered their creative expression. This and numerous other studies were the basis for Teresa Amabile's formulation of the Intrinsic Motivation Hypothesis (IMH), which in its 1983 version runs: 'the intrinsically motivated state is conducive to creativity, whereas the extrinsically motivated state is detrimental.'[25]

Subsequent research complicated the picture. In one study, a group of children were given intrinsic-motivation training, using 'immunisation' techniques. They were taught how to maintain their intrinsic interest in a task, despite the offer of rewards, by being shown videos of children talking about how to maintain intrinsic interest, and then by discussing this in groups with a teacher. If these children were then offered a reward, the creativity of their stories was actually enhanced relative to those who had the same training but who were offered no reward, and also relative to those who were offered a reward but no training.[26] So contra the IMH, extrinsic motivation can actually enhance creativity. This and similar studies led Amabile to reformulate her hypothesis as the Intrinsic Motivation Principle (IMP): 'Intrinsic motivation is conducive to creativity; controlling extrinsic motivation is detrimental to creativity, but informational or enabling extrinsic motivation can be conducive, particularly if initial levels of intrinsic motivation are high.'[27] So

[24] Mark R. Lepper, David Greene and Richard E. Nisbett, 'Undermining Children's Intrinsic Interest with Extrinsic Reward: A Test of the "Overjustification" Hypothesis', *Journal of Personality and Social Psychology* **42** (1973), 129–137.
[25] Amabile, op. cit, 107. This book updates and incorporates Amabile's 1983 book, *The Social Psychology of Creativity*. The quoted passage is from the earlier incorporated book.
[26] Beth A. Hennessey, Teresa M. Amabile and Margaret Martinage, 'Immunizing Children against the Negative Effects of Reward', *Contemporary Educational Psychology* **14** (1989), 212–227 (see esp. Study 1).
[27] Amabile, op. cit., 119.

the claim is that some ('synergistic') extrinsic motivations enhance creativity, since they support intrinsic motivations (for instance, they enhance the subject's sense of being self-determining, or they give information about what is working and what is not) and other ('non-synergistic') extrinsic motivations undermine creativity, particularly where the offer of a reward tends to suggest control over the subject's behaviour. One of IMP's adherents claims that it is now so well empirically supported that it is 'an undisputed principle' in social psychology.[28]

Does this evidence show that creativity is a (fully-fledged) virtue? The first problem is that the claim concerns only probabilistic causal influence: intrinsic motivation is 'conducive' to, i.e., tends to promote, creativity, whereas non-synergistic extrinsic motivation is 'detrimental' to, i.e., tends to reduce, creativity. But for a trait to be a virtue it is *necessary* that the agent have the appropriate intrinsic motivation. Being motivated to perform an act for the sake of kindness does not *tend* to make the act kind; rather, having that aim is *necessary* for the act to be kind. And being motivated by self-interest in performing a kind act is not just detrimental to the act's being kind: rather, in so far as that is one's motivation, one is not kind, and if it is one's sole motivation, one is not kind at all. So the empirical, causal, claims are too weak to support the necessary connections required for the existence of a virtue.

However, this way of construing IMP assumes that synergistic extrinsic motivations are capable of *independently* motivating creative actions, as well as motivating them by enhancing intrinsic motivations. But if one holds that synergistic extrinsic motivations work *only* by enhancing intrinsic ones, then it follows that intrinsic motivations are necessary for creativity: since creativity is a disposition, a trait, it requires some motivation; synergistic extrinsic motivations on their own cannot motivate it, since they work only by enhancing intrinsic motivations; hence an intrinsic motivation must be present for creativity to exist. And this enhancement construal of IMP seems to be how Amabile, at least at some points, understands IMP. For instance, she refers to 'the intrinsic motivation that is essential for creativity.'[29] That requires the enhancement, rather than the independence, construal of IMP. Amabile also states that 'the first

[28]   Beth A. Hennessey, 'The Creativity-Motivation Connection' in James C. Kaufman and Robert J. Sternberg (eds.), *The Cambridge Handbook of Creativity* (Cambridge: Cambridge University Press, 2010), 346.
[29]   Amabile, op. cit, 121.

(problem identification) and third (response generation) stages of the creative process, where the *novelty* of the outcome is importantly determined, may require intrinsic motivation that is unencumbered by any significant extrinsic motivation.'[30] Since there is no creativity without the generation of novel responses, it follows that intrinsic motivation may indeed be required for creativity. And that would support the claim of creativity to be a fully-fledged virtue.

So construed, though, IMP goes considerably beyond what is warranted by the evidence that Amabile marshalls. What her evidence shows is that sometimes extrinsic motivations reduce creativity (the magic marker case) and sometimes enhance it (the immunisation case). Neither kind of case shows that intrinsic motivations are necessary to creativity. The case required to prove that would be one where people who are completely lacking in intrinsic motivation for some task, when offered rewards of some kind, were incapable of producing anything creative. Not only is no evidence of this kind offered, but it is also highly implausible as a psychological claim. For instance, it would mean that George is a psychological impossibility, even though we have no problem in making sense of him. It would also mean that a student who took a required course for credit, but who lacked all intrinsic interest in the subject, would be incapable of producing creative work in the course, even though getting the high grades that he desired depended partly on his producing creative work.

There is even some experimental evidence against IMP understood in its enhancement version. Robert Eisenberger and Linda Rhoades gave 115 students taking an introductory psychology module a class assignment of producing five creative titles for a short story about popcorn being cooked in a pan. One half of the class was also offered a financial reward for coming up with creative titles. The students offered the financial reward produced more creative titles than those who were not offered a reward.[31] Some of these titles were rather good: 'The Little Kernel That Could', 'The Golden Years', 'Coming Out' and 'Growing Pains'. But all these students were acting from extrinsic motivations (this was true even of the ones who were not promised a reward: this was a class assignment) and there is no reason to think that they had any intrinsic interest in producing short story titles: they were, after all, taking a psychology class, not a creative writing one. Yet they produced something

---

[30] Ibid., 118.
[31] Robert Eisenberger and Linda Rhoades, 'Incremental Effects of Reward on Creativity', *Journal of Personality and Social Psychology* **81** (2001), 728–741. The case is their Study 3.

Berys Gaut

creative. Of course, the supporter of the enhancement construal could maintain that they *must* have had some intrinsic interest in writing titles, but unsupported psychological speculation does not warrant any claim, let alone one about what is essential.

There is a second reason why the psychological evidence does not support the (fully-fledged) virtue view. This concerns how the notion of an intrinsic motivation is defined in the psychological literature. Amabile in 1983 defined it thus: 'Persons who engage in an activity for its own sake are intrinsically motivated; persons who engage in an activity to achieve some goal external to task engagement are extrinsically motivated.'[32] With its reference to engaging in an activity for its own sake this definition is clearly related to the notion of intrinsic motivation as I have characterised it. But it is also puzzling: what would we mean, for instance, if we said that we went walking for its own sake, or did some cooking for its own sake? To make sense of this we have to identify some characteristic of the action that the agent finds desirable.[33] So we have to specify the kind of reason the agent has more exactly: for instance, she engages in *pleasurable* activity for its own sake, i.e., for sake of the pleasure she takes in it. And likewise, for each value characteristic that the agent might pursue for its own sake: e.g., she engages in a *challenging* activity for its own sake, i.e., for the sake of the challenge it provides; or a *cognitively interesting* activity for its own sake, i.e., for the sake of its cognitive interest. The definition we developed earlier was used to characterise the kind of intrinsic motivation that a virtuous agent must have: she performs a *virtuous* action for its own sake, for the sake of virtue: that is, she performs an action because it is virtuous and this is her ultimate end. On Amabile's definition this is only one kind of intrinsic motivation and her definition allows for a wide range of kinds of intrinsic motivation. So even if the psychological evidence showed that intrinsic motivations were necessary for creativity, this would not show that the *kind* of intrinsic motivation that is necessary for a disposition to be a fully-fledged virtue is required to be creative. Even if one showed, for instance, that enjoying some activity were necessary to be creative in it, this would not prove that creativity is a virtue, since this would require showing that one must act with the ultimate aim of being creative. Suppose that psychological tests of the Abelam showed that they had to enjoy their wood-carving in order to be creative in it; this would

[32] Amabile, op. cit., 109.
[33] See G. E. M. Anscombe, *Intention*, 2nd ed. (Cambridge, Mass.: Harvard University Press, 2000).

200

not show that creativity is a virtue, since, as we noted, they are creative without aiming to be so.[34]

Amabile later refined her definition:

> We define as *intrinsic* any motivation that arises from the individual's positive reaction to qualities of the task itself; this reaction can be experienced as interest, involvement, curiosity, satisfaction, or positive challenge. We define as *extrinsic* any motivation that arises from sources outside of the task itself; these sources include expected evaluation, contracted-for reward, external directives, or any of several similar sources.[35]

If we read the list of five ways in which a reaction can be positive as complete, then the problem is that the definition is set up so that the intrinsic motivation of creativity – aiming at creativity as an ultimate end – does not figure at all, so that showing that a motivation satisfies one of these conditions *cannot* show that creativity is a virtue. And if we read it as a list of open-ended conditions, then as with the earlier definition, showing that intrinsic motivation in some of these senses is necessary to be creative does not entail that the intrinsic motivation is of the right kind to constitute creativity as a virtue.

So the evidence produced by Amabile's research programme does not show that creativity is a virtue. Proponents of the programme also sometimes overstate its claims. Hennessey, for instance, glosses IMP as holding that 'Intrinsic motivation is conducive to creativity, and extrinsic motivation is almost always detrimental.'[36]

However, that sits ill at ease with the fact, as we noted earlier, that competition and rivalry are common between creative people in various domains, from arts to sciences; that there are institutional structures in many domains, such as academia, that give overt rewards to creative results and moreover appear to produce them; and that there are prizes, including literary, architectural and philosophical ones, which are intended not just to mark creative achievement but also to foster it. Much of the research programme's data

---

[34] A more general way to bring out this point is by noting that to show that someone has to be motivated by pleasure in some activity does not show that she is acting from virtue in that activity, even if the activity is in conformity to virtue. For instance, if being motivated to run from pleasure were necessary for someone to participate in sponsored charity runs, this would not prove that she was exercising a virtue in so doing, for she might simply be running out of enjoyment in running, and regard the fact of charity sponsorship as a useful excuse for running.

[35] Ibid., 115.

[36] Hennessey, op. cit., 346.

comes from work on schoolchildren and undergraduates. But if we turn to the world of high-end creativity associated with professionals, the existence of extrinsic rewards of various kinds is endemic and given how creative some of these people are, the evidence does not suggest that extrinsic motivation is 'almost always' detrimental to creativity. Rather, it suggests that it can be very helpful. Given the years of preparation that are required to acquire the expertise needed for creativity in a domain, how long it can take to achieve creative success and how many utterly dispiriting failures someone may have to endure before she does so, it is easy to explain why *any* motivation, extrinsic or intrinsic, can help someone to get through the hard times. However much one loves one's subject, faced with continual failure, or self-agonising doubts about one's ability to pull off an achievement, or paralysing uncertainty about how to proceed, the thought that one may not just fail in some creative endeavour that one values, but may also lose one's job or forfeit one's career if one does so, is bound, like hanging, to concentrate the mind wonderfully.

5. Conclusion

I have argued that creativity is not a fully-fledged virtue, since an appropriate intrinsic motivation is not essential to it. Creativity can, and probably almost invariably does, proceed from mixed motivations, both intrinsic and extrinsic, but there is no reason why it cannot proceed from purely extrinsic reasons, or, for that matter, purely intrinsic ones. This is consistent with creativity's being a virtue in weaker senses that have a place in our language and theoretical reflections, as what I have termed a dispositional excellence, and more weakly an excellence. Whether we should restrict the term 'virtue' only to what I have called a fully-fledged virtue is largely a matter of stipulation and little hangs on it. What does matter, and what I claim to have shown, concerns the relation of creativity to motivation. Creativity can proceed from extrinsic motivations, and in that respect it is different from paradigm moral virtues such as kindness and fairness. Creativity turns out to be more complex in its structure and also more multifarious in its instances than it would be were it an example of a paradigm case of virtue. So those virtue-theoretic accounts of creativity that try to model it on fully-fledged virtues will fail.

University of St Andrews
bng@st-andrews.ac.uk

Creativity, Virtue and the Challenges from Natural Talent, Ill-Being and Immorality

MATTHEW KIERAN

1. Introduction

We praise and admire creative people in virtually every domain from the worlds of art, fashion and design to the fields of engineering and scientific endeavour. Picasso was one of the most influential artists of the twentieth century, Einstein was a creative scientist and Jonathan Ive is admired the world over as a great designer. We also sometimes blame, condemn or withhold praise from those who fail creatively; hence we might say that someone's work or ideas tend to be rather derivative and uninspired. Institutions and governmental advisory bodies sometimes aspire, claim or exhort us to enable individual creativity, whether this is held to be good for the individual as such or in virtue of promoting wider socio-economic goods. It is at least a common thought that people are more self-fulfilled if they are creative and society more generally is held to be all the better for enabling individual creativity.[1]

In what follows I shall outline a virtue theoretic account of exemplary creativity that makes sense of how and why we think in this way.[2] If we are interested in a robust account of creative excellence we need to look at the underlying psychological mechanisms that enable individuals to be imaginative, surprising or original (and those which undermine them). I will suggest that what it is to be a

---

[1] See, for example, 'All Our Futures: Creativity, Culture and Education', *Report to the Secretary of State for Education and Employment and the Secretary of State for Culture, Media and Sport*, May 1999, National Advisory Committee on Creative and Cultural Education.

[2] See in this light in particular Linda Zagzebski, 'Exemplarist Virtue Theory', *Metaphilosophy* **41** (1–2), 2010, 41–57, as well as Jason Baehr, *The Inquiring Mind* (Oxford: Oxford University Press, 2011) and Robert C. Roberts and W. Jay Wood, *Intellectual Virtues* (Oxford: Oxford University Press 2007) for distinct but related conceptions of intellectual virtue.

doi:10.1017/S1358246114000241   © The Royal Institute of Philosophy and the contributors 2014
Royal Institute of Philosophy Supplement **75** 2014

Matthew Kieran

creatively excellent person depends – amongst other things – upon certain admirable character traits such as curiosity, courage and perseverance. Creative virtues are admirable character traits that ground creative excellence and contribute to individual flourishing. Once the view is laid out the rest of the paper will be devoted to apparent objections to this view emerging from the psychological and philosophical literature: challenges based on claims concerning natural talent, ill-being and immorality.

2. Creativity and Virtue

It is an intellectual orthodoxy that creativity requires the production of something novel and valuable.[3] How to disambiguate novelty and value is much disputed but virtually everyone agrees that creativity must meet these conditions. According to Boden, psychological creativity involves 'coming up with a surprising, valuable idea that's new to the person who comes up with it.'[4] Thus we can recognize that a 6 year old's drawings or a student's essay are psychologically creative – produce something of value and novel to them – without thereby making any grand claims about historical originality. Historical creativity, Boden argues, just is a special case of psychological creativity. If an idea is historically creative then at its strongest 'that means that (so far as we know) no one else has had it before: it has arisen for the first time in human history.'[5] Moreover a creative person is someone who possesses the agential skills, abilities and dispositions that enable creative thought and action.[6] Thus a psychologically robust characterization of creativity needs to give an account of the kind of mechanisms and traits that enable people to be creative. We are also naturally interested in what constitutes and enables creative excellence. We praise and admire those who excel

---

[3] See, for example, Margaret Boden, *The Creative Mind: Myths and Mechanisms*, 2nd ed., (London: Routledge, 2004), 1, Berys Gaut, 'Creativity and Imagination' in Berys Gaut and Paisley Livingston (eds.) *The Creation of Art* (Cambridge: Cambridge University Press 2003), 151, Richard E. Mayer, 'Fifty Years of Creativity Research', in Robert J. Sternberg (ed.), *Handbook of Creativity* (Cambridge: Cambridge University Press, 1999), 450 and Dustin Stokes, 'Minimally Creative Thought', *Metaphilosophy*, **42**, 2011, 658–681.
[4] Margaret Boden, 'Creativity in a Nutshell', in *Creativity and Art* (Oxford: Oxford University Press, 2010), 30.
[5] Op. cit. Boden note 2.
[6] Op. cit. Gaut and Stokes note 2.

creatively – precisely because so doing is a particular kind of achievement – and many of us strive to be more creative at what we do.

Minimally to be a creative person requires drawing on the kinds of knowledge, capacities and skills that for creatures like us are required to arrive at purposively or realize non-accidentally that which is new and worthwhile in a given domain. At least for creatures such as ourselves certain traits of mind or character are also required in order to a) acquire such knowledge, capacities and skills and b) in order to deploy such knowledge, capacities and skills appropriately in the face of different challenges across many different kinds of situations over time to arrive at or realize that which is new and valuable. The relevant traits include dispositions of mind or character that are admirable or praiseworthy (i.e. virtues).[7]

To take one example Van Gogh was an exemplary creative person to the degree that he persevered at his art despite lack of support, formal training and the challenges he faced in acquiring the technique required to paint as he desired. He was also extremely resilient in coping with indifference and failure, showed courage in persevering despite much criticism and showed great critical self-honesty in identifying his own weaknesses and what he needed to work on. Moreover, Van Gogh's curiosity and open mindedness explain the ways in which he sought out non-orthodox artistic styles, experimenting and exploring their various effects in arriving at his mature style. Had Van Gogh lacked curiosity, critical self-honesty, perseverance and fortitude, amongst other traits, it is hard to see how he could have acquired the skills required to achieve what he did (especially given he showed no great talent to start with). Even given the requisite skills it is hard to see how Van Gogh would have used them to achieve what he did without resilience and courage in the face of critical indifference and derision. Whilst Van Gogh may be an extreme case in his exemplarity, a creative saint if you like, this is no different in kind from less extraordinary cases. At least to the extent someone is creatively ambitious, she should seek to be, amongst other things, critically self honest about where weaknesses in technique or argument lie, resilient in the face of failure, humble enough to take criticism, courageous enough to stand up to contempt or ridicule, curious enough to explore new problems and solutions. Such traits are creative virtues in the sense that they are admirable or praiseworthy excellences of mind or character

---

[7] See Matthew Kieran, 'Creativity as a Virtue of Character' in Scott Barry Kaufman and Elliot Samuel Paul (eds.), *The Philosophy of Creativity* (New York: Oxford University Press, 2014), 125–144.

that enable creative achievement in the face of different challenges or pressures as one's life unfolds.

It is consistent with the view that people can be creative whilst lacking such virtues. Creativity as such is not a virtue. People can get very lucky, act out of character or the inter-action between someone's non-virtuous character and particular situational pressures may be highly conducive to doing something creatively. We may admire such achievements in all sorts of ways but the creative character manifested will be less than fully exemplary. Moreover, in such cases, it will be the case that the relevant person will not tend to strive for or be able to achieve creative excellence robustly across relevantly different kinds of situations. Hence, at least to the extent one is creatively ambitious, it is best to acquire and strive to realize creative virtues to enable creative achievement. If you can only commit to working on or realizing that which meets with popularity, then it will be difficult, at least in many situations, to do something that is significantly new and worthwhile. Why? Since doing so often meets with criticism, indifference or incredulity given that being creative involves being unconventional, going against that which is fashionable or confounding people's expectations.

Consider Thom Yorke on making Radiohead's breakthrough album:

> [TY] When people rip each other off but don't add anything original to the equation, it's painful because you can hear the anxiety of the creator wanting to be loved. . . everybody goes through that period of imitating other things because you're worried, you want to be liked.
>
> [Interviewer] When do you think you were liberated from that?
>
> [TY] *The Bends.* For the first time ever, we had two months just working on 12 tunes, not seeing anybody, and that was all we did. We went into the studio with John Leckie and the A&Rs and management would turn up, and say, 'Where's the hits?' There was a half-hour period following that where everyone wobbled and then we were like, 'F**k you! You're banned!' and we pulled out all the phones. Then the anxiety was gone. The excitement of it being our choice and the fact that no one else was making songs like us was liberating.[8]

This is no different from other areas of life. Whilst it may be easy to be honest where the environment presents no difficulties and being so

---

[8]   Tim Noakes, 'Splitting Atoms: Thom Yorke Interview', *Dazed and Confused*, February, 2013.

always leads to approval or social inclusion, it is more difficult to be honest where it meets with rejection. Similarly, whilst fortitude or perseverance may not always be required when everything is going well, nonetheless across a range of situations such traits are required to confront various kinds of challenges (e.g., where we face ridicule, boredom, difficulty, repeated failure, anxiety and self doubt).

What might a taxonomy of the cluster of creative virtues look like? Curiosity is perhaps the master virtue required for creative excellence. Why think this? Due to the role that novelty plays. In general curiosity involves the disposition to learn and understand, to play, to make, experience or master something new in ways which drives the identification of questions worth asking or tasks worth approaching. Amongst other things curiosity motivates people to consider how problems can be conceptualized differently, why things may not be better done otherwise and set new problems or challenges for themselves. Hence curiosity is bound up with the desire to explore, experiment and acquire the mastery that is required to be creative. Perseverance is also required. Curiosity devoid of perseverance would incline someone to give up when the going gets tough. Creative excellence requires hard work and thus the disposition to be steadfast in persisting purposefully in the face of difficulties or discouragement. Idle curiosity does not get anyone very far. A distinct but related creative virtue is courage. Whilst this may be obvious in the face of oppression courage is often required to face up to indifference, ridicule, derision or other pressures in the pursuit of creative vision and goals. Creative failures of nerve are sometimes just a matter of being too afraid to face up to or deal with anticipated negative responses. Resilience too is an important creative virtue given the need to cope with misfortune, hardship, challenges and failure. Self-belief or assurance combined with perseverance, courage and resilience enable curiosity to flourish across the many different challenges and set backs that arise in striving to be creative. Whilst courage and resilience may both be bound up with self-belief such assurance had better not be deluded in ways that block openness or receptivity to criticism. Thus humility is also required in order to be open to the possibility of error, deficiencies or inadequacy. A closely related virtue is critical self-honesty about what one is doing and why. It is one thing, for example, to know that pursuing acclaim for its own sake may be problematic, it is quite another to realize and acknowledge that one has been so motivated.

In addition to creative virtues being admirable and causally enabling creative achievement there is also reason to hold that they contribute toward living a good life. They most obviously enhance

Matthew Kieran

what an agent can achieve in at least two ways. First, where an agent is driven to question, strive for imaginative approaches and seek new solutions she is more likely to achieve more worthwhile results in a given domain. Second, creative virtues render an agent's creativity more robust across situational differences (for the reasons given above). Putting matters this way gives a rather consequentialist flavour to the role that creative virtue plays in a good life. Creative virtue gets better results and better results give rise to a better life (at least in so far as one values bringing about better results in some given domain). Whilst true enough there is, however, more to the idea than this. The possession and exercise of creative virtue inherently contributes to leading a happier, more fulfilled life.

A very direct route to this claim would be to identify creative activity as pleasurable especially where this is undertaken for its own sake. Csikszentmihalyi argues that creative activity paradigmatically involves what he terms 'flow' experiences where an agent is, amongst other things, maximally absorbed in an activity pursued for its own sake (at least given that the challenges posed are finely balanced in relation to the agent's skill level).[9] This lends itself to the thought that creative virtue does not just lead to better results but gives rise to greater enjoyment in the creative activity itself. A more enjoyable life is, ceteris paribus, a happier, more fulfilling life.

However, whilst significant, the joy to be had in creative activity may rate pretty low down on the hedonic scale – at least for some – given how mundane and frustrating much creative activity is. Moreover the pleasure to be had is often highly dependent upon the recognition of the value of achievement and how one is implicated in it. We take, for example, greater pride in cases where we have come up with an original idea ourselves as opposed, say, to executing another's original idea. We also take pride in activity involving courage, resilience, perseverance or resistance to taking an easy route. It is a familiar point that hypothetical experience machine cases – *Matrix* style simulations of pleasurable experiences and successful lives – are unsatisfactory because the achievements are not real. There is no contact with underlying reality.[10] It is a less familiar though surely equally significant point that what matters is not just that the achievements are real but the extent to which they manifest

---

[9]   See Mihaly Csikszentmihalyi, *Creativity: Flow and the Psychology of Discovery and Invention* (New York: Harper Collins, 1996) and his 'Happiness and Creativity', *The Futurist*, September-October, 1997, 8–12.
[10]   This is the point of Robert Nozick's experience machine thought experiment in *Anarchy, State and Utopia* (New York: Basic Books), 42–45.

our capacities and excellences of character. A good or flourishing human life involves activity that exercises and cultivates human capacities and traits for the right sort of reasons in praiseworthy or admirable ways. In so far as cultivating creative capacities and excellences of character tend toward the production of worthwhile things in good ways they will be conducive to happiness or flourishing. In other words to the extent that someone is creatively excellent they will tend to thrive and be more fulfilled in doing what they do well.

I have briefly sketched a conception of exemplary creativity that yields a psychologically explanatory account of what it is to be a creatively excellent person that speaks to intuitions about why the relevant traits are admirable and praiseworthy. There is also some reason to think that possessing creative virtue partly constitutes and tends toward the realization of a more fulfilled life. In what follows we will look at three distinct challenges that put pressure on conceiving of exemplary creativity in this way.

3. The Natural Talent Attribution Error

Mozart was a composer in childhood, Picasso's drawings at the age of thirteen were truly exceptional and Mary Shelley started writing *Frankenstein* when she was nineteen. Creative excellence can easily seem to be something that only a relative few can achieve because it depends upon exceptional natural gifts or talents. There is, moreover, a strong intellectual tradition that holds natural (or unnatural) talent is the major source of creative genius. Plato's *Ion* characterizes creativity as the upshot of divine inspiration[11], Dryden used 'genius' to denote a 'gift of Nature' that 'must be born, and never can be taught'[12], Immanuel Kant considered genius to be 'the talent (natural endowment) that gives the rule to art'[13] and Francis Galton took his studies to show that genius really is a matter of heredity.[14] Even at the most minimal level natural talent or endowment is standardly taken to explain creative achievements. A widely cited survey of music teachers found that three-quarters of those surveyed believed that children could not do well at music unless they

---

[11]   Plato's *Ion*, 533c9–535a2, has Socrates characterizing poets as being akin to prophets in being non-rationally, divinely inspired.
[12]   John Dryden, *Epistle to Congreve*, 1693, l. 60.
[13]   Immanuel Kant, *Critique of Judgement*, Section 46.
[14]   Francis Galton, *Hereditary Genius: An Inquiry Into Its Laws and Consequences* (London: Macmillan and Co., 1869).

Matthew Kieran

had special, innate gifts (and the teachers selected pupils on this basis).[15] Indeed, the identification of creative excellence with natural talent underlies a wide variety of programmes aimed at picking out naturally gifted children to enhance their creative potential. There is not much point, the challenge goes, in encouraging everyone to be creatively excellent or virtuous, given that, at least for most people, creative potential is naturally somewhat limited. Moreover, if all that is required for creative excellence is talent plus hard work it is unclear what significant role if any the creative virtues as conceived above have to play. In what follows I will argue that the presumption that creative excellence requires exceptional natural talents is flawed. This is not to deny that natural gifts have a role to play. Nonetheless, most possess at least some creative potential that can be cultivated more or less excellently.

One influential line of thought holds that human beings are naturally curious about the world. Even at a basic developmental level we tend to delight in the development and exercise of our intellectual, practical and creative capacities. This provides the platform from which more skillful creative thought and activity can be cultivated. Thus some have argued that the fundamental problem may lie with educational systems that 'teach to test' alongside associated work or organizational practices.[16] According to Sir Ken Robinson teaching to test tends to alienate us from some of the natural pleasures to be had in learning for ourselves, stifle curiosity and undermine the psychological importance of learning being its own reward. Some work in developmental psychology seems to suggest that children would be much more curious and creative were it not for certain pedagogical practices. In other words pedagogy structured toward passing standardized tests that focus on narrow skill and knowledge sets may tend to stifle curiosity. By way of illustration in one experiment children exposed to direct pedagogical demonstration seemed to focus almost exclusively on the illustrated function of an object. By contrast children merely presented with an object tended to engage much more in wider exploration and were thus more likely to discover new information.[17] In a related but distinct experiment one group of children were presented with a recognized knowledgeable teacher

---

[15] M. Davis, 'Folk Music Psychology', *The Psychologist*, 7 (12), 1994, 537.
[16] See Ken Robinson, *Out of Our Minds: Learning to Be Creative* (Oxford: Capstone, 2001).
[17] Elizabeth Bonawitz, Patrick Shafto, Hyowon Gweon, Noah D. Goodman, Elizabeth Spelke and Laura Schulz, 'The Double-Edged

who demonstrated action sequences leading to a particular outcome whereas a distinct group were presented with a naïve demonstrator. Those children in the naïve demonstrator condition were far more likely to find new shorter action sequences to the same outcome i.e. find a new solution.[18] It might thus be thought that enhancing people's creativity depends less upon exceptional talent and more upon reforming pedagogical and socio-institutional practices that undermine the creative potential of many.

Whilst there is much to this line of thought we should take care before generalizing from the idea that pedagogical practices may undermine exploratory learning and curiosity at developmental stages to the idea that everyone would otherwise naturally be much more creative than they are. First, the experimental evidence is itself rather mixed.[19] Second, even if in developmental terms creativity naturally seems to emerge as an upshot of curiosity, playfulness and problem solving, nonetheless exploratory play and curiosity are costly. Once we know how to meet our needs and take on projects that cost time, energy and commitment, it might be quite natural for open-ended curiosity and playfulness to diminish.[20] For many purposes it is often easier to seek out the testimony or know-how of others. We quite rightly value predictability and good enough competence (as opposed to originality and excellence) in many things. Hence, above a certain level of competence, creative apathy – at least with respect to most things – may be a very natural state of affairs indeed.

What this points to is a need to distinguish natural (or the natural basis for) creativity from acquired creative virtue. Natural creativity may emerge as an upshot of development that enables us to master

---

Sword of Pedagogy: Instruction Limits Spontaneous Exploration and Discovery', *Cognition*, **120** (3), September, 2011, 322–330.

[18] Daphna Buchsbaum, Alison Gopnik, Thomas L. Griffiths, Patrick Shafto, 'Children's Imitation of Causal Action Sequences is Influenced by Statistical and Pedagogical Evidence', *Cognition*, **120** (3), September 2011, 331–340.

[19] See Angeline S. Lillard, Matthew D. Lerner, Emily J. Hopkins, Rebecca A. Dore, Eric D. Smith and Carolyn M. Palmquist, 'The Impact of Pretend Play on Children's Development: A Review of the Evidence', *Psychological Bulletin*, **139** (1), 2013, 1–34.

[20] See Alison Gopnik, *The Philosophical Baby* (New York: Farrar, Straus and Giroux, 2009) for the idea that our adult minds tend to become comparatively more attention focused, project driven, inhibited and conservative.

our physical and social environment. Acquired creativity – the kind of creativity upon which creative excellence depends - involves cultivating the expertise and traits required to excel in a given domain. Perhaps acquired creativity only speaks to the desires of a minority (though I suspect many if not most people would desire to be more creative given the right kind of opportunities). If this is right, then the claim that everyone would be more creative were it not for certain pedagogical and organizational practices might be too strong. Nonetheless, even if that claim is too strong, creative achievement, as we shall see, is non-accidentally tied to the cultivation of virtues and need not require exceptional talent.

Whilst Van Gogh is acknowledged as a master of twentieth century art, going from mere novice to greatness in ten years flat, what is less remarked upon is the fact that he was not particularly talented to start with. A felicity for calligraphic ink drawing apart, Van Gogh's initial work was extremely crude, clumsy and flat. As the art critic Robert Hughes puts it:

> Anyone could have been forgiven for looking at his early work and passing it by. Perhaps no artist who got as good as Vincent has ever started out so bad. Not just bad, but worthy bad, which is (if anything) worse. Even today, you'd hardly want one as a present, unless it was from someone you didn't want to offend. Those dogged, I-share-your-suffering images of ground-down peasant women and Dutch cloggies grouped around the sacramental potato, done in glum, awkward homage to Jean-François Millet and English social-consciousness painters such as Luke Fildes, all testify that sincerity, on its own, is not an artistic virtue. Gazing at early Van Gogh, at that murky stuff from the mid-1880s, you thirst for some signs of style - and there are none, or none that count.[21]

Van Gogh is far from being an aberration. To cite a few artistic case studies, Francis Bacon's naturalistic figuration was poor, much of Jackson Pollock's career consisted in underwhelming pastiches of others and Mark Rothko's early work suggested a modest talent at best. Closer to home, in a period of four years the Sistema Scotland project took Raploch in Scotland, one of the most deprived council estates in the U.K., from a position where one child on the estate was learning a musical instrument to a full blown orchestra consisting of 450 children (80% of the primary age youngsters on the estate).

---

[21] Robert Hughes, 'The Genius of Crazy Vinnie', *The Guardian*, Thursday, 27 October, 2005.

Indeed the children's orchestra attained what might seem intuitively to be an unbelievably high level as demonstrated by its various public performances, including the opening public performance of the London 2012 Olympics festival with the Simón Bolívar Symphony Orchestra of Venezuela.[22] The phenomenon of great creative achievement emerging from unpromising or naturally modest beginnings is far from restricted to the artistic domain. Darwin was thought by his family and teachers to be 'a very ordinary boy, rather below the common standard in intellect'[23], Edison was famously considered stupid by his teacher, the young Einstein was thought to be slow, later being rejected by the Zurich Polytechnic School, and the Nobel laureates Luis Alvarez and William Shockley were both turned down, at different times, from the same research programme because their IQ scores were too low for them to count as gifted.

What enables those who aren't especially naturally gifted to become exemplars of creativity? A wide ranging in depth interview study of 120 highly achieving individuals in music, art, academics and sport foregrounds several factors including introduction in a playful manner at a young age alongside significant practical and emotional support.[24] Immersion at a time when individuals develop a love or passion for the chosen domain is key. This foundation enables individuals to go on to the precision and integration stages crucial for excellence.[25] The study provides 'strong evidence that no matter what the initial characteristics (or gifts) of the individuals, unless there is a long and intensive period of encouragement, nurturance, education, and training, the individuals will not attain extreme levels of capability in these particular fields.'[26]

Consonant with this work empirical studies on the acquisition of high levels of expertise from music to chess suggest that extensive experience is required to attain reliably superior performance. The initial phase of the Sistema Scotland project, Raploch, started children playing string instruments five mornings a week at summer school and built from there. Thousands of hours of practice,

[22]   Charlotte Higgins, 'Big Noise Orchestra's Classical Music Proves Instrumental in Social Change', *The Guardian*, Wednesday, 20th June, 2012, p. 1.
[23]   *The Autobiography of Charles Darwin 1809–1882* (London: Collins, 1958), p. 28.
[24]   Benjamin Bloom (ed.), *Developing Talent in Young People* (New York: Ballantine Books, 1985).
[25]   Lauren A. Sosniak, 'Phases of Learning' in op. cit. note 19, 409–438.
[26]   Op. cit. note 19, 3.

Matthew Kieran

development and refinement are required to attain the level of expertise needed to be creatively excellent in most domains. Yet it is not just the sheer number of hours and dedication that matters. Only certain types of experience count toward significantly improved performance and creative excellence. The highest achieving performers spend the highest number of hours on *deliberate* practice.[27]

Why is deliberate practice required? Addressing tasks or challenges leads agents to focus on consciously attempting to generate and co-ordinate actions. Increased experience gives rise to increased automaticity that also brings a concomitant loss of conscious control and a hardened inability to adjust intentionally. The advantage of this process is that it yields enhanced automatic performance up to a certain level. The disadvantage is that once such processes are automatized further extensive experience fails to yield any significant improvement in performance above the level attained. *Deliberate* practice involves seeking out demanding tasks that require problem solving to combat the effects of automaticity and thus involve refining the cognitive and motor mechanisms required for continued improvement. Deliberate practice is required to acquire the independent motor and cognitive representational capacities for controlling, monitoring and evaluating creative performance. Indeed such improvements are associated with changes in the cortical mapping of musicians, enhanced finger flexibility, greater memory capacity, increased speed in the 'instinctive' representation of moves and skilled anticipation:

> Improvements are caused by changes in cognitive mechanisms mediating how the brain and nervous systems control performance and in the degree of adaptation of physiological systems of the body... Continued attempts for mastery require that the performer always try stretching performance beyond its current capabilities, to correct some specific weakness while preserving other successful aspects of function.[28]

Creative excellence is much more a function of immersion and the right kind of hard work than is commonly presumed. Furthermore,

[27] K. A. Ericsson, R. Th. Krampe and C. Tesch-Römer, 'The Role of Deliberate Practice in the Acquisition of Expert Performance', *Psychological Review*, **100**, 1993, 363–406.

[28] K. A. Ericsson, 'The Influence of Experience and Deliberate Practice on the Development of Superior Expert Performance', in K. A. Ericsson, N. Charness, P. J. Feltovitch and R. R. Hoffman (eds.), *The Cambridge Handbook of Expertise and Expert Performance* (Cambridge: Cambridge University Press, 2006), 700.

working hard in the right kinds of ways and acquiring the kind of expertise required for developing creative excellence, which involves pushing at the limits of whatever creative stage one is at, requires the cultivation or possession of persistence, patience, curiosity, the desire to experiment, the courage to be open to failure, resilience, critical self honesty about where one's weaknesses lie and so on. It is no accident that Van Gogh, Darwin and Edison were, amongst other things, passionate, curious, courageous, critically self-honest, persistent and resilient, or that the Raploch children were immersed in a disciplined yet playful environment that cultivated passion, enjoyment in the activity for its own sake, persistence, resilience, aspiration, self-reliance and self-confidence.[29] The natural talent attribution error is the tendency to over attribute the role that natural talent plays in creative achievement and under attribute the role that immersion, the right kinds of deliberate practice and cultivating virtues plays in acquiring the abilities to be creatively excellent. Hence it is sometimes all too easy to underestimate people's creative potential and the extent to which they can be creative in some particular domain.

4. Creativity and Ill-Being

A distinct challenge arises from thinking that certain psychological disorders may be a 'price to be paid' for creative excellence. The association of creativity with depression, madness or melancholia reaches as far back as Aristotle and is most strongly identified with the Romantics. Contemporary culture draws upon and reinforces folk assumptions about the mad scientist or tortured artist whilst biographies of figures such as Van Gogh, Sylvia Plath or Alan Turing speculate about the links between the subject's mental condition and creativity. If creative excellence often non-accidentally depends upon psychological disorders, then it looks like creative achievement can be the workings of involuntary capacities and conditions that seem constitutive of ill-being. At least indirectly this may seem to put pressure on a virtue account of exemplary creativity given that a) the workings of such conditions and the capacities thereby enabled do not seem to be tied up with virtues of mind or character and b) such seem to undermine rather than promote well-being.

---

[29] See the Scottish Government Social Research Report, 'Evaluation of Big Noise, Sistema Scotland' (Edinburgh: Crown Copyright, Queen's Printer for Scotland, 2011).

Why think there is such an interesting relation? The literature positing such relationships is vast so we will look at three of the most cited classic sources with respect to depression (given the most robust evidence for an association is taken to be between creativity and in particular bipolar depression).

The psychiatrist Arnold M. Ludwig studied 1004 biographies of historically eminent figures in various domains from the arts and sciences to business (identified via reviews from the *New York Times Book Review* 1960 – 1990).[30] As diagnosed the percentages of those suffering from some kind of mental disorder included 87% of poets, 77% of fiction writers, 51% of social scientists and 28% of natural scientists. The clinical psychologist Kay Jamison studied 36 major poets from Britain and Ireland in the period 1705–1805 including figures such as Blake, Byron, Shelley and Keats. Jamison retrospectively diagnosed over 50% of the poets identified as having suffered from mood disorders with thirteen (over 33%) probably suffering from manic depression. Six poets, including Clare and Cowper, were committed to madhouses or the lunatic asylum, ostensibly at least twenty times the committal rate of the general populace at the time.[31] In a separate study of forty-seven contemporary British writers and artists who had won major prizes in their fields, Jamison found 38% of the total sample had been treated for mood disorders with 63% of playwrights requiring some kind of treatment for depression and 33% of poets having been given medical treatment for depression (and the only ones requiring medical intervention for mania).[32] This study seems consonant with an earlier study by Nancy Andreason that found 80% of 30 creative writers identified had experienced significant depressive episodes compared with only 30% of 30 matched control subjects with similar IQs from normal jobs.[33]

There are grounds for skepticism. Retrospectively diagnosing historical figures with varying mental illnesses is a subfield in its own right (Van Gogh, for example, has been the subject of at least 30 differential diagnoses).[34] Yet we should be extremely cautious,

[30]   Arnold M. Ludwig, *The Price of Greatness: Resolving the Creativity and Madness Controversy* (New York: Guildford Press, 1995), 149.

[31]   Kay Redfield Jamison, *Touched with Fire: Manic Depressive Illness and the Artistic Temperament* (New York: Free Press, 1993), 61–72.

[32]   Op. cit., 76.

[33]   Nancy C. Andreasen, 'Creativity and Mental Illness: Prevalence Rates in Writers and Their First-Degree Relatives,' *American Journal of Psychiatry*, **144** (10), 1987, 1288–92.

[34]   Dietrich Blumer, 'The Illness of Vincent Van Gogh', *American Journal of Psychiatry*, **159** (4), 2002, 519–526.

especially in the realm of mental illness. Consider how difficult it is even in normal circumstances to reach diagnoses of mental illness. Clinical observation, exploratory therapy, background medical histories and a range of physical or psychological tests are often needed to arrive at initial diagnoses. A patient's response to initial treatment then provides the basis for diagnostic revision or refinement. Contrast this with the paucity of the right kind of information we typically have with respect to historical figures. Even with respect to more contemporaneous people, where there are often journals, more detailed records and the testimony of various friends or enemies, many clinicians would often be wary about identifying behaviour patterns as symptomatic of particular mental illness' on such a basis. Perhaps, to take the case cited, Van Gogh was just a particularly irascible, moody person driven by a passion for art, subject to poverty and the onset of disordered episodes prompted by drinking far too much absinthe.[35] In historical cases it can be hard to tell what condition someone really suffered from or indeed what constitutes cause and effect.

The sample for many such studies based on biographical materials are also subject to various kinds of selectional and informational biases.[36] One such is what I will term the 'Elizabeth Taylor effect'. Elizabeth Taylor the actress had eight marriages, suffered alcoholism, mental illness and was subject to religious conversion. Biographies, journalistic and television pieces on her life seem innumerable despite hardly anyone watching her movies any more. By contrast when the husband of Elizabeth Taylor the novelist, compared by Anne Tyler to Jane Austen and considered one of the best English novelists of the twentieth century by Kingsley Amis[37], approached a friend, the writer Elizabeth Jane Howard, to write a biography, Howard declined the offer since 'she led a life that contained very little incident.'[38] With respect to figures of comparative stature in the same field there is a natural tendency to cover and constantly return to the lives of those with highly dramatic personalities, relationships and events. This perhaps explains why the number of

[35] Ibid.
[36] Jonathan Hurlow and James H. MacCabe, 'Paradoxes in Creativity and Psychiatric Conditions', in N. Kapur (ed.), *The Paradoxical Brain* (Cambridge: Cambridge University Press, 2011), pp. 289–300.
[37] Benjamin Schwarz, 'The Other Elizabeth Taylor', Books Section, Editor's Choice Column, *The Atlantic*, September 2007, http://www.theatlantic.com/magazine/archive/2007/09/the-other-elizabeth-taylor/306125/.
[38] Neel Mukherjee, 'A Fiendish Mood: The Mid-Century Novels of 'the other Elizabeth Taylor', *Boston Review*, Jan/Feb 2008, Fiction Section, http://bostonreview.net/BR33.1/mukherjee.php.

books covering Picasso's life far outweighs those covering the more straightforward Matisse. Creatively excellent but mundane lives tend to get far less attention than the wildly dramatic. Identifying achievers and their mental conditions via biographies or renowned stories may skew the sample toward dramatic lives rather than creatively excellent ones as such. Moreover, interviews and self-reports may be subject to worries about evidence distortion given that creative subjects' self-conception may be bound up with a rather romanticized notion of tortured, suffering artists. In different ages artists were often expected to behave as guildsmen or gentlemen scholars and may thus perhaps have conceived of themselves and acted rather differently. It could also be that behaviour taken to be indicative of mental illness might just be symptomatic of what is involved in striving for high achievement, breaking with social norms or being open to experience and a sensation seeker. Artists in contemporary society often work in far greater isolation than scientists, take greater risks, experiment with life more and are often expected to be romantic and moody. Many of these factors, rather than creativity as such, may show up directly or indirectly as exhibiting or resulting in behavior often associated with depressive illness. We also know that the poverty stricken tend to be disproportionately afflicted with mental illness and differential results from those in natural science through to poets may reflect such underlying life conditions i.e. perhaps poets tended to be poorer or less socio-economically secure. A higher incidence of mental illness in creative artists may be due to greater exposure to life conditions that precipitate mental illness rather than a function of any deeper intrinsic connection between mental illness and creativity. Alternatively perhaps writers are often drawn towards fiction or poetry in order to work through and ameliorate underlying psychological conditions or for reasons unrelated to what makes them creative.[39]

Whilst the above is hardly an exhaustive review of the evidence available it should give us pause for thought. On the evidence cited from some of the classic studies in the field there are good reasons to doubt there is a significant link between creativity and mental illness. Perhaps the idea that there is such a link taps into a socio-historically contingent conception of the artist as tortured genius but this may well be a damaging myth rather than reality.

[39] See Berys Gaut, 'Creativity and Rationality', *Journal of Aesthetics and Art Criticism*, **70** (3), 2012, 264–265 which makes many of these points and gives an extended treatment of this point in a closely related though perhaps less sceptical discussion of much of the same evidence.

Nonetheless it does not follow that there is no reason to think there might be such a link. A recent investigation into scholastic achievement (not straightforwardly to be identified with creativity) and susceptibility to bipolar disorder used prospective data in a whole population cohort study.[40] The grades of all individuals who finished compulsory school in Sweden, aged 15–16 (class 9), from 1988 – 1997, were taken as a measure of scholastic achievement and were compared with hospital admission data for the individuals for psychosis from the ages of 17–31. Amongst the study's findings it turned out that those with excellent school performance were virtually four times more likely to be at risk from bipolar disorder than those with average grades (interestingly this was male specific). Let us, for the sake of argument, assume that, as with academic performance, something similar might show up with respect to creative achievement in this kind of study. If aspects intrinsic to mental illness are held to enhance rather than diminish people's creative capacities, then creative excellence may appear to be – at least sometimes – independent of virtue. Moreover, at least to the extent that creative achievement is enabled by conditions of ill-being then creative excellence might thus be the enemy of happiness rather than its hand servant.

So let us assume for the sake of argument that there is some link between creativity and mental illness. But in virtue of what we might ask? How might conditions of ill-being have psychological effects that promote creativity? A brief and non-exhaustive typology of mechanisms and benefits that may accrue might include:

i)   Capacity enhancement. The workings of the imagination, pattern recognition and the capacity to generate associations often go into overdrive in mania phases of depression and schizophrenia. Jamison argues that the creative capacity of writers is enhanced due to mania's fluency, flexibility and connectivity of thought whilst mild depressive phases are suitable for critical editorial development.[41] In addition it could be that certain cognitive distortions associated with depression lend themselves to more creative conceptualization or expression.[42]

[40]   James H. MacCabe, Mats P. Lambe, Sven Cnattingius, Pak C. Sham, Anthony S. David, Abraham Reichenberg, Robin M. Murray and Christina M. Hultman, 'Excellent School Performance at Age 16 and Risk of Bipolar Disorder', *British Journal of Psychiatry*, **196**, 2010, 109–15.

[41]   Jamison op. cit., 105–118.

[42]   Gaut op. cit., 265, and K. M. Thomas and M. Duke, 'Depressed Writing: Cognitive Distortions on the Work of Depressed and Non-

ii)   Framing enhancement conditions. Differences in negative background psychological states and vulnerabilities framing an agent's imaginative activity may lead to enhanced creativity. There is some evidence to suggest that just as social rejection may enhance creativity so too might dispositional vulnerability to negative emotions.[43] Whilst there are various competing explanations available at least one possibility might be that background negative emotional states may enhance alertness, focus and perception (as might be expected if negative emotional states are associated with threat identification).

iii)   Enhanced rumination. Self-focused recursive thinking is associated with mania and depression.[44] It could be that self-concerned rumination aids creativity in certain circumstances, especially in domains such as art, literature or music where self-expression or psychological states are themselves often part of the subject matter.[45] By contrast we might add that ruminative self-concern might prove to be a distraction rather than a benefit in contrasting domains or activity. Rumination on one's sadness may enhance musical expression or the literary articulation of such in lyric poetry, whilst it may do nothing for one's ability to construct logical theorems or perform calculations.

iv)   Enhanced motivation. Depression – at least in its milder forms or as someone comes out of a depressive state – may prompt people to address problems, dissatisfactions or underlying unhappiness and thus ultimately lead to more creative activity. Aversion to depressive states may,

Depressed Poets and Writers', *Psychology of Aesthetics, Creativity and the Arts* **1** (4), 2007, 204–218.

[43]   M. Akinola and W. B. Mendes, 'The Dark Side of Creativity: Biological Vulnerability and Negative Emotions lead to Greater Artistic Creativity', *Personality and Psychology Bulletin*, **34** (12), 2008, 1677–1686.

[44]   Sharmin Ghaznavi and Thilo Deckersbach, 'Rumination in Bipolar Disorder: Evidence for an Unquiet Mind', *Biology of Mood and Anxiety Disorders*, 2012, **2** (2), 1–11.

[45]   P. Verhaeghen, J. Joormann and R. Khan, 'Why We Sing the Blues: The Relation Between Self-Reflective Rumination, Mood and Creativity', *Emotion* **5**, 2005, 226–232.

at least where the cause is not perceived as being hopeless, prompt greater exertion to avoid staying in or sliding back into painful emotions. Thus depression may under certain circumstances lead people toward becoming more creative. By contrast mania is more particularly associated with excitability and a drive for novelty seeking which may enhance creative activity.[46]

However, even if there are such interesting links between creativity and mental illness note that the kind of connections as spelt out are indirect. It is not mental illness as such that enhances creativity but, putatively, certain underlying capacities or psychological states associated with mental illness. Moreover, depression and bipolar depression typically seem to be extremely bad for creativity (given depressed people tend to be aversive rather than approach orientated and distrust their judgement, capacities or worth). Virginia Woolf could barely write when depressed, Van Gogh was unable to paint when in seemingly similar states and Coleridge suffered a deeply paralyzing writer's block for years due to anxiety. Depression is associated with low self-worth and a marked tendency to jump to conclusions about the uselessness or futility of what one is doing. Such a state is hardly conducive to good judgement, perseverance or resilience in creative activity. Moreover in bipolar depression the depressive state oscillates with mania whilst being associated with high self-regard, systematic over-estimation about what is achievable and future orientated fantasizing. Such a state makes it much harder to judge what is worthwhile and tends toward the uptake of large numbers of tasks that typically remain incomplete. A manic phase in bipolar depression may tend to generate all sorts of wild ideas only a few of which may have anything worth developing. Even then, the generation of an idea is one thing, but working out which one to develop, having the perseverance to do so, the resilience to overcome set backs and the courage to expose the idea to peer or public evaluation is quite another. Neither the depressive or manic state typically seems conducive to the kind of judgement or perseverance tied up with creative excellence. There are particular points where milder episodes or manic phases on the rise to full blown mania may facilitate productivity through quicker information

[46] Alice W. Flaherty, 'Frontotemporal and Dopaminergic Control of Idea Generation and Creative Drive', *Journal of Comparative Neurology*, **493** (1), 2005, 147–153.

processing or less need for sleep.[47] Yet it should be emphasized that the psychological conditions identified tend to undermine the ability to realize creative excellence with much stability or reliability, if at all, unless the conditions are manageable (which will itself be individually variable and often a huge achievement). Manic episodes are followed by depressive crashes and in clinical terms the aim is to prevent the mania in the first place (especially given the lack of responsiveness to anti-depressants). The point is that where someone's condition is not manageable – and such conditions tend to be deeply disordering and undermining of good functioning - then a disorder's contribution to someone's creative achievement will tend to be negative whilst any positive contribution will be extremely fragile and intermittent at best.

Creative excellence neither requires the possession of psychologically destabilizing conditions nor is guaranteed by such, especially given that such conditions typically undermine creative achievement. Moreover, making use of the benefits of any associated creative enhancements will typically require mastery, the right kind of motivation, curiosity, courage, perseverance and resilience amongst other things. In other words creative virtues have a crucial role to play in the exercise of judgement, deployment of skill, evaluation, purposiveness, exploration and development of an idea identified as worthwhile in order for the idea to be realized creatively. Doing so well depends upon and is facilitated by traits of mind and character such as persistence, the courage to overcome anxiety, the curiosity to experiment with and try out the idea in various ways and so on (indeed some of the virtues may be required to a greater degree than by normal subjects in particular cases where, for example, someone's depression is tied up with say anxiety and fear of failure).

We should not over romanticize the relationship between creativity and ill-being. If there is a significant link, which we have some reason to doubt, then it is a misfortune that creative capacities, where manageable, may be enhanced at particular times by conditions that synchronically tend to undermine psychological functioning and creative activity. This does not refute the idea that creative virtue tends towards a happier, more fulfilled life. It would, however, compromise or at least require refinement of the simple claim and should push us to think through matters in more detail. If the connection is a strong one then we might expect that, on the whole, creative people (or a

---

[47]   Jonathan Hurlow and James H. MacCabe, 'Paradoxes in Creativity and Psychiatric Conditions', in N. Kapur (ed.), *The Paradoxical Brain* (Cambridge: Cambridge University Press, 2011), pp. 291–3.

significant sub section thereof) will tend to be less happy than those who are not. Nonetheless, this is consistent with creative people being more fulfilled to the extent that, other things being equal, they pursue and achieve something novel and worthwhile with their lives. Thus perhaps the kind of fulfillment that creativity aims for should come with a health warning. The successful pursuit of creative fulfillment may leave us prone to a potentially significant cost to happiness. Yet this remains consistent with the claim that a life of creative virtue still tends toward a more fulfilling life than many others. An unqualifiedly happy, flourishing creative life may require not just excellence but also good fortune.

5. The Challenge from Immorality

Creative excellence often seems closely tied to morally defective character traits. Infamously Bob Dylan stole extremely rare folk records from a friend, claiming he needed them for his musical development, and John Lennon once said 'you have to be a bastard to make it man and the Beatles were the biggest bastards on earth.'[48] More generally Feist's meta-analysis of empirical studies on personality and creative achievement from 1950–1995 found that

> Creative people are more autonomous, introverted, open to new experiences, norm-doubting, self-confident, self-accepting, driven, ambitious, hostile, and impulsive . . . [the] largest effect sizes are on openness, conscientiousness [negatively correlated], self-acceptance, hostility, and impulsivity.[49]

By far the most significant effect sizes are openness to experience, which seems consonant with the virtue account of exemplary creativity, and lack of conscientiousness, which seems in tension with it. Interestingly creative scientists came out with a stronger negative correlation to conscientiousness than non-creative scientists and creative people in the arts were found to be even less conscientious than creative scientists.

Now we should be rather wary of what exactly is being measured here. Conscientiousness measures range over indicators taken to

---

[48]   As excerpted from a radio documentary on The Beatles, *Feedback*, Radio 4, BBC Radio 4, 20th August 2010.
[49]   Gregory J. Feist, 'A Meta-Analysis of Personality and Scientific and Artistic Creativity', *Personality and Social Psychology Review*, **2** (4), 1998, 299.

manifest a lack of honesty, disorganization, tendency to meet agreed deadlines and turning up to work. It is not obvious that such behaviours relate to the same trait. Why presume that disorganization is related to dishonesty? Moreover, perhaps some creative people score negatively on certain dimensions of conscientiousness due to a range of characteristics including achievement orientation, perfectionism, autonomy and norm variation. Plumbers or builders might tend to score just as negatively given they too tend to be autonomous, self-organized and operate under looser punctuality conventions (without thereby being dishonest).

However in a series of recent studies Gino and Ariely focus specifically on honesty.[50] Subjects were identified as more or less creative using a wide variety of measures such as self-description, self-report activities, accomplishments and self-report cognitive styles. The first study involved a visual perception task, a problem solving task and a multiple choice task where subjects could earn more by cheating. In the visual perception task, for example, subjects were shown 100 slides with squares divided diagonally with red dots either side. There were always more dots on the left side but in 50 slides (the measure of dishonesty) matters were more ambiguous thus affording opportunity for creative misinterpretation to yield greater pay off. The study found that 'the measures of creative personality were positively and significantly correlated with the level of dishonesty on each of the three tasks. . . We did not find evidence of a link between creativity and intelligence or a link between intelligence and dishonesty.'[51] The second study found that subjects subconsciously primed for creative thinking tended to cheat more in word tasks accruing small amounts of money. The third and fourth studies used creatively primed and non-primed subjects rolling dice where self-reported results accrued monetary rewards. Non-primed subjects reported an average dice roll of 3.5 whereas primed subjects reported an average of 5. In the fifth study subjects identified as more dispositionally creative were not significantly affected by creative primes with respect to either creative performance or dishonest behaviour. Thus, the authors argue, dispositionally creative people do not need a creative prime to be more creative or dishonest than normal subjects. Exactly what is going on remains unclear. It could be that creativity in such a scenario is bound up with imaginativeness,

[50] Francesca Gino and Dan Ariely, 'The Dark Side of Creativity: Original Thinkers Can Be More Dishonest', *Journal of Personality and Social Psychology*, **102** (3), 2012, 445–459.
[51] op. cit., 449.

risk taking, competitiveness, self-interest or some admixture thereof whilst apparent dishonesty is construed as legitimate in such game playing situations. Nonetheless the studies are strongly suggestive so for the sake of argument let us assume the studies identify a significant, general correlation between the lack of an aspect of conscientiousness, specifically genuine dishonesty, and creativity. Gino and Ariely hypothesize that greater creativity 'may lead people to take unethical routes when searching for solutions' and 'lead to greater dishonesty by increasing individuals' ability to justify their immoral actions'.[52] Creativity thus seems to pull away from or at least be in tension with ethical behaviour.

We should ask ourselves just how much of a challenge this really is though. Would we be surprised, for example, if traits that tend toward courage such as resilience, risk taking and self-assurance, facilitate lying? If so, would we think this shows courage is at odds with honesty? Surely it is only a deep psychological challenge if the traits that tend toward the appropriate acquisition of or acting from one virtue are psychologically inconsistent with doing so with respect to another. There is no obvious reason to think this is the case with respect to creativity and honesty. Children enjoy imaginative play and are often motivated to make stories up to avoid punishment or accrue gains. But we do not take this to show anything deep about the incompatibility of imaginativeness versus honesty as opposed to the importance of a good developmental environment for children. Moreover, we need to distinguish the basis for what we might think of as a natural or rough basis for virtue from acquired virtue or virtue proper. In isolation certain natural or rough trait tendencies may help ground intellectual, moral or creative achievements. However, unlike virtue proper, such tendencies are prone to certain kinds of errors either in isolation or in combination. Someone who always tells the truth might naturally tend to ride roughshod over the feelings of others, sometimes inappropriately, just as someone who is always compassionate may sometimes act unjustly. Similarly, someone who is very creative might tend to be rather imaginative with respect to truth telling, again sometimes inappropriately. All this shows is that certain trait tendencies (like temperaments) may form the raw material out of which we acquire or refine virtue even though such tendencies are not the same as full or proper virtue.[53]

[52]   op. cit., 454–55.
[53]   Aristotle, *Nicomachean Ethics*, VI, 1144 b 4–6 makes something like this distinction. For contrasting elaborations as to what this distinction amounts to see Susan Wolf, 'Moral Psychology and the Unity of the

Matthew Kieran

Virtue generally consists in seeing where, when and why certain kinds of thoughts, responses or actions are appropriate for the right kinds of reasons. Exemplary creativity thus partly consists in seeing where being creative and how so is appropriate and thus seems to depend upon a cluster of virtues which are an admixture of virtues of mind and virtues of character. This is to deny what we might term an independence thesis i.e. the possession of any one virtue is independent of any other. It also involves a stronger claim than the consistency claim made above i.e. possession of some one virtue tied up with creative excellence is consistent with the possession of any other virtue such as honesty. It is to claim that possession of a given virtue will be inter-related to and depend upon the possession of some others.

Whilst most philosophers who appeal to some account of virtue, such as Aristotle, Aquinas or Hume[54], hold to some version of an inter-dependence claim, albeit in systematically distinct ways, it is not obvious that everyone does. Positive psychology sometimes proceeds on the basis that one virtue or positive psychological character trait can be studied independently of others (or in relation to one contrast trait). Yet there seems to be good reason to hold that the independence thesis is false and that this must be so in particular with respect to exemplary creativity.

As we saw above, amongst other virtues, creative excellence depends upon curiosity, perseverance, courage, self-assurance, resilience, self-honesty and humility. If someone lacks curiosity then there will tend to be a marked disinterest in the kind of exploration subserving creative excellence. Where someone lacks courage there will tend to be an aversion to exposing the self, thoughts or work to critical exposure. Curiosity partially enhances the possession of courage in giving an interest in and motivation to seek critical exposure. By the same token self-honesty is required for creative excellence and is closely intertwined with humility. Clear-sightedness about our weaknesses or lacks enables us to identify what we need to work on and why. Yet admitting to being mistaken or inadequate can be

---

Virtues', *Ratio* **20**, 2007, pp. 145–167 and Gopal Sreenivasan, 'Disunity of Virtue', *Journal of Ethics* **13** (2/3), 2009, esp. pp. 198–200.

[54] Aristotle, *Nicomachean Ethics*, VI, 1144 b 30 – 1145 and Thomas Aquinas, *Disputed Questions on Virtue*, On the Cardinal Virtues, Article 2, Hause and Murphy edition (New York: Hackett, 2010), 232–241, Marie A. Martin, 'Hume on Human Excellence', *Hume Studies*, **XVIII** (2), pp. 383–400.

difficult given that we naturally like to think highly of ourselves. Hence humility is required to be open to the possibility of mistakes or error which is itself tied up with self-honesty about the state of one's work or what needs to be worked on in order to get better. What it is to be a creatively excellent person partly depends upon and is constituted by the possession of inter-related clusters of virtues. Note that whilst the inter-dependency claim commits us to clusters of virtues it does not entail the unity of the virtues (though it is consistent with it). Whilst Aristotle and Aquinas held that none of the virtues are strictly speaking possible for an individual without possessing the others, subscribing to the interdependence claim does not entail commitment to the unity thesis. In other words possessing some cluster of virtues, such as those required for exemplary creativity, *may* require only the possession of certain virtues or types of virtues as distinct from the possession of all. It could be, for example, that creative excellence does not require or depend on the possession of kindness, charity or other particular moral traits. Whilst creative excellence partly depends upon critical self-honesty, it may not require the kind of honesty tied up with respecting the niceties of property rights. This may give a rather different inflection to the phrase 'good artists borrow, great artists steal'.

Putting matters thus refines the challenge from immorality. Perhaps, the challenge now goes, there is some reason to think that creative excellence might be *in principle* at odds with (at least certain aspects of) moral excellence. In other words perhaps there are clusters of virtues that are disordered in relation to one another. Co-opting Williams's fictional simplification of Gaugin's life brings this out (the following is not the purpose to which Williams puts the case).[55] Williams' Gaugin is characterized as prioritizing his creative drive above the demands of morality by abandoning his wife in France for the artistic life in Tahiti. It is common to hold that the dictates of morality should trump other interests so, presumably, a morally good person would neither be morally praiseworthy nor happy in abandoning his wife. Yet in the scenario as characterized the pursuit of exemplary creative excellence seemingly must come at the expense of moral excellence (or vice versa). The pursuit of creative excellence may thus seem to be in principle at odds with the pursuit of moral excellence.

Even as refined the challenge remains overstated. There are many ways suppressed premises or assumptions built into the scenario may

[55] Bernard Williams, 'Moral Luck' in his *Moral Luck: Philosophical Papers 1973–1980* (Cambridge: Cambridge University Press), 20–39.

be disambiguated. Whilst Williams' Gaugin may judge the situation is such that he has to choose between his wife and artistic development it could be that there is no such in principle conflict. Rather than jettison his wife perhaps the fictional Gaugin would have done better to try and work things out with his wife so that both aims could be pursued. Alternatively if Gaugin really would have been so unhappy staying with his wife perhaps it was morally better for him to go (rather than stay and ruin his wife's life as well as his own). More fundamentally what is the nature of the putative conflict here? If the point is that there are some circumstances where pursuing different virtues or excellences may conflict then it is unclear why this is a challenge for a virtue theoretic account of exemplary creativity. Life is often such that due to circumstance there is not enough time or opportunity to pursue all the excellences one desires. Why think the Gaugin case points to anything more fundamental than this? The pursuit of creative excellence as such does not preclude marital fidelity or adherence to moral excellence more generally. Perhaps one or both parties to the marriage were ignorant, foolish or made a mistake. We all make mistakes and circumstances sometimes do not favour us. All this points to is the fact that previous mistakes or some circumstances are such that pursuing certain excellences sometimes comes at the cost of forgoing others (and this is just as true within the moral domain as it is across domains). Fair enough. What this does not yet show is that there is a deep in principle conflict between exemplary creativity and moral excellence (though it may tend to make pursuing them conjointly much more difficult in various circumstances).

Gaugin's artistic aims were praiseworthy and valuable. What about more radical cases where someone apparently manifests creative excellence whilst serving ignoble ends? Terrorists, torturers or certain city financiers, for example, might possess the creative virtues sketched above whilst realizing them in bringing about physically, economically and morally destructive ends. If someone can possess creative virtues in unjustifiably wiping out human lives or the illicit distribution of financial risk and capital then surely something has gone wrong in conceiving of exemplary creativity as being bound up with virtue? Virtue in general surely precludes malevolence and the pursuit of immoral ends.

There are various possible moves open here. A modest position would be to hold that the possibility of the ethically vicious yet creatively virtuous person is compatible with the inter-dependency and consistency claims made above. The devil may or may not have all the best tunes, but perhaps he can possess exemplary creative virtue in the service of evil. There is only a significant challenge, the defender of such a modest position might suggest, on the assumption that a virtue theoretic approach must be committed to the unity of the virtues. As we have seen above this need not necessarily be the case. Indeed, the defender of the modest position might suggest that disavowing the unity thesis whilst holding onto some version of the consistency and inter-dependency claims may help to explain why we feel torn about such cases. A more robust position would hold that what is praiseworthy in the creative terrorist or dubious financier case is the creative excellence manifest *given* the evaluatively problematic ends. Nonetheless, at least to the extent that the agent is purposively devoted towards ends that are themselves morally problematic, the value of what is achieved is marred or defective. Thus the overall excellence of creative character shown in achieving those ends may thereby be defective or diminished. We may judge that a research scientist such as Diederik Stapel was creative in various respects. His ideas for experimental studies were very often novel, interesting and worthwhile. Yet to the extent Stapel systematically made up results, publishing large numbers of 'top tier' psychology papers with fictitious evidence, he manifested creative vice rather than virtue.[56] Similarly the financier or entrepreneur who knowingly creates and sells dud financial instruments or products may display all sorts of creative excellences along various dimensions but can only be praiseworthy at best in some qualified sense and certainly remains less than exemplary in terms of full creative virtue. The robust position holds that full creative virtues must be cognizant of and directed toward good ends and values that really are worthwhile in the right sorts of ways. Whichever way one goes here, the modest and more robust positions involve cashing out virtue approaches to creative excellence in distinct ways. The former involves adhering to a virtue conception of exemplary creativity whilst holding that human virtues generally may be disordered whilst the latter involves holding to a conception in which creative virtues in principle fit with (and in the extreme case are bound up with) the virtues more generally involved in leading a good human life.

6. Conclusion

I started out by sketching a general virtue theoretic approach to traits of mind and character as psychological mechanisms that underwrite and partly constitute creative excellence. Creative virtues were

[56]   Yudhijit Bhattacharjee, 'The Mind of a Con Man', *New York Times*, Magazine, April 26, 2013.

Matthew Kieran

taken to be a cluster of inter-related admirable traits such as curiosity, courage, self-honesty, humility and perseverance. Three empirically motivated indirect challenges to such a virtue theoretic conception of creative excellence were then articulated, based on claims concerning natural talent, ill-being and immorality. I have argued that the first two challenges rested on over stated assumptions concerning the role that natural talent and mental illness play in the constitution or promotion of creative excellence. The third challenge projected tensions between isolatable trait tendencies or circumstances, falsely, onto putatively fundamental conflicts between moral and creative excellence. Nonetheless, working through these challenges forced us to refine our understanding of the nature, commitments and shape virtue approaches to creative excellence might or should take.[57]

University of Leeds
m.l.kieran@leeds.ac.uk

[57] I would like to thank in particular Matthew Broome, Gregory Currie, Dominic Lopes, James MacCabe, Sam Wren-Lewis and audiences at the Inter-University Center, Dubrovnik, University of British Columbia, University of Hertfordshire, University of Nanterre–Paris X and the RIP 'Philosophical Aesthetics and the Sciences of Art?' conference, Leeds, for valuable critical comments and discussion. Grateful acknowledgement is made to the AHRC 'Method in Philosophical Aesthetics: the Challenge from the Sciences' project and the Leverhulme Trust.

Music and Cognitive Science

ROGER SCRUTON

It has always been controversial to make a sharp distinction between the philosophical and the psychological approaches to aesthetics; and the revolution brought about by cognitive science has led many to believe that the philosophy of art no longer controls a sovereign territory of its own. To take one case in point: recent aesthetics has addressed the problem of fiction, asking how it is that real emotions can be felt towards merely imagined events. Several philosophers have tried to solve this problem by leaning on observations in psychology – Jenefer Robinson, for example, exploring the domain of pre-conscious and non-rational responses, and Greg Currie, invoking simulation theory from the realm of cognitive science. I am not yet persuaded that either has succeeded in solving the philosophical question: but the fact that such sophisticated and well-informed philosophers should begin from studies in empirical psychology says much about how the subject of aesthetics has changed since the early days of linguistic analysis.

If philosophy has any rights in this area, however, one of them is to identify nonsense, and especially nonsense that arises when practitioners of first-order disciplines seize upon the jargon of some science in order to take an unwarranted second-order standpoint. It often seems as though cognitive science and neuroscience are now fulfilling a career need that was in a previous generation fulfilled by the postmodern theory machine. Here is Ian Cross, a respectable musicologist, taking advantage of cognitive science jargon to re-define his subject matter:

'Musics are cultural particularisations of the human capacity to form multiply-intentional representations through integrating information across different functional domains of temporally extended or sequenced human experience and behaviour, generally expressed in sound.'[1]

That is a case where we might very well call for some philosophical first aid. The unexplained plural of 'musics', the use of 'representations' to transfer our attention from the thing heard to the process

---

[1]   In Isabelle Peretz and Robert J. Zatorre, eds., *The Cognitive Neuroscience of Music*, Oxford, OUP, 2003.

doi:10.1017/S1358246114000277   ©The Royal Institute of Philosophy and the contributors 2014
Royal Institute of Philosophy Supplement **75** 2014

of hearing it; the jargon, the running together of experience and behaviour and – emerging from all this like the rabbit from the hat – the extraordinary suggestion that music, whether singular or plural, is not necessarily expressed in sound. Cross is not talking about the art of sound as we know it, but about a neural process that 'integrates information' across 'different functional domains' of 'temporally extended or sequenced human experience or behaviour'. That description, in so far as it is meaningful, applies to every kind of human perception, and does nothing to distinguish music – or musics – from dinner parties and football games.

Behind Cross's nonsensical definition, however, I sense the encroachment of some real and interesting theories. First, there is the adaptation theory of the human mind, which tells us that our capacities to experience and act upon the world are the product of millennia of adaptation. Secondly there is the computational theory of the brain, according to which the brain is an information processing device that acts like a digital computer, to transform input to output through the recursive operation of quasi-syntactical algorithms. Thirdly there is the modular theory, which assigns specific 'domains' to independent capacities that evolved in order to 'process' them. All three theories have a following among philosophers, the second and the third featuring in the philosophy of Fodor as the basis for a naturalistic understanding of the mind.[2] And there are ways in which all of them might have an impact on the philosophy of music.

The adaptation theory will not concern me in what follows. Whether we follow Steven Pinker in considering music to be 'evolutionary cheese-cake', whose attractions are a by-product of other and more important adaptations, or whether we believe, with Geoffrey Miller, that musicality confers an independent reproductive advantage on the genes that produce it, the fact is that such theories have little or no bearing on the nature and meaning of music.[3] The case is exactly like mathematics. It could be that mathematical competence is a by-product of other and more useful adaptations; or it could be that it is an adaptation in its own right. But neither theory tells us what mathematics is, what numbers are, what mathematical truth

[2] Jerry A. Fodor, *Representations: Philosophical Essays on the Foundations of Cognitive Science*, Cambridge Mass., MIT Press, 1981.
[3] Steven Pinker, *How the Mind Works*, New York, Norton, 1997, p. 534. Geoffrey Miller, 'Evolution of Human Music through Sexual Selection', in Nils L. Wallin, Björn Merker and Steven Brown, eds., *The Origins of Music*, Cambridge Mass., MIT Press, 2000.

is, or what mathematics really means. All the philosophical questions remain when the evolutionary account is called in. And the same is true of most of the problems that concern philosophers of music.

Matters are otherwise with the computational theory of the brain. There is no doubt that this has cast light on the understanding of language. And it is not implausible to suggest that, if the computational theory goes some way towards explaining language, it might go some way towards explaining music too. For it reminds us that music is not sound, but sound organised 'in the brain of the beholder'. Musical organisation is something that we 'latch on to', as we latch on to language. And once the first steps in musical comprehension have been taken we advance rapidly to the point where each of us can immediately absorb and take pleasure in an indefinite number of new musical experiences. This recalls a fundamental feature of language, and not surprisingly results from linguistics have been transferred and adapted to the analysis of musical structure in the hope of showing just how it is that musical order is generated and perceived, and just what it is that explains the grip that music exerts over its devotees.

We should recognise here that music is not just an art of sound. We might combine sounds in sequence as we combine colours on an abstract canvas, or flowers in a flowerbed. But the result will not be music. It becomes music only if it also makes *musical sense*. Leaving modernist experiments aside, there is an audible distinction between music and mere sequences of sounds, and it is not just a distinction between *types* of sound (e.g. pitched and unpitched, regular and random). Sounds become music as a result of organisation, and this organisation is something that we perceive and whose absence we immediately notice, regardless of whether we take pleasure in the result. This organisation is not just an aesthetic matter – it is not simply a *style*. It is more like a grammar, in being the precondition of our response to the result *as music*. We must therefore acknowledge that music (or at any rate, tonal music of the kind familiar to the Western listener) has something like a syntax – a rule-guided process linking each episode to its neighbours, which we grasp in the act of hearing, and the absence of which leads to a sense of discomfort or incongruity.

Of course there are things called music which do not share this syntax – modernist experiments, African drum music, music employing scales that defy harmonic ordering, and so on. But from mediaeval plainsong to modern jazz we observe a remarkable constancy, in rhythmical, melodic and harmonic organisation, so much so that one extended part of this tradition has been singled out as 'the common practice' whose principles are taught as a matter of course in classes of music appreciation. This phenomenon demands an explanation.

Leonard B. Meyer, in an influential book (*Emotion and Meaning in Music*, Chicago 1956), argued that we understand music by a kind of probabilistic reasoning, which endows musical events with varying degrees of redundancy. The common practice has emerged from a steady accumulation of conventions and expectations, which enable listeners to predict what follows from what, and which give rise to the distinctive 'wrong note' experience when things go noticeably astray. This suggestion was taken forward by Eugene Narmour, to produce what he called the 'implication-realization model' of musical structure.[4] And more recently David Temperley has applied Bayesian probability theory to standard rhythms and melodies, in order to 'model' the way in which listeners assign meter and tonality to sequences.[5]

Temperley's work raises three questions: what is a 'model'? When is a model 'adequate' to the data? And what might the discovery of an adequate model show, concerning our understanding and appreciation of music? A model that can be rewritten as an algorithm could programme a computer to recognise (or should we say 'recognise'?) metrical order and key. Such a model can be tested against human performance, and if it successfully predicts our preferences and decisions, it offers the beginning of a theory of musical cognition. It suggests an account of what goes on in the brain, when listeners identify the metrical and tonal structure of the piece they are listening to. And that seems to be the aim of Temperley's reflections, especially in his earlier work, in which he develops a computational system for the analysis of music, and uses that system to represent patterns and sequences that are 'preferred' by habituated listeners.[6]

However, others use the term 'model' more loosely, to mean any way of representing the musical surface that displays the perceived connections among its parts, and which suggests a way in which we grasp those connections, whether or not consciously. In this sense the circle of fifths, chord-sequence analysis and the old charts of key relations are all partial 'models' of our musical experience. They enable us to predict, up to a point, how people will respond

---

[4] *The Analysis and Cognition of Basic Melodic Structures*, Chicago 1990.
[5] *Music and Probability*, MIT Press, 2007.
[6] See David Temperley, *The Cognition of Basic Musical Structures*, Cambridge Mass., MIT Press, 2001, and also Temperley's web-site, which offers access to the Melisma Music Analyzer, a program developed by Temperley and Daviel Sleator.

to changes of key and to accidentals in a melody, and they also suggest musical 'constants' on which a composer can lean when constructing the harmonic framework of a piece. But they do not aim to reduce musical understanding to a computational algorithm, nor do they offer anything like a complete theory of musical cognition, that will explain how we assemble a coherent musical surface from our experience of its parts. Rather, they describe the surface, by identifying the salient features and the perceived relations between them.

Things would look a little different, however, if we could take the idea of a musical 'syntax' literally. Linguistics attempts to model language use and comprehension in ways that lend themselves to computational analysis. If we could extend to the realm of musicology the advances made in psycholinguistics, therefore, we might be nearer to explaining what goes on, when people assemble the notes that they hear into coherent structures. Inconclusive research by the neuroscientists suggests that 'although musical and linguistic syntax have distinct and domain-specific syntactic representations, there is overlap in the neural resources that serve to activate these representations during syntactic processing'.[7] This – 'the shared syntactic integration resource hypothesis' – would be of considerable interest not only to evolutionary psychology but also to musicology, if it could be shown that the syntactic processes involved in the two cases work in a similar way. The neurological research does not show this. But there is a kind of speculative cognitive science that suggests that it might nevertheless be true, and that a 'grammar' of tonal music could be developed which both resembles the grammar of language, and can also be rewritten as a computational algorithm.

One goal of Chomsky's generative grammar has been to explain how speakers can understand indefinitely many new utterances, despite receiving only finite information from their surroundings. Formal languages like the predicate calculus provide a useful clue, showing how infinitely many well-formed formulae can be derived by recursion. If natural languages are organised in the same way, then from a finite number of basic structures, using a finite number of transformation rules, an infinite number of well-formed sentences could be extracted. Understanding a new sentence would not be a mystery, if speakers were able to recuperate from the string of uttered words the rule-governed process that produced it. Likewise the widespread capacity to latch on to new music without any guidance other than that already absorbed through the ear, could be

[7] Aniruddh D. Patel, *Music, Language and the Brain*, Oxford, OUP 2008, p. 297.

explained if musical surfaces were the rule-governed products of a finite number of basic structures, which might be partly innate, and partly acquired during the early years of acculturation.

Certain aspects of music have been modelled in ways that suggest such a generative grammar. If metrical organisation proceeds by division, as in Western musical systems, then surface rhythms can be derived from basic structures by recursion and also understood by recuperating that process. This is made into the basis of a generative grammar of metrical rhythm by Christopher Longuet-Higgins and C.S. Lee[8]. Others have made similar first shots at grammars for pitch organisation.[9]

Such small scale proposals were quickly displaced by the far more ambitious theory presented by Fred Lerdahl and Ray Jackendoff in their ground-breaking book, *A Generative Theory of Tonal Music* (1983). Their argument is bold, ambitious and detailed, and although things have moved on in the thirty years since the book first appeared, it has lost none of its relevance, and continues to be called upon by musicologists, music theorists and philosophers of music, in order to develop or make use of the analogy between linguistic and musical understanding. Lerdahl and Jackendoff recognise at many points, however, that this analogy is stretched, and that Chomskian linguistics cannot be carried over wholesale into the study of tonal music. Syntax, they recognise, does not in music point towards semantics, as it does in language. Moreover, the hierarchical organisation that Lerdahl and Jackendoff propose is an organisation of individual musical objects, such as notes and chords, and not, as in Chomsky, of grammatical categories (verb, noun-phrase, adverb etc.). There are no grammatical categories in music. Moreover, while we can distinguish 'structural' from 'subordinate' events in music, there is much room for argument as to which is which, and there is no one hierarchy that determines the position of any particular event. An event that is structural from the 'time-span' point of view might be metrically subordinate and also a prolongation of some other event in the hierarchy of tension and release. Still, the various hierarchies identified by Lerdahl and Jackendoff capture some of our firmer intuitions about musical importance. The task

[8] 'The Rhythmic Interpretation of Monophonic Music', in Longuet-Higgins, *Mental Processes: Studies in Cognitive Science*, Cambridge MA, MIT Press 1987.
[9] For example D. Deutsch and J. Feroe, 'The Internal Representation of Pitch Sequences in Tonal Music', *Psychological Review* 1981, **88**, 503–522.

is to show that there are transformation rules that derive the structure that we hear from a more deeply embedded structure, and do so in such a way as to explain our overall sense of the connectedness of the musical surface.

To grasp the point of the generative theory of tonal music it is important to distinguish two kinds of hierarchy. A generative hierarchy is one in which structures at the level of perception are generated from structures at the 'higher' level by a series of rule-governed transformations. Perceivers understand the lower level structures by unconsciously recuperating the process that created them, 'tracing back' what they see or hear to its generative source. By contrast a cumulative hierarchy is one in which perceived structures are repeated at different temporal or structural levels, but in which it is not necessary to grasp the higher level in order to understand the lower. For example, in classical architecture, a columniated entrance might be contained within a façade that exactly replicates its proportions and details on a larger scale. Many architectural effects are achieved in that way, by the 'nesting' of one aedicule within another, so that the order radiates outwards from the smallest unit across the façade of the building. This is not an instance of 'generative' grammar in the sense that this term has been used in linguistics, but rather of the amplification and repetition of a separately intelligible design. It is true that the order of such a façade is generated by a rule, namely 'repeat at each higher scale'. But we understand each scalar level in the same way as every other. You recognise the pattern of the entrance; and you recognise the same pattern repeated on a larger scale in the façade. Neither act of recognition is more basic than the other, and neither depends on the other. In *The Aesthetics of Music*[10] I argue that many of the hierarchies discerned in music, notably the rhythmic hierarchies described by Cooper and Meyer[11], are cumulative rather than generative, and therefore not understood by tracing them to some hypothetical 'source'. In the case of rhythm there are generative hierarchies too, as was shown by Christopher Longuet-Higgins, writing at about the same time as Cooper and Meyer. But it seems to me that, in the haste to squeeze music into the framework suggested by linguistics, writers have not always been careful to distinguish the two kinds of hierarchy. Music, in my view, is more like architecture than it is like language, and this means that repetition, amplification, diminution and

---

[10]   Oxford, OUP, 1997, p. 33.
[11]   *The Rhythmic Structure of Music*, Chicago 1960.

augmentation have more importance in creating the musical surface than rule-guided transformations of some structural 'source'.

The place of semantics in the generation of surface syntax is disputed among linguists, and Chomsky has not adhered to any consistent view in the matter. As a philosopher, however, influenced by a tradition of thinking that reaches from Aristotle to Frege and Tarski and beyond, I would be surprised to learn that deep structure and semantics have no intrinsic connection. Language, it seems to me, is organised by generative rules not by chance, but because that is the only way in which it can fulfil its primary function, of conveying information. Deep structures must surely be semantically pregnant if the generative syntax is to shape the language as an information-carrying medium – one in which new information can be encoded and received. Without semantically pregnant deep structure language would surely not be able to 'track the truth', nor would it give scope for the intricate question-and-answer of normal dialogue. A syntax that generates surface structures from deep structures is the vehicle of meaning, and that is why it emerged.

Take away the semantic dimension, however, and it is hard to see what cognitive gain there can be from a syntax of that kind. In particular, why should it be an aid to comprehension that the syntactical rules generate surface structures out of concealed deep structures? This question weighs heavily on the generative theory of music, precisely because (as Lerdahl and Jackendoff recognize) music is not about anything in the way that language is about things or in the way that figurative painting is about things. Indeed, musical organisation is at its most clearly perceivable and enjoyable in those works, like the fugues of Bach and the sonata movements of Mozart, which are understood as 'abstract' or 'absolute', carrying no reference to anything beyond themselves. The 'aboutness' of music, for which we reserve words like 'expression' and 'feeling', is a matter of what Frege called tone, rather than reference.

You might say that a hierarchical syntax would facilitate the ability to absorb new pieces. But this ability is as well facilitated by rules that link surface phenomena, in the manner of the old rules of harmony and counterpoint, or by the techniques of local variation and embellishment familiar to jazz improvisers. What exactly would be added by a hierarchical syntax, that is not already there in the perceived order of repetition, variation, diminution, augmentation, transposition and so on? Perhaps it is only in the case of metrical organisation that a generative hierarchy serves a clear musical purpose, since (in Western music at least) music is measured out by division, and divisions are understood by reference to the larger units from which they derive.[12]

There is a theory, that of Schenker, which offers to show that harmonic and melodic organisation are also hierarchical, and Lerdahl and Jackendoff acknowledge their indebtedness to this theory. According to Schenker tonal music in our classical tradition is (or ought to be) organised in such a way that the musical surface is derived by 'composing out' a basic harmonic and scalar progression. This basic progression provides the background, with postulated 'middle ground' structures forming the bridges that link background to foreground in a rule-governed way. Musical understanding consists in recuperating at the unconscious level the process whereby the background *Ursatz* exfoliates in the musical surface.

Objections to Schenker's idea are now familiar. Not only does it reduce all classical works, or at least all classical masterpieces, to a single basic gesture. It also implies formidable powers of concentration on the listener's part, to hold in suspension the sparse points at which the *Ursatz* can be glimpsed beneath the surface of a complex melodic and harmonic process. Moreover, it leaves entirely mysterious what the *benefit* might be, either in composing or in listening to a piece, the understanding of which involves recuperating these elementary musical sequences that have no significance when heard on their own.

More importantly, the whole attempt to transfer the thinking behind transformational grammar to the world of music is a kind of *ignoratio elenchi*. If music were like language in the relevant respects, then grasp of musical grammar ought to involve an ability to produce new utterances, and not just an ability to understand them when produced by someone else. But there is a striking asymmetry here. All musical people quickly 'latch on' to the art of musical appreciation. Very few are able to compose meaningful or even syntactically acceptable music. It seems that musical understanding is a one-way process, and musical creation a rare gift that involves quite different capacities from those involved in appreciating the result.

Here we discover another difficulty for theories like that of Lerdahl and Jackendoff, which is that they attempt to cast what seems to be a form of aesthetic preference in terms borrowed from a theory of truth-directed cognition. If understanding music involved

---

[12]   Note, however, that there are musical traditions which measure musical elements by addition and not division, notably the Indian traditions studied by Messiaen. See my 'Thoughts on Rhythm', in *Understanding Music*, London, Continuum, 2009.

recuperating information (either about the music or about the world) then a generative syntax would have a function. It would guide us to the semantically organised essence of a piece of music, so that we could understand what it says. But if music says nothing, why should it be organised in such a way? What matters is not semantic value but the agreeableness of the musical surface. Music addresses our preferences, and it appeals to us by presenting a heard order that leads us to say 'yes' to this sequence, and 'no' to that. Not surprisingly, therefore, when Lerdahl and Jackendoff try to provide what they regard as transformation rules for their musical grammar, they come up with 'preference rules', rather than rules of well-formedness.[13] These 'rules' tell us, for example, to 'prefer' to hear a musical sequence in such a way that metrical prominence and time-span prominence coincide. There are over a hundred of these rules, which, on examination, can be seen not to be rules at all, since they do not owe their validity to convention. They are generalisations from the accumulated preferences of musical listeners, which are not guides to hearing but by-products of our musical choices. Many of them encapsulate aesthetic regularities, whose authority is stylistic rather than grammatical, like the norms of poetic usage.

The formal languages studied in logic suggest, to a philosopher at any rate, what might be involved in a generative grammar of a natural language: namely, rules that generate indefinitely many well-formed strings from a finite number of elements, and rules that assign semantic values to sentences on the basis of an assignment of values to their parts. Nobody, I believe, has yet provided such a grammar for a natural language. But everything we know about language suggests that rules distinguishing well-formed from ill-formed sequences are fundamental, and that these rules are not generalisations from preferences but conventions that define what speakers are doing. They are what John Searle calls 'constitutive' rules. Such rules have a place in tonal music: for example the rule that designated pitches come from a set of twelve octave-equivalent semitones. But they do not seem to be linked to a generative grammar of the kind postulated by Lerdahl and Jackendoff. They simply lay down the constraints within which a sequence of sounds will be heard as music, and outside which it will be heard as non-musical sound. Moreover these constitutive rules are few and far between, and far less important, when it

---

[13]   Likewise, the theory of musical cognition advanced by David Temperley in his earlier work, *The Cognition of Basic Musical Structures, op. cit.,* is formulated in terms of 'preference rules'.

comes to saying how music works, than the résumés of practice that have been studied in courses of harmony and counterpoint.

This brings me to the crux. There is no doubt that music is something that we can understand and fail to understand. But the purpose of listening is not to decipher messages, or to trace the sounds we hear to some generative structure, still less to recuperate the information that is encoded in them. The purpose is for the listener to follow the musical journey, as rhythm, melody and harmony unfold according to their own inner logic, so as to make audible patterns linking part to part. We understand music as an object of aesthetic interest, and this is quite unlike the understanding that we direct towards the day-to-day utterances of a language, even if it sometimes looks as though we 'group' the elements in musical space in a way that resembles our grouping of words in a sentence.

This does not mean that there is no aspect to musical grammar that would deserve the sobriquet 'deep'. On the contrary, we recognise long-term tonal relations, relations of dependence between episodes, ways in which one part spells out and realises what has been foretold in another. These aspects of music are important: they are the foundation of our deepest musical experiences and an endless source of curiosity and delight. But they concern structures and relations that are created in the surface, not hidden in the depths. The musical order is not generated *from* these long-term relations as Schenker would have us believe, but points *towards* them, in the way that architectural patterns point towards the form in which they culminate. We come to understand the larger structure as a result of understanding the small-scale movement from which it derives.

One of the strengths of *A Generative Theory of Tonal Music* is that it emphasizes these long-term relations, and the way in which the listener – especially the listener to the masterworks of our listening culture – hears the music as *going somewhere*, fulfilling at a later stage expectations subliminally aroused at an earlier one. The mistake, it seems to me, comes from thinking that these perceived relations define a hidden or more basic structure, from which the rest of the musical surface is derived. The perceived relations should rather be seen as we see the relation between spires on a Gothic castle. The pattern made by the spires emerges *from* the supporting structures, but does not generate them.

So where does this leave the cognitive science of music? Thanks to Turing and 'information technology' a particular image of mental processes has taken hold in philosophy. According to this image all mental processes of which understanding is a crucial component are syntactical operations, in which the 'logic gates' of the brain open and close in obedience to algorithms that link input to output in ways that fulfil the cognitive needs of the organism. This powerful image feeds from our own attempts, in computer technology, to 'reverse engineer' the human cortex. A telling instance is provided by the digital image, transmitted from camera lens to computer screen. The image on the screen is composed of coloured pixels, which are themselves generated digitally, from information supplied by the camera, and transferred algorithmically to the screen. There is no miracle involved in this process, nor would it be a miracle if something similar occurred, by way of transferring information from the retina of the eye to the optical centres of the cortex.

However, the image on the screen is not just an array of pixels: it is an image *of* something – of a woman, say. It has the crucial 'about-ness' that has so often eluded the theories of psychology, and which requires an act of what might be called 'semantic descent': the passage from the data to their interpretation. Moreover, although this act of interpretation depends on processes in the brain, it is not the brain but the person who grasps the result of it. The computational theory that explains the transfer of the image from the lens to the screen offers no explanation of what goes on, when that image is interpreted as the image of a woman.

Moreover, the woman in the picture may be imaginary. I may see the woman while believing there is no such woman. And even in the case of photographs, where the assumption is that there is or was just such a scene as the scene portrayed, standing in a causal relation to its image on the screen, the normal person does not think that the things he sees in that image are actually *there* where he sees them, on the screen.

Imaginary objects, like mathematical objects, and other objects that slip without trace through causal networks, pose well-known problems for naturalistic theories of the mind. But they also remind us that we cannot dispense with philosophy. Such objects raise a question about intentionality that must be solved *prior* to cognitive science, if we are to know what shape our cognitive science is to have. We want to know how it is possible for a mental state to be of or about something that is believed not to exist – how a mental state can contain an apprehension of the nothingness of its own object, so to speak. And we want to know how such a mental state can connect with the steady flow of our thoughts and desires, and the developing thread of our emotional life, even though it tells us nothing directly about the world around us. Greg Currie's suggestion, that in the work of the imagination we run our mental states 'off-line', seems to me to be more a description of the problem than a solution to it.[14] For what is the ground for thinking that the 'on-line' mental state of believing that p is importantly similar to its off-line version of imagining that p? And in what way similar? You don't provide a cognitive science of the mind by using computer science as a source of metaphor.

As I earlier suggested, music is not a representational art form, and musical understanding is in that respect quite unlike our understanding of pictures – it does not involve, as the understanding of pictures involves, the recuperation of an imaginary world. Nevertheless, we do not perceive music simply as sequences of sounds: there is, as Lerdahl and Jackendoff and many others remind us, an act of synthesis, of mental organisation, involved in hearing sounds as music, and this is the equivalent in auditory perception of the moment of 'semantic descent' to which I referred earlier. We do not simply hear the sounds that compose the musical work. We hear sequences of pitched sounds, and we hear *in* those sounds a musical process that is supervenient on the sounds although not reducible to them. I have argued this point at length in *The Aesthetics of Music*. Music involves movement in a one-dimensional space, in which there are fields of force, relations of attraction and repulsion, and complex musical objects like melodies and chords that occupy places of their own. It exhibits opacity and transparency, tension and release, lightness and weight and so on. I have argued that there is an entrenched metaphor of space and movement underlying all these features of music. Some – notably Malcolm Budd[15] – dispute my claim that this metaphor is as deeply entrenched as I suppose it to be. But, as I have argued else-where,[16] the alternative view – that the parameters of musical movement and musical space can be described in the literal language of temporal progression – must also concede that musical understanding involves grasping activity, movement, attraction and repulsion, and a host of other phenomena that are not reducible to sequential ordering or to any other physical features of the sounds in which they are heard. Those features are part of what we perceive, when we hear music, and someone who merely hears sequences of pitched sounds – *however accurately* – does not hear music. (You could have absolute pitch and still not hear music. Some birds are like this.)

The great question, then, is what cognitive science can tell us, about hearing and understanding music. I earlier gave arguments

[14] *Arts and Minds*, Oxford, Clarendon Press 2004, chapters 9 and 10.
[15] Malcolm Budd, 'Musical Movement and Aesthetic Metaphors', *British Journal of Aesthetics*, 2003.
[16] *Understanding Music*, London, Continuum, 2009, ch. 4 'Movement'.

for dismissing the view that there is a generative syntax of music. But it is clear that music is organised in the ear of the beholder, and that all those features to which I have just referred, whether or not based in entrenched metaphors, are features of the organisation that we impose upon (or elicit in) the sequences that we hear. So how should the cognitive science proceed? One thing is clear: it cannot proceed simply by adapting cognitive science models from other areas, such as the cognitive science of language. We have to start from scratch. But there is very little scratch to start from, at least in the work of those cognitive scientists who have attended to this problem. Thus Aniruddh Patel, who has made a consistent effort to summarise the relevant findings of neuroscience, begins his discussion of melody from the following definition: melody is 'a tone sequence in which the individual tones are processed in terms of multiple structural relationships'.[17] But what is a tone? Is it identical to a pitched sound, or something that is heard *in* a pitched sound? What kind of 'relationships' are we talking about, and why describe them as 'structural'? You can see in this very definition a host of short cuts to the conclusion that music is processed in something like the way language is processed, and that 'processed' is just the word we need – the very word that suggests the algorithms of computer science. But maybe it is not like that at all. How would we know? Surely it is exactly here that philosophy is needed.

The first thing that a philosopher ought to say is that we understand music in something like the way we understand other art forms – namely, imaginatively. *Pace* Budd and others, I believe that when we hear music we hear processes, movements, and relations in a certain kind of space. This space is what is represented in our standard musical notation, and it is one reason why that notation has caught on: it gives us a clear picture of what we hear, unlike, say, the graph notation used by lutenists or the fret-board notation for the guitar, which give us a picture of the fingers, rather than the tones. If we adhere to the strict sense of 'model' that I referred to earlier, according to which a model is the first step towards a computational algorithm, then it is clear that no model can make use of the phenomenal space that is described by ordinary musical notation. A space in which position, movement, orientation and weight are all metaphors is not a space that can feature in a computer program, or indeed in any kind of theory that seeks to explain our experience, rather than to describe its subjective character. It is a space that is *read into, imposed upon, elicited in,* sounds when perceived by a

17   *Music, Language and the Brain*, p. 325.

certain kind of perceiver – one who is able to detach his perceptions from his beliefs, and to put normal cognitive processes on hold (or 'off line', to use Currie's metaphor).

Here is a point at which we might wish to step in with a long suppressed protest against the ambitions of cognitive science. Musicology, we might say, is or ought to be a humanity and not a science. It is not a prelude to a theory of musical cognition, whatever that may be. It is devoted to describing, evaluating and amplifying the *given* character of musical experience, rather than to showing how musical preferences might be tracked by a computer. Hence the one-dimensional pitch space in which *we*, self-conscious and aesthetically motivated listeners, situate melodic and harmonic movement, is the real object of musical study – the thing that needs to be understood in order to *understand music*. But this one-dimensional pitch space is not a space in which the physical events that we hear as music actually occur. An account of 'auditory representations' which offers to explain what goes on when we hear music will therefore not be an account of anything that occurs in that imaginary space. No account of auditory sequences and their 'processing' in the brain will be an account of what occurs in the imaginary space of music.

I shall conclude with a few observations that suggest, to me at least, that the philosophy is needed before the cognitive science can begin, and that the premature desire for an explanation may actually distort our account of the thing that needs to be explained. First, there is an asymmetry in music between the listener's, the composer's and the performer's competence. You can acquire a full understanding of music even though you cannot compose, and even though you cannot perform. I have already touched on this point, but it would surely have to be developed philosophically prior to any attempt at a cognitive science of musical appreciation.

Secondly, there is a kind of freedom in musical perception which parallels the freedom in the perception of aspects in the visual arts, but which is absent from ordinary cognitive processes. In the Müller-Lyer illusion the apparent inequality of the lines remains even after the subject knows that the lines are of the same length – proof, for some psychologists, of the modular nature of our sensory and intellectual processes, which deliver independent information about one and the same state of affairs. In the case of aspect perception, by contrast, appearances can change under the influence of thought, and will change if the right thinking is brought to bear on them. The nude in Titian's *Venus of Urbino* changes appearance if you imagine her to be looking at a lover, a husband, or merely a curious observer. How you see her depends upon how you think of her size, which in turn depends on how you think of the size of the bed on which she is lying. And so on. In the case of music the structural relations to which Patel refers are multiply adaptable to the needs of musical thought. Melodies change according to our conception of where upbeats end, where phrases begin, which notes are 'intruders' and which part of the flow, and so on. And it is one reason why performers are judged so intently, namely that how they *play* can influence how we *hear*.

Thirdly, we do not hear music as we hear other sounds in our environment. Music is heard as *addressed* to us. We move with it, regard it as calling on our attention, making demands on us, responding to our response. Enfolded within the music there lies an imagined first-person perspective, and to listen with full attention is to relate to the music as we relate to each other, I to Thou. Musical movement is a kind of action, and the 'why?' with which we interrogate it is the 'why?' of reason and not the 'why?' of cause. Hence the imagined space of music is a 'space of reasons', to use Wilfrid Sellars's well known idiom, and what we hear in it we hear under the aspect of freedom. This feature is integral to the meaning of music, and is one reason why we wish to speak of understanding and misunderstanding what we hear, regardless of whether we can attach some separately identifiable meaning to it. No doubt cognitive science will one day tell us much about the forms of inter-personal understanding. But it will have to advance well beyond the theory of auditory perception if it is to complete the task.

Those features, it seems to me, demand philosophical exegesis. They ask us to look at the phenomenon itself, to identify just what makes an experience of sound into an experience of *music*. Only when we have clarified that question, can we go on to ask questions about the neural pathways involved and the way the sounds are 'processed' by them.

But there is, I think, a more important topic that opens here, and one that must be the subject of another article. Even if we came up with a theory about the processing of music, it would not, in itself, be an account of musical understanding. Indeed, it would tell us as little about the meaning and value of music as a cognitive model of mathematical understanding would tell us about the nature of mathematical truth. All the real problems, concerning what music means, why we enjoy it, and why it is important to us, would remain untouched by such a theory. For they are problems about the experience itself, how that experience is profiled in our own first-person awareness, and what it means. Meaning is opaque to digital processing, which passes the mystery from synapse to synapse as a relay team passes the baton, or as the algorithm passes the image in my earlier example. The crucial moment of 'semantic descent' certainly occurs. But it involves the whole cognitive and emotional apparatus, and achieves an act of understanding of a kind that has yet to find its place in the computational theory of the mind. But here we are in deep water, and there are as many philosophers who will disagree with that last sentence (Fodor, for instance) as there are who will agree with it (Searle, for instance).

Ethics and Public Policy Center, Washington D.C. and
the University of Oxford
rogerscruton@mac.com

Aesthetics as a Normative Science

GORDON GRAHAM

1.

It is well known that we owe the term 'aesthetics' in its philosophical sense to the 18th century German philosopher Alexander Baumgarten. The eighteenth century's interest in aesthetics, however, pre-dated the invention of the term. In 1725, Francis Hutcheson published an *Inquiry into the Original of Our Idea of Beauty and Virtue*[1]. This may be said to be the first sustained and significant work in philosophical aesthetics as we now know it. Hutcheson's volume preceded Baumgarten's by 10 years, and within Scotland it inaugurated a series of philosophical writings on taste and beauty that continued for almost a century. Contributors included major philosophical figures like David Hume, Thomas Reid and Adam Smith, as well as influential figures less well known today such as Alexander Gerard, George Turnbull and Lord Kames.

This considerable flurry of philosophical activity was not confined to aesthetics, of course. Indeed it is important to see that the exploration of aesthetics was simply one aspect of the commanding project of the times – the 'science of human nature'. In the introduction to his *Treatise of Human Nature*, Hume declares that 'in the four sciences of *Logic, Morals, Criticism*, and *Politics* is comprehended almost everything . . . which can tend either to the improvement or ornament of the human mind' and that 'the only solid foundation for [these] sciences must be laid on experience and observation'[2]. The word 'improvement' is important here, because the aim of the science of mind was, in a broad sense, practical. It sought to understand the faculties of the human mind in order to make better use of them. Hume was in many ways at intellectual odds with his Scottish contemporaries, but in this passage he is articulating a conception of philosophy that all of them shared. The incorporation of 'Criticism' within the

---

[1] Francis Hutcheson, *An Inquiry into the Original of Our Idea of Beauty and Virtue*, edited by Wolfgang Leidhold (Indianapolis: Liberty Fund, 2008)

[2] David Hume, *A Treatise of Human Nature*, edited by David fate Norton and Mary J Norton, (Oxford: Clarendon Press, 2007), 4

doi:10.1017/S1358246114000216   ©The Royal Institute of Philosophy and the contributors 2014
Royal Institute of Philosophy Supplement **75** 2014

Gordon Graham

'science of human nature' was a standing assumption, because its inclusion struck them all as obvious.

What does it mean to seek a foundation for aesthetics in experience and observation? The supposition of the Scottish philosophers was that the 'taste' by which we appreciate and enjoy beautiful things, is one of our 'intellectual powers'[3]. To understand it correctly, we must determine just how the mind works with regard to this particular power. To do that, we have to draw the relevant data both from the introspection of our own experience and the observation of human beings at large, including the structure of natural languages and the sentiments expressed in literature. In short, the task of aesthetics is to arrive at general principles based upon facts about the characteristic operations of the human mind. 'Moral philosophy' so conceived was modeled on 'natural philosophy' as revolutionized by Newton, but it had the additional value of being applicable to deliberation and action. It promised genuine enlightenment, not simply by uncovering true empirical generalizations, but by using these in the education and improvement of our faculties, including the faculty of 'taste'. Empirical observations were to replace both dogmatic pronouncements from self or socially appointed authorities and the abstractions of rationalistic philosophers. In short, moral philosophy so conceived was normative as well as descriptive. Even Hume, despite his strictures on deriving 'ought' from 'is', looked to the science of human nature as the means by which both the superstition born of ignorance and the dogmatism born of 'revealed' theology might be ameliorated.

Though the Scottish philosophers who wrote on these matters did not use (or know) the term 'aesthetics', their conception of the project in hand is undoubtedly very similar to Baumgarten's. Kant, who thought highly of Baumgarten, and used his book on metaphysics as a student text, nevertheless raises a fundamental objection to Baumgarten's conception of aesthetics, an objection to which the Scottish philosophers also seem vulnerable. In a note to Part I of the *Critique of Pure Reason* he writes:

> The Germans are the only people who currently make use of the word 'aesthetic' in order to signify what others call the critique of taste. This usage originated in the abortive attempt made by Baumgarten, that admirable analytical thinker, to bring the critical treatment of the beautiful under rational principles, and so to raise its rules to the rank of a science. But such endeavours are

---

[3] 'Taste' is included by Reid in his *Essays on the Intellectual Powers of Man* (1785) rather than the corresponding volume on the 'Active Powers'

fruitless. The said rules or criteria are, as regards their chief sources, merely empirical, and consequently can never serve as determinate *a priori* laws by which our judgment of taste must be directed. On the contrary, our judgment is the proper test for the correctness of the rules. For this reason it is advisable either to give up using the name in this sense of critique of taste, and to reserve it for that doctrine of sensibility which is true science. . . . or else to share the name with speculative philosophy, employing it partly in the transcendental and partly in the psychological sense[4].

Kant here appeals to a deep division between the empirical study of human beings and the discipline of critical philosophy, a division that his writings did much to make orthodox. If such a division holds, then the idea of empirically studying the way the human mind responds to beautiful things as a way of educating and improving aesthetic sensibility is a mistake. From the Kantian (or perhaps post-kantian) point of view, it does not seem possible to identify the distinctive way in which the mind responds to beauty without first determining what the beautiful is. Trying to do so amounts to seeking a correlation between two things – the mind and its objects – in the absence of one of them. If 'our judgment is the proper test for the correctness' of any rules of criticism we might formulate, the most straightforward role observation can perform is generalize about the things people take delight in. Psychological preferences, however, are not the same as rational judgments. Logic cannot be grounded in psychology because people commonly reason fallaciously. Similarly, human beings can take genuine delight in disfiguration as well as embellishment, in kitsch as well as beauty.

Kant, of course, did not rest content with criticizing his contemporaries' attempts at an aesthetic science. Instead, he pursued the method of transcendental philosophy. In the *Critique of Judgment* he elaborates an alternative conception of the mind's operation with respect to beauty, an account of 'taste' and imagination that has proved very much more influential than Baumgarten's. For present purposes it is important to note that this Kantian alternative raises a further objection to aesthetics as a normative science. Famously the third *Critique* separates aesthetic judgment from practical reason (the subject of the second *Critique*), and declares judgments of taste to have as their object the *form* of purposiveness, but without *actual* purpose. It is in Kant's defense of this contention,

[4]   Immanuel Kant, *The Critique of Pure Reason*, translated Norman Kemp Smith, (London: Macmillan, 1929), 66

arguably, that the anti-utilitarian slogan 'art for art's sake' finds its most sophisticated philosophical articulation.

If Kant is correct on this score, then 'aesthetic science' of the kind the Scottish philosophers aimed to engage in is mistaken on *two* counts. Not only does it seek a psychological foundation that cannot serve its purposes, it also has normative ambitions that cannot be realized. Obviously, it is not simply the 18th century Scots to whom these objections apply. They hold equally well against all empirical studies of aesthetic experience that aim to inform either philosophical aesthetics or practical criticism. If Kant's point is a good one, then while the much greater sophistication of contemporary psychological research methods might produce a more powerfully explanatory 'doctrine of sensibility', they can contribute no more to philosophical aesthetics or practical criticism than could Baumgarten's unhappy hybrid.

2.

My purpose in this paper is not to discuss Kant, but to explore the challenge he articulates (or something like it) in the context of the Scottish Enlightenment's own debates. *Pace* Kant, there is a plausible account to be given of a normative 'science' of aesthetics grounded in empirical observation. But just what that grounding is, is a matter of debate between the Scottish philosophers, and there is light to be shed on the issue by comparing aesthetics with another 18th century conception – 'moral science'. For this too was intended to be both descriptive of human nature and normative for human conduct.

A good place to start the comparison is Hume's famous essay 'Of the Standard of Taste'. In this essay Hume attempts, with considerable ingenuity, to reconcile two seemingly opposing phenomena. Everyone agrees, he thinks, that taste is necessarily a subjective matter. Yet no one really subscribes to the apparent implication of this contention – that about matters of taste there can be no disputing. On the contrary, people regularly engage in debate and argument, they invoke the ideas of good and bad taste, and they seek to persuade and dissuade each other. But if taste is indeed a subjective matter of what pleases and displeases, how could there be a *standard* of taste by which some 'pleasings' are to be declared better than others? Either we simply record what people in general find pleasing, or, like Kant, we find some way of determining what they *ought* to find pleasing.

Hume's resolution of the problem he sets himself, is to affirm that

> though the principles of taste be universal, and nearly, if not entirely, the same in all men; yet few are qualified to give judgment on any work of art, or establish their own sentiment as the standard of beauty. The organs of internal sensation are seldom so perfect as to allow the general principles their full play . . . They either labour under some defect, or are vitiated by some disorder; and by that means excite a sentiment which may be pronounced erroneous[5].

Judgments of beauty, then, are indeed subjective sentiments. But if such sentiments are to be 'just', we need not only a faculty of taste, but the education of that faculty. This requires

> strong [common] sense, united to delicate sentiment, improved by practice, perfected by comparison, and cleared of all prejudice. [The satisfaction of these conditions] can alone entitle critics to this valuable character; and the joint verdict of such, wherever they are to be found, is the true standard of taste and beauty[6].

In short, only the correctly situated and properly educated person can be said to respond to beauty in accordance with truly universal principles of taste. The vast majority of people, when they declare that they are pleased by the beauty of something, are either ignorant of these principles or applying them defectively. They are truly expressing their sentiments, certainly, but their sentiments are 'erroneous' since they arise from imperfect apprehension.

On Hume's account of the matter, morality stands in a special relationship to the aesthetic. We can admire artistic products or representations without qualification even if they feature scientific beliefs, religious practices or social fashions that we now regard as absurd. Moreover, as Hume's no less famous essay 'Of Tragedy' argues, art that powerfully portrays a level of suffering that would normally distress us, can nevertheless prompt aesthetic pleasure. But, we cannot do the same for artistic representations of what we regard as grossly immoral. Paintings, poems or dramas that depict vindictive cruelty or pornographic sensuality cannot please a well educated aesthetic taste.

> The poet's *monument more durable than brass*, must fall to the ground like common brick or clay, were men to make no

---

[5] David Hume, 'Of the Standard of Taste', *Essays Moral, Political and Literary*, (Oxford: Oxford University Press, 1963), 246
[6] Ibid., 247

allowance for the continual revolutions of manners and customs, and would admit nothing but what was suitable to the prevailing fashion. Must we throw aside the pictures of our ancestors, because of their ruffs and farthingales? But where the ideas of morality and decency alter from one age to another, and where vicious manners are described, without being marked with the proper characters of blame and disapprobation, this must allow to disfigure the poem, and to be a real deformity. I cannot, nor is it proper I should, enter into such sentiments; and however I may excuse the poet on account of the manners of his age, I can never relish the composition[7].

Opinions differ on whether Hume successfully resolves the problem he has set himself. Here, I want only to highlight two puzzles relevant to the present topic. First, there is something rather odd about Hume's contention *both* that the principles of taste are universal, *and* that only a small minority of people ever apply them accurately. Furthermore, though it may be, as he contends, that the passage of time reveals an enduring standard of taste, its universality, he thinks, must necessarily be qualified by the character of the individual, and the *mores* of different cultures. Character and culture lead even educated and open minded people to diverge considerably in their aesthetic judgments and artistic preferences. So in what sense, exactly, is the standard of taste 'universal', and why identify it as part of human *nature*?

The second puzzle is this. Hume thinks that we can, and should, set aside distorting conditions. We should, for instance, pass judgment on the liveliness of a painting only if we are seeing it in the right light, and we should avoid the anachronism of judging the past by the standards of the present. But why should precisely the same point not apply to moral apprehension? If we overlook 'the ruffs and farthingales' when considering the portraits of previous ages, why can we not overlook the slavery or violence that also marked them? Indeed, to move to modern examples, what is preventing us from divorcing Nazi or Soviet art from the objectionable ideologies that gave rise to them, so that our aesthetic sensibilities can 'relish' these 'compositions'? The question is made more pressing by Hume's strange claim that moral defects are *real* aesthetic deformities. If everything rests on sensibility, how could 'morality' generate 'reality' on his picture?

---

[7]   Ibid., 252

3.

As in other contexts, Hume's account of these matters may be contrasted with that of his greatest contemporary critic – Thomas Reid. Reid was no less committed to the project of the science of human nature than Hume, but he thought that Hume was misled into pursuing it in the wrong way by his implicit subscription to a (broadly) Lockean conception of mind. It is this background conception that inevitably leads Hume to skeptical conclusions. Accordingly, Reid often expounds a view that, while strikingly similar to Hume's, reverses the role of certain key concepts. Such may be said to be the case here. 'Taste' is the subject of the eighth and final essay in Reid's *Essays on the Intellectual Powers of Man*. In it, he asserts that

> Our judgment of beauty is not indeed a dry and unaffecting judgment, like that of a mathematical or metaphysical truth. By the constitution of our nature, it is accompanied with an agreeable feeling or emotion, for which we have no other name but the sense of beauty. This sense of beauty, like the perceptions of our other senses, implies not only a feeling, but an opinion of some quality in the object which occasions that feeling[8].

This, evidently, is very close to Hume's view of the matter – but with a crucial difference. Where Hume supposes that the feeling gives rise to our 'opinion', Reid thinks it is the opinion that gives rise to the feeling. For Hume, we judge something beautiful *because* we find it aesthetically pleasing, which means that any proposition about its beauty (or ugliness) will be an *expression of* feeling. For Reid, on the contrary, we delight in those things we first *judge* to be beautiful, and are repelled by those we judge to be ugly. It is this anterior exercise of judgment that *determines* the feeling. His principal argument in favor of this alternative is an observation about linguistic usage.

> If it be said that the perception of beauty is merely a feeling in the mind that perceives, without any belief or excellence in the object, the necessary consequence of this is that when I say VIRGIL's Georgics is a beautiful poem, I mean not to say anything of the poem, but only something concerning myself and my feelings. Why should I use a language that expresses the contrary of what I mean? . . . Even those who hold beauty to be merely a feeling in the person that perceives it, find themselves under

---

[8]   Thomas Reid, *Essays on the Intellectual Powers of Man* edited by Derek R. Brookes, (Edinburgh: Edinburgh University Press, 2002), 578

a necessity of expressing themselves, as if beauty were solely a quality of the object, and not of the percipient.

No reason can be given why all mankind should express themselves thus, but that they believe what they say. It is therefore contrary to the universal sense of mankind, expressed in their language, that beauty is not really in, the object, but is merely a feeling in the person who is said to perceive it[9].

For Reid then, judgment is primary and feeling is secondary in just this sense; it is because we judge something beautiful that agreeable feelings arise within us, and because we judge something ugly that we experience revulsion. Of course, causal primacy does not necessarily mean temporal priority. As a matter of experience, judgment and feeling may appear instantaneously. Indeed, that may be what lends plausibility to Hume's sentimentalist view of the matter. Still, Reid's alternative account enables him to make more sense of the puzzle with which Hume wrestles. 'Delicacy of taste' is a matter of sophisticated judgment, not refined feeling. The 'agreeable feeling' that accompanies judgments of beauty 'by the constitution of our nature', is truly universal and never in itself 'erroneous'. But *contra* Hume, it is most readily experienced, and hence most evident, in simple, 'instinctive' judgments that require no complex thought processes. It is the 'rational' judgments involved in, for instance, the appraisal of major works of art, that are more likely to go wrong and, in the absence of the necessary knowledge and sophistication, likely to result in uncertainty of thought and feeling.

What is it that we are judging? Reid is struck by the great variety of things to which 'beautiful' can be applied.

Beauty is found in things so various, and so very different in nature, that it is difficult to say wherein it consists, or what there can be common to all the objects in which it is found. . . we find beauty in colour, in sound, in form, in motion. There are beauties of speech, and beauties of thought; beauties in the arts, and in the sciences; beauties in actions, in affections, and in characters. In things so different, and so unlike, is there any quality, the same in all, which we may call by the name of beauty? What can it be that is common to the thought of a mind, and the form of piece of matter, to an abstract theorem, and stroke of wit? . . . But why should things so different be called by the same name? This cannot be without a reason[10].

---

[9]   Ibid., 577
[10]   Ibid., 591–2

Reid thinks there is a reason, and that it is to be found in the special pleasure we get in contemplating all the things we judge to be beautiful. This pleasure, though, is not the apprehension of some common property – beautifulness – which can mysteriously inhere in objects as diverse as flowers, poems, faces and mathematical proofs. Rather, it is a manifestation of our natural admiration for excellence. The delight we take in beauty arises from our judging something to be excellent by the standards of its kind. 'The thought of a mind, the form of piece of matter, an abstract theorem' can all be beautiful because they can all achieve distinctive kinds of excellence. Excellence is a natural 'norm'. So, *contra* Hume, we cannot derive a 'standard of taste' by surveying our feelings, or even the feelings of an educated minority. But happily, we do not need to. Excellent things both *do* please us and *ought* to please us, just because they are excellent. Their excellence is not a projection of our feelings, which would carry the absurd implication that believing something to be excellent actually makes it so. Their excellence is a function of the kind of thing that they are.

Some excellent things are simple – a flawless shade of blue, for example – and others are complex – a theatrical production, an orchestral composition. There is still this question of course. What makes the perception of excellence, and the delight it occasions, a judgment of *beauty*? In answer to this question, Reid connects beauty with morality, though in a quite different way to Hume. Where Hume holds that, somewhat arbitrarily, moral turpitude must undermine aesthetic delight, Reid sees an essential connection between the moral and the aesthetic. It is to be found in the fact that the most fundamental object of delighted approval is moral excellence. Beauty is first and foremost a characteristic of morally lovely people (a contention reflected in the familiar expression 'a beautiful personality'). It is by analogical extension that we call many other things beautiful, because they too, in their different ways, exemplify excellence.

By Reid's account, then, feeling matters because judgments of beauty, unlike judgments of truth, are not 'dry and unaffecting'. Nevertheless, taste is not itself a 'sentiment' but the exercise of our rational faculty as we assess degrees of excellence. Reid thus places beauty at the heart of human life, and in principle he seems to offer a rather better integrated account of ethics and aesthetics than Hume's contingent invocation of a moral veto on aesthetic approval. The main point here, though, is not to vindicate Reid over Hume, but to provide an avenue into exploring the potential analogy between the 'moral science' of the 18th century and a corresponding 'aesthetic

Gordon Graham

science'. Reid, I shall suggest, lays the foundations for a reasonably promising parallel.

4.

Though all the major philosophers of the Scottish Enlightenment regarded their inquiries in moral philosophy as in some way connected with practical ethics, they were at the same time acutely aware of an important tension, memorably described by George Davie as the need 'to respect the instincts of the farmer as against the sophistication of the philosopher, and initiate a sort of dialogue between the vulgar and the learned'[11]. This necessity arises because 'common sense' (Reid's preferred term) or 'natural belief' (Hume's) has a foundational role in the 'science of human nature', conceived as the formulation and assessment of scientific theories and explanations. But how exactly is the theorizing of the 'learned' to be related to the natural belief or common sense of the 'vulgar'? The issue is especially important with respect to morality, for while moral *philosophy* is necessarily the occupation of an intellectually motivated few, moral *agency*, with equal necessity, is the province of all human beings. Precisely the same point can be made about beauty. Aesthetic theory may be an intellectual specialty confined to experts; the appreciation of beauty is an important dimension of everyday life.

The relation of aesthetic theory to artistic activity (broadly conceived) is not addressed by the Scottish philosophers as explicitly as the division between moral philosophy and practical ethics. In *The Theory of Moral Sentiments*, for example, Adam Smith tells us that 'in treating the principles of morals there are two questions to be considered. First, wherein does virtue consist? . . . And secondly, by what power or faculty of the mind is it that [virtue] whatever it be, is recommended to us'[12]. Hume draws a similar distinction, but reflects at greater length on the relevant methodological differences.

> Moral philosophy, or the science of human nature, may be treated after two different manners; each of which has its peculiar merit, and may contribute to the entertainment, instruction and reformation of mankind. The one considers man chiefly as born for action; and as influenced in his measures by taste and

[11] George E Davie, *A Passion for Ideas: Essays on the Scottish Enlightenment* Vol. II, (Edinburgh: Polygon, 1994), 41–2
[12] Adam Smith, *The Theory of Moral Sentiments*, edited by Knud Haakonssen, (Cambridge: Cambridge University Press, 2002), 313–4

258

sentiment; pursuing one object, and avoiding another, according to the value which these objects seem to possess, and according to the light in which they present themselves. As virtue, of all objects, is allowed to be the most valuable, this species of philosophers paint her in the most amiable colours; borrowing all helps from poetry and eloquence. . . They make us feel the difference between vice and virtue; they excite our sentiments; and so they can bend our hearts to the love of probity and true honor. . . . The other species of philosophers consider man in the light of a reasonable rather than an active being, and endeavour to form his understanding more than cultivate his manners. They regard human nature as a subject of speculation; and with a narrow scrutiny examine it, in order to find those principles which regulate our understanding, excite our sentiments, and make us approve or blame any particular object, action or behavior[13].

It is in relating the connection between these two 'species' of philosophy that Hume draws his famous distinction between the painter and the anatomist.

An artist must be better qualified to succeed . . . who . . . possesses an accurate knowledge of . . . the operations of the understanding, the workings of the passions, and the various species of sentiment which discriminate vice and virtue. How painful soever this inward search or enquiry may appear, it becomes, in some measure, requisite to those, who would describe with success the obvious and outward appearances of life and manners. The anatomist presents to the eye the most hideous and disagreeable objects; but his science is useful to the painter in delineating even a VENUS or an HELEN. While the latter employs all the richest colours of his art; . . . he must still carry his attention to the inward structure of the human body. Accuracy is, in every case, advantageous to beauty, and just reasoning to delicate sentiment. In vain would we exalt the one by depreciating the other[14].

Hume's analogy is a captivating one but it does not quite answer to the issue in hand. Let us agree, if only for the sake of argument, that accuracy is indeed advantageous to beauty. This may make painters importantly reliant on scientific anatomy, but it does not make them

[13] David Hume, *An Enquiry concerning Human Understanding* edited by Tom L Beauchamp (Oxford: Oxford University Press, 1999), 87
[14] Ibid., 90

Gordon Graham

contributors to the science of the human body. Their paintings are not a different way of investigating the body that brings a different kind of anatomical understanding. Rather, they apply the knowledge that anatomical study provides in the first place, in order to *present* it in a different way. By extension, then, moralists do not add to our philosophical understanding of morality; they find attractive and persuasive ways of inculcating the moral principles that philosophers formulate. In short, Hume's analogy does not reflect a *division within* philosophy or the science of human nature, but rather a *contrast between* science and rhetoric. The first is concerned with investigation, the second with persuasion.

Like Smith and Hume, Reid has his version of the distinction when he contrasts a 'system of morals' with a 'theory of morals'

> A system of morals is not like a system of geometry, where the subsequent parts derive their evidence from the preceding, and one chain of reasoning is carried on from the beginning. . . . It resembles more a system of botany or mineralogy, where the subsequent parts depend not for their evidence upon the preceding, and the arrangement is made to facilitate apprehension and memory, and not to give evidence.
>
> . . . . . .
>
> By the theory of morals is meant a just account of the structure of our moral powers; that is, of those powers of mind by which we have our moral conceptions and distinguish right from wrong in human actions. This indeed is an intricate subject, and there have been various theories and much controversy about it in ancient times. But it has little connection with the knowledge of our duty; and those who differ most in the theory of our moral powers, agree in the practical rules of morals which they dictate[15].

The last sentence is crucial. Moral philosophers are notorious for radical differences of opinion. These differences arise from the 'intricacy' of their subject, and contrast with the near unanimity among ordinary people on general principles of justice, truthfulness, integrity and so on. If moral agency relied on a theory of morals, it would be a very chancy matter confined to a few intellectuals. To come within the purview of all (except infants, the senile and the

---

[15]   Thomas Reid, *Essays on the Active Powers of Man* ed Knud Haakonssen and James A Harris, (Edinburgh: Edinburgh University Press, 2010), 281–2

insane), it must depend upon a faculty of judgment that does not require special intellectual expertise.

On the face of it, Reid's distinction seems to confine moral 'science' to the activities of intellectuals no less than Hume's. This is not quite right, however. Ordinary moral thinking is not theoretical by his account, but it can be systematic. The difference is illustrated by Reid's contrast between geometry and botany. From time to time, botanists discover new plants. Discovery is not the principal purpose of their science, however, which is rather the devising of systems of classification and relation. Botanists do not uncover or reveal a new dimension of experience; they begin with our existing knowledge of the world of plants and seek to organize in ways that will reveal interesting connections and parallels within it. The aim is to heighten our appreciation of both its structure and variety, the latter being the aim that drives the search for new plants. Botany is a science, but it is a different science to the newer discipline of plant biology. Plant biology is an explanatory rather than a classificatory discipline, one that aims to develop ever more sophisticated theories of the genetic processes within plants.

Considered in the light of this parallel, we can regard 'moral science' as the pursuit of a a *system* of morals. Such a system is a way of organizing the moral 'data' that present themselves to ordinary consciousness without any special investigation, basic moral 'intuitions', the point of which is to make us more aware of the structure and variety of our moral judgments. Reid's lectures to his students on practical ethics (which, significantly, he never published in his lifetime) are of just this nature. He observes that practical ethics is 'level to all capacities' in just this sense:

> There is hardly any moral Duty which when properly explained and delineated, does not recommend itself to the heart of every candid and unbiased Man. For every man has within him a touchstone of Morals . . . which approves of what is Right and condemns what is wrong, when it is fairly represented and considered without prejudice. . . .

The problem is that:

> Mens private interests, their passions, vicious habits and inclinations do often blind their understandings and bias their judgment. . . It is therefore of great consequence to those who would judge right in matters of their own Conduct or that of others, to have the Rules of Morals fixed & settled in their minds before

Gordon Graham

they have occasion to apply them to cases wherein they may be interested[16].

On this account a system of morals is a normative science. It is a science in being the intellectual activity of organizing our moral convictions in order to maximize coherence and consistency and minimize prejudice. It is normative because it guides practical activity. Adapting some phrases of Wittgenstein's we might say, a system of morals (in contrast to a theory of morals) does not uncover new information that enables us to say 'Now I know some moral truths'. Rather it assembles reminders of what we already know, and organizes them in ways that enable us to say 'Now I know my way around the moral life'.

5.

Could this conception of 'moral science' provide the model for a normative science of aesthetics? Adapting Reid, this would require the identification of a 'touchstone' of beauty within us which approves of what is beautiful and and condemns what is ugly, at least when it is properly represented and considered without prejudice. This sounds remarkably close to Hume's 'Standard of Taste', but it is in fact importantly different. Here as elsewhere, on one level Reid's and Hume's views are close, but on another diametrically opposed.

One significant difference is this. Hume's 'standard' takes the form of a sentiment that is found to be common to a small subset of human beings whose 'taste' has been fashioned and refined by experience. His 'rules of art' simply capture this shared sensibility. Simply applying them, and thereby correctly second guessing the opinion of 'experts', is wholly inadequate because refined taste is a necessary condition of aesthetic pleasure properly so called. Reid's 'touchstone', by contrast, is a natural faculty of appreciation whose operation is evident in children no less than adults.

> Some objects strike us at once, and appear beautiful at first sight, without any reflection, without our being able to say why we call them beautiful. . . Something of this kind there seems to be . . . in children; nor does it end with infancy, but continues through life[17]

Such immediate responses, according to Reid, are corrected or justified as we try to 'specify [the] perfection which justifies our

[16] Thomas Reid, *On Practical Ethics* ed Knud Haakonssen, (Edinburgh: Edinburgh University Press, 2007), 10–11
[17] Op. cit., note 7, 596

judgment'[18]. This perfection lies in the object, and not in our response to it, however refined. An important implication for present purposes is the contrasting role of reason in Hume and Reid.

Having declared 'morals and 'criticism' to be 'sciences' in the *Treatise*, Hume returns to the topic in the first *Enquiry*. But their classification as sciences is now heavily qualified.

> Morals and criticism [he tells us here] are not so properly objects of the understanding as of taste and sentiment. Beauty, whether moral or natural, is felt more properly than perceived. Or if we reason concerning it, and endeavour to fix its standard, we regard a new fact, the general taste of mankind, or some such fact, which may be the object of reasoning and enquiry[19].

This passage contrasts sharply with Reid on the same topic.

> Our moral and rational powers justly claim dominion over the whole man. Even taste is not exempted from their authority; it must be subject to that authority in every case where we pretend to reason or dispute about matters of taste; it is the voice of reason that our love or our admiration ought to be proportioned to the merit of the object. When it is not grounded on real worth, it must be the effect of constitution or of some habit or casual association[20].

It seems obvious that anything we might call a 'science' of criticism must involve the exercise of reason, and both Reid and Hume suppose this to be the case. For Reid, 'in a poem, in a picture, in a piece of music, it is real excellence that pleases a good taste'[21]. Accordingly, the aim of a science of taste must be to trace the structure of perfection, and he contends that it is the ability to do this that unites the critic and the artist. 'The most perfect works of art have a beauty that strikes even the rude and ignorant; but they see only a small part of that beauty which is seen in such works by those who understand them perfectly, and can produce them'[22]. On this account, then, aesthetics truly is a normative science since it is the exercise of critical reason that both deepens our appreciation of art works and guides our artistic creativity.

---

[18] Ibid.
[19] Op. cit note 12, 210
[20] Op.cit., note 7, 614
[21] Op. cit., note 7, 601
[22] Op. cit., note 7, 595

Gordon Graham

The science of 'reasoning and enquiry' that Hume's conception holds out to us, on the other hand, could only encompass facts about psychological responses – 'the general taste of mankind, or some such fact' – and never the phenomena to which they are responses. It is a science that could be (and perhaps is) pursued with much greater rigor and sophistication by modern empirical psychology than was the case with the relatively primitive introspective psychology of Hume's day. Yet even this much more sophisticated type of psychology is necessarily divorced from anything properly called normative 'criticism', and the attempt to found aesthetic norms on this sort of 'experience and observation' can only result in absurdity. This result is demonstrated by the example of *America's Most Wanted* (1994), one of a number of what we might call' nationally preferred' paintings produced by Vitaly Komar and Alexander Melamid. All of the 'most wanted' paintings are based on extensive empirical research into aesthetic preferences, and each picture aims to combine the most frequently declared preferences in a single work. Ironically, the result, as Arthur Danto observes, is a painting that we cannot really imagine anyone wanting – *as a painting*. *America's Most Wanted*, for example, is a realistic rendering of a lakeside scene that includes, among other popular preferences, George Washington and a hippopotamus! Danto thinks that construed as a 'performance piece by Komar and Melamid which consists in opinion poll, the painting, the publicity, etc. . . . [*America's Most Wanted*] is probably a masterpiece'. It is a 'work about people's art without being people's art at all . . . "post-modern, humorous and iconic" as one observer said'[23].

If *America's Most Wanted* does indeed qualify for these commendatory epithets, it is not because of its connection with the aesthetic preferences that careful empirical investigation has shown to be widespread. It is because the painting has achieved excellence of a quite different kind. As a painting it is bad; as a visual *reductio ad absurdum* it is brilliant. The absurdity it reveals, however, is one embodied in a certain conception of how aesthetics might be founded on 'experience and observation'. *America's Most Wanted* thus serves to confirm, in two ways, this conclusion. If indeed there can be a normative science of aesthetics, its nature must be as Reid and not as Hume conceives it.

Princeton Theological Seminary
gordon.graham@ptsem.edu

[23]   Danto, Arthur C, *After the End of Art; Contemporary Art and the Pale of History*, (Princeton: Princeton University Press, 1997), 216